JIM MANTHORPE (seen here on Mont de la Saxe, Grandes Jorasses in the background) is a wildlife cameraman and writer. He has written and updated dozens of Trailblazer guidebooks over the years, from Ladakh to Canada. Based in the Scottish Highlands, he has a particular love for wild places and wildlife and has filmed eagles, otters and orcas for various BBC shows including *Springwatch*.

He is also the author of *Scottish Highlands Hillwalking* and the *Great Glen Way*, both from Trailblazer.

Author

Tour du Mont Blanc
First edition 2008; this second edition July 2018

Publisher: Trailblazer Publications
The Old Manse, Tower Rd, Hindhead, Surrey, GU26 6SU, UK
www.trailblazer-guides.com

British Library Cataloguing in Publication Data
A catalogue record for this book is available from the British Library

ISBN 978-1-905864-92-8

© **Jim Manthorpe** 2008, 2018
Text, maps and photographs unless otherwise credited

The right of Jim Manthorpe to be identified as the author of this work has been asserted
by him in accordance with the Copyright, Designs and Patents Act 1988

Editor: Clare Weldon; **Layout & proofreading**: Daniel McCrohan
Cartography: Nick Hill; **Index**: Daniel McCrohan
Illustrations: p52, Nick Hill; line drawings on pp53-55, and p57 are from
A Guide to Chamonix and the Range of Mont Blanc by Edward Whymper (London,
1896); the line drawing on p56 is from *A Handbook of Mr Albert Smith's Ascent of
Mont Blanc*, illustrated by William Beverley (London, 1852)

Acknowledgements

I'd like to thank the Trailblazer team for their tireless work and attention to detail,
particularly Bryn Thomas for making it possible for me to write and travel. I'm also
grateful to Clare Weldon for the thorough editing, Daniel McCrohan for layout and
proofreading and to Nick Hill for his excellent map skills. Thanks are also due to Nick
Jeggo for his knowledge and enthusiasm, to the staff at the Chamonix tourist office
and the ephemeral friends I met on the trail and to the readers who wrote in with
suggestions, in particular Annie Lord. Finally, a big thank you and a big hug to Claire,
Oren and Zara for allowing me to explore... and allowing me to come home.

A request

The author and publisher have tried to ensure that this guide is as accurate and up to date
as possible. However, things change even on these well-worn routes. If you notice any
changes or omissions that should be included in the next edition of this guide, please
email or write to Jim Manthorpe at Trailblazer (address above). You can also contact us
via the Trailblazer website (🖳 www.trailblazer-guides.com). Those persons making a
significant contribution will be rewarded with a free copy of the next edition.

Warning – mountain walking can be dangerous

Please read the notes on mountain safety on pp38-46.
Every effort has been made by the author and publisher to ensure that the information
contained herein is as accurate and up to date as possible. However, they are unable to
accept responsibility for any inconvenience, loss or injury sustained by anyone as a result
of the advice and information given in this guide.

Updated information will shortly be available on: 🖳 **www.trailblazer-guides.com**

Photos – Front cover: The descent into the Trient Valley from Fênetre d'Arpette
This page: Hikers heading for Col du Bonhomme. **Overleaf**: On the trail for Col Sapin.

Printed in China; print production by D'Print (☎ +65-6581 3832), Singapore

Tour du
Mont Blanc

PLANNING – PLACES TO STAY – PLACES TO EAT

50 large-scale trail maps and guides to
Chamonix, Courmayeur & Argentière

JIM MANTHORPE

TRAILBLAZER PUBLICATIONS

Contents

Contents

For Claire, Oren and Zara

Introduction

INTRODUCTION

Mont Blanc, that grand marvel, not only of Europe, but of the whole world.
Francis Trench, *A Walk Round Mont Blanc*, 1847

In 1767 a scientist by the name of Horace Bénédict de Saussure walked around the massif of Mont Blanc, looking for a route to the summit of the unclimbed mountain. Since then many thousands of trekkers have followed in his bootsteps and some have gone on to follow him to the top of the mountain itself. Others are just content to enjoy the startlingly beautiful Mont Blanc massif with Mont Blanc itself as the centrepiece.

At 4808m (15,777ft), Mont Blanc, the highest mountain in western Europe and one of the most famous mountains in the world, does not stand alone. The snow-dome sum-

> **At 4808m (15,777ft), Mont Blanc is the highest mountain in western Europe**

mit is the highest point of a spectacular massif of peaks stretching 60 miles by 20 miles. The heights of Mont Blanc and its adjacent peaks, such as the Grandes Jorasses and Mont Dolent, allow for the development of vast glaciers that slip from the high slopes and through the side valleys. Some might dare to say that this is the most magnificent

Above: The route is well waymarked; you're unlikely to get lost.
Opposite: On the Mont de la Saxe ridge (see p114) above the Italian Val Ferret.

mountain scenery in Europe. You may even be forgiven for thinking, at times, that the Alps are like a mini Himalaya.

The trail (105 miles, 168km) that circumnavigates the massif, passing through France, Italy and Switzerland, is the most popular long-distance walk in Europe.

The trail (105 miles, 168km) circumnavigates the massif, passing through France, Italy and Switzerland,

Anyone who has completed it will understand why; for every day the beauty of the mountains, valleys and forests is a constant and welcome companion. On the last day of the circuit, when your feet complete the circle around the icy massif, you'll undoubtedly feel that every tiring climb – and there are a few – will have been worth the effort.

Those responsible for planning the present-day course of the trail deserve a big pat on the back; throughout its route the Tour takes in some of the most magical viewpoints, largely by avoiding the deep valley floors and, instead, sticking to the high slopes opposite the massif. The result is a grandstand view across the valleys and onto the snowy peaks.

The superb landscape is not all that the Tour has to offer. Passing through three countries means there is plenty of cultural interest too. French is widely spoken, even in Italy, and most of the staff in the service industry can speak English. Nevertheless, they will appreciate it if you at least try to speak the local tongue. So, if you are not already a linguist, remember to brush up on your schoolboy or schoolgirl French and Italian; a 'bonjour' here and a 'bon giorno' there will usually bring a smile.

The trail is waymarked and poses few difficulties. That

It's a strenuous trek involving significant ascents and descents, crossing high passes and, in places, passing over rough ground.

said, it is a strenuous trek involving significant ascents and descents, crossing high passes and, in

Left: Mont Blanc massif seen from the Grand Balcon Sud.
Overleaf: Lac Blanc in the Aiguilles Rouges. If you follow the Lac Blanc variente (the alternative route from Tête aux Vents to La Flégère, see p154) you could stay by this beautiful lake at the perfectly-placed *Refuge du Lac Blanc*.

places, passing over rough ground. Despite this, there are plenty of home comforts on offer after a hard day's trek. The trail passes through some beautiful villages, all of which offer good-value accommodation and restaurants for tired, hungry walkers. There is also a fantastic network of mountain huts providing food and lodging in the remoter spots. While those who prefer to camp can do so at organised campsites and, occasionally, outside the refuges.

A trek along the Tour du Mont Blanc (TMB), be it the whole thing or just a few kilometres, is a wonderful way to experience the Alpine environment and is within the capabilities of any reasonably fit person. So, read on, get inspired and start trekking.

When to go

The trekking season in the Alps is short. Snow blocks the passes until at least early June and sometimes until late June. If you don't mind a bit of deep snow at altitude, June is a great month to go because you will get there before most of the other trekkers. July and August are the most popular months, the trail is at its most snow-free and the Alpine wildflowers are at their best.

(Opposite) Top: The little chapel on the edge of Ferret (see p124) in the Swiss Val Ferret. **Bottom**: Alpage de la Peule (see p122) is a working farm that offers simple demi-pension dormitory accommodation.

Above: Bivvying at Refugio Bertone above Courmayer. On this walk you can camp or bivvy or else stay in refuges and hotels for more comfort.

Above: Refugio Elisabetta (see p101), in the Vallon de la Lée Blanche, is spectacularly perched at an altitude of 2195m, one to two hours' walk from or to Col de la Seigne.

Above: Alp Bovine, (1987m, see p135) set high above the Rhone valley, is a spectacular place to stop for lunch.

September is when the first snow falls but it usually melts quite quickly. Don't discount September: it is a beautiful month and the crowds have all but disappeared. That said, be prepared for some cold nights and the possibility of winter weather. Most mountain refuges open in mid-June but some not until the end of the month so be sure to check in advance. The refuges usually stay open until mid-September. You will likely need to book a bed in advance during July and August as they tend to be full every night.

❑ **LATE SNOW PATCHES**

In June large semi-permanent snow patches can still be present on the higher passes. They are not usually difficult to cross but they can be very exposed with long drops below them. If you don't feel comfortable negotiating these wintry remnants it may be wise to walk the trail later in the summer when most of them will have melted. The earlier in the season, the more likely it is that you will have to cross some large patches of snow.

The following high passes hold snow well into the summer: Col du Bonhomme, Col de la Croix du Bonhomme, Col des Fours, Col de la Seigne, Grand Col Ferret and Fenêtre d'Arpette. You can check real time trail conditions at ⌨ www.autourdumont blanc.com and ⌨ www.valledutrail.com.

Above: The final approach over late snow patches to the Fenêtre d'Arpette (2665m, p138).

Opposite: The Mer de Glace (see p152) is the second longest glacier in the Alps but has been melting at an alarming rate owing to climate change. Signs indicate the former extent of the glacier and chart its retreat over the last couple of centuries.

NIVEAU DU GLACIER
LEVEL OF THE GLACIER
1820

WEATHER AND CLIMATE (see also pp43-6)

June to August boasts some beautiful weather. Days tend to be sunny and warm, nights cool and clear. Daytime temperatures are 20-30°C at 1000m, about 10°C lower at 2000m. Sometimes it can be uncomfortably hot at lower altitudes, making long ascents with a heavy rucksack a sweaty business. One or two wet days per week is normal but you'd be unlucky to have a completely wet holiday. The downside to warm, sunny weather in the mountains is that it invariably leads to afternoon thunderstorms. These are particularly common later in the summer. It is always a good idea to get your day's walk done by lunchtime to avoid any such storms, which at best can leave you with a pile of soggy clothing and at worst fry you alive on a ridge if a bolt of lightning scores a direct hit.

Your motto should be: be prepared for anything. On one occasion in Chamonix in mid-August I enjoyed a morning of sunshine and temperatures of 32°C followed by a night of dramatic thunderstorms and floods, finished off the following day with more wet weather, a top temperature of 14°C and snow falling down to 1700m.

For more on mountain weather and safety, see p38.

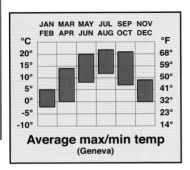

Average max/min temp
(Geneva)

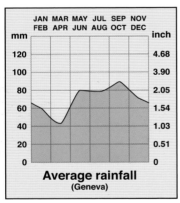

Average rainfall
(Geneva)

Photos (following pages)
● **Opposite, top:** The view east from the Fenêtre d'Arpette (2665m, see p138).
Bottom: Col du Bonhomme (2329m, see p92).
● **Overleaf, top**: The view from the Col de la Seigne (2516m, see p100), on the French-Italian border, looking over the Vallon de la Lée Blanche. **Bottom, left**: The welcoming waters of Lac de Champex (see p131). **Right**: Climbing to the Tête aux Vents above Argentière (see p150 and Map 36) is very steep and has fixed ladders in places. There's an alterative route (p153) if you don't have a head for heights.

PLANNING YOUR TREK

1

With a group or on your own?

Trekkers who walk alone will have a completely different experience to those in a group but one approach is not necessarily better than the other. If you are the gregarious type and enjoy the camaraderie that goes with a group hike in the mountains the choice is obvious and you should hook up with some friends. If you don't have any like-minded mountain-loving pals get in touch with one of the numerous commercial outfits who run guided and self-guided trips (see p18).

Some people may find that sharing a trek with a group of strangers, or even friends, detracts from the 'wilderness' experience. The great thing about walking the Tour alone is that you get the best of both worlds; you can spend most of the day trekking alone, making the most of the peace, quiet and solitude and then, in the evening, when you start to feel like a bit of a loner, you can enjoy a drink in a refuge or bar with other trekkers.

In fact the Tour is such a popular trek that if you are after some serious solitude you may be disappointed. Invariably you bump into the same people each day so, unless you are happy to be a cantankerous hermit, you may as well just talk to the blighters.

WALKING ALONE

Walking alone in the mountains is often frowned upon because it is thought to be more dangerous. Should you have an accident, who will call for help? In practice those who walk alone are far more aware of their own vulnerability and consequently they take fewer risks. People in groups often develop a false sense of security. A person is more likely to push themselves beyond their limits in a group, either for fear of letting their peers down or to try to impress them. If you want to walk alone, walk alone and don't let anyone suggest you are being irresponsible by doing so. But if you do walk alone you should bear in mind the following points:

● Let somebody know your planned route for the day
● Let somebody know your estimated arrival time at your destination

---

(Opposite) Top & middle: Maison Vieille and its cosy interior, Col Chécroui (1956m, see p104). **Bottom, left**: Suspension bridge at Glacier de Bionnassay (p81). **Right**: The chapel of Notre Dame de la Gorge (p87): the point where the road through the valley ends and the trail to the Col du Bonhomme begins.

● Be adequately equipped (see pp28-32)
● Check the weather forecast and be prepared to abandon a day's walk if it's bad
● Know what to do in the event of an accident (see pp42-3)

WITH A GROUP

The previous points apply equally to those walking with a group, be it with friends or a commercial organisation. The obvious advantages of walking with a group of friends is the chance to share a wonderful experience and get to know each other even better. Booking with a trekking agency, whether for a self-guided walk or a guided walk, is for those who want someone else to organise all the accommodation and meals. The trekking agencies listed below offer both guided and self-guided treks on the Tour du Mont Blanc. However, some companies do not cover the whole trail so check before you book.

Making a booking in the UK
● **Alpine Exploratory** (☎ 0131-247 6702, 🖳 alpineexploratory.com) Offers treks from July to mid September, staying in hotels and refuges on a half-board basis. You can walk the whole Tour over eleven days or just the southern or northern sections over four days.
● **Explore** (☎ 01252-883624, 🖳 explore.co.uk) Offers a popular eleven-day trek in groups of ten to sixteen. The price covers all accommodation and local transport and most of your food.
● **Icicle Mountaineering** (☎ 01539-442217, 🖳 icicle-mountaineering.ltd.uk) This outfit has a choice of walks aimed at different levels of fitness and stamina. Their 'Classic TMB' is not for the faint-hearted, covering every step of the Tour in just seven days. On the more leisurely 'Luxury TMB' takes ten days.
● **Macs Adventure** (☎ 0141-530 1794, 🖳 macsadventure.com) Another company that gives you a choice of styles; you can walk just a few sections of the Tour or do the whole circuit at a slow or fast pace.
● **Mountain Kingdoms** (☎ 01453-844 400, 🖳 mountainkingdoms.com) Thirteen days, taking in some of the spectacular variante routes. Unlike most trekking companies this one follows the trail in a clockwise direction. Most meals and accommodation included, as well as luggage transfer.
● **Salamander Adventures** (☎ 01273-256753, 🖳 salamanderadventures.co.uk) Nine-day fully-guided trek with a group of up to fourteen. Accommodation is included in the price as well as airport transfers and most of your food.
● **Sherpa Expeditions** (☎ 0800-008 7741, 🖳 sherpaexpeditions.co.uk) Sherpa arrange self-guided holidays on the Tour du Mont Blanc over eight or fourteen days. They also do an eight-day guided walk covering the highlights of the circuit while skipping the less inspiring sections by bus.
● **Treks and Trails** (☎ 01539-567 477, 🖳 treksandtrails.co.uk) Twelve-day guided trek including half board and packed lunches.

Making a booking in continental Europe
● **Elite Mountain Guides** (☎ +33 (0)6 38 85 20 43, 🖳 elitemountainguides .com) Guided walk of the TMB over ten days.

● **Happy Tracks** (☎ +41 (0)44 586 8754, 🖳 happytracks.net) Based in Switzerland, they offer a nine-day trek covering most of the TMB.
● **Macs Adventure** (☎ 00-353 1531 4570, 🖳 macsadventure.com) See above.

North America
● **Alpine Interface** (☎ 1-800 368 5056, 🖳 alpineinterface.com) Based in Canada, they have two TMB trekking holidays to offer; one taking eight days and the other six, neither of which covers the whole route. Both include half-board hotel accommodation and transfers to/from Geneva.
● **Explore** (☎ USA 1-800 715 1746, CAN 1-888 216 3401, 🖳 explore.com) See p18.
● **Macs Adventure** (☎ 1-844 858 5892, 🖳 macsadventure.com/us/) See p18.
● **Ryder Walker** (☎ 1-888 586 8365, 🖳 ryderwalker.com) Ten-day itinerary staying in top-end hotels.

Getting there

GETTING TO GENEVA/CHAMONIX
By air
Geneva, in Switzerland, has the most convenient airport for getting to the start of the walk. Swiss (🖳 www.swiss.com) operate daily direct flights to Geneva from many parts of the world, though not at the time of writing from Australia or New Zealand. However, connecting flights via either Asia or the USA are readily available. Most national airlines in the UK, mainland Europe, the USA and Canada operate direct daily flights to Geneva.

If you do fly from somewhere in Europe, budget airline EasyJet (🖳 www.easyjet.com) is probably the least polluting option as they tend to cram people in rather than fly half-empty planes. They fly to Geneva from 35 other cities in Europe.

❏ **Airport transfer services**
The following companies will pick you up from Geneva Airport at a pre-arranged time and drop you off at your accommodation in Les Houches or Chamonix. They will do the same (in reverse) on your return trip to the airport. Journey times are about 90 minutes from the airport to Chamonix. Fares depend on how many others are booked into the bus/taxi but they all charge similar prices (€19-40/UK£17-36/US$22-47pp one-way).

AlpyBus ☎ (UK) +44 (0)1509-213 696, (Switzerland) +41 (0) 227 232 984, 🖳 www.alpybus.com; **ChamExpress** ☎ (UK) +44 (0) 1743-817305, (France) +33 (0)4 80 96 50 08, 🖳 www.chamexpress.com; **Chamonix Cabs** ☎ +33 (0)6-79 01 46 02, 🖳 www.chamonixcabs.com; **Cham Van** ☎ (France) +33 (0)6-32 24 03 94, (UK) +44 (0) 845-154 8415 🖳 www.cham-van.com; **Geneva Chamonix Transfers** ☎ +33 970 448 699, 🖳 www.geneva-chamonix-transfers.com. **Mountain Drop-offs** ☎ +44 (0)20-7043 4874, 🖳 www.mountaindropoffs.com; **Ouibus** 🖳 www.ouibus.com.

See below for details of the bus from Geneva Airport to Chamonix or Les Houches and the box on p19 for other transfer options.

> ❏ **EU nationals**
> Remember that you need a passport to enter Switzerland.

By train

If travelling from somewhere in Europe you might want to consider the ecofriendly option of travelling overland rather than flying. Travellers **from the UK** can take one of the frequent Eurostar (🖳 eurostar.com) services from London St Pancras to Paris Gare du Nord (about 2½ hours) and then the Lyria TGV **train** from Paris Gare de Lyon to Geneva; this runs four to five times a day and takes about 3½ hours. For further information contact Voyages SNCF (🖳 uk.voyages-sncf.com/en), the European distribution channel of French railways (SNCF).

Other useful websites for finding out about rail services to Geneva (or Chamonix) from places in **mainland Europe** are those operated by the national railways: Swiss Federal Railway (🖳 sbb.ch), France's SNCF (🖳 sncf.com); Italy's Trenitalia (🖳 trenitalia.com) and Germany's Deutsche Bahn (🖳 bahn.de).

From Geneva it is best to go to Chamonix by bus rather than train as for the latter it is necessary to go first to Martigny (see below).

By coach

Eurolines (🖳 eurolines.com) serve 500 destinations in Europe, including Chamonix, so there is bound to be a way to get there from where you live. However, coach travel is the slowest option and not necessarily the cheapest.

GETTING FROM GENEVA/CHAMONIX TO LES HOUCHES

The start of the Tour du Mont Blanc is in Les Houches but Chamonix, being the hub of the valley, is a good place to head to first so that you can stock up on supplies and find your feet – which you will need on the trek!

For transfers from Geneva airport to Les Houches or Chamonix see the box on p19. You should book in advance to guarantee a seat and arrange a pick-up time. If you haven't booked a seat you might get lucky by asking them if they have space when you get to the airport terminal, though this is of course the riskier option. To reach Chamonix by train from Geneva you need to take one of the frequent services to Martigny (1½-1¾ hours) and from there change onto the Chamonix and Les Houches service (see p22). This option, however, takes longer than both the bus and the airport transfer services.

> ❏ **Marathon du Mont Blanc**
> Every year, in the last week of June, the trails around the Chamonix valley echo to the footsteps of hundreds of runners competing in one of many races. The routes vary in length from three to 80km and take place over a four day period. It is worth checking the details at 🖳 www.montblancmarathon.net if you plan to walk the Tour at this time of year, as some of the races do occupy the TMB trail, particularly around the Aiguilles Rouges and Aiguillette des Posettes regions.

Getting around

PUBLIC TRANSPORT – A SUMMARY

Public transport around the Mont Blanc massif and particularly in the Chamonix valley is excellent, which makes it quite easy to pick off a few day and weekend walks and still be able to get back to where you started (see 'Highlights – day and weekend walks', box p60).

Chamonix Valley
It's easy to get around the Chamonix valley with regular trains and buses running up and down throughout the summer. Chamonix Bus operates from the end of April to the end of December. Mont Blanc Express Train operates services linking Le Fayet in France and Martigny in Switzerland (with a change at the French–Swiss border). For a taxi call Taxi Besson +33 (0)4-50 93 62 07, ⌨ www.taxi-montblanc.com

Les Contamines
To get to Les Contamines you should catch a train to Le Fayet. From the railway station in Le Fayet a bus operates six times a day (July and August) up the valley to Les Contamines.

Chamonix to Courmayeur
If you are staying in Chamonix, the bus that runs through the Mont Blanc tunnel is useful for getting to the Italian side of the massif for some day walks. Buses operate from the end of June to the start of September (six or seven buses a day). Tickets must be bought in advance from the ticket office outside the railway station in Chamonix or at the bus station in Courmayeur.

Champex
Getting to Champex from the Chamonix valley is not as difficult as it first appears thanks to the efficient French and Swiss public transport systems. Eleven trains operate daily from Chamonix to Martigny (changing at Le Châtelard-Frontière) but be sure to catch one that corresponds with one of the 15 connecting train services from Martigny to Orsières. From Orsières a bus climbs the steep road to Champex seven times a day.

PUBLIC TRANSPORT – THE DETAILS

The frequency of buses and trains around the Mont Blanc massif varies from one area to the next. Buses and trains in the Chamonix valley are frequent and reliable while Les Chapieux to the south is a bit of a public transport black hole. Courmayeur and Chamonix are linked by a daily bus service through the Mont Blanc tunnel, which enables those staying in Chamonix to pop over (or through) to Italy for a day or two's walk.

PLANNING YOUR TREK

The Swiss segment of the walk is served by famously reliable trains and buses. Getting from Chamonix to Champex, for example, is quite straightforward by train and by bus, despite the need to change at both Martigny and Orsières. Also in Switzerland, the Val Ferret is well served by a bus that runs to the head of the valley and back from Orsières.

There are also a number of cable car and mountain railway routes which may be of use to the Mont Blanc trekker, particularly in the Chamonix valley.

The following list gives the main public transport information for road, rail and cable-car routes close to the Tour du Mont Blanc. **The details given are for summer (July and August) only**: however, some services may operate in other months as well. **The timetable information** below was correct at the time of research but is **subject to change**. For accurate times contact the relevant company or check the timetables, available at bus stations, train stations and tourist information centres, before travelling. This information should be used in conjunction with the public transport map on pp24-5.

Chamonix Bus
(France ☎ 04-50 53 05 55, 💻 www.chamonix.montblancbus.com)
A Glacier des Bossons-Chamonix–Les Praz–Argentière–Le Tour (Line 2)
Daily, every half hour.
First bus from Glacier des Bossons: 6.50am; last bus 8.20pm
First bus from Le Tour: 6.55am; last bus 8.25pm

B Les Chosalets–Argentière–Col des Montets (Line 21)
Daily 6 per day
First bus from Les Chosalets: 9.20am; last bus 5.20pm
First bus from Col des Montets: 9.32am; last bus 5.32pm

C Les Praz-Chamonix–Les Pélerins–Les Houches-Le Prarion (Line 1)
Daily, every half hour.
First bus from Les Praz: 6.42am; last bus 8.12pm
First bus from Le Prarion: 6.55am; last bus 8.25pm

Chamon'nuit (nightbus) Le Prarion-Les Houches-Chamonix-Les Praz-Argentière
end Jun-Aug, daily 4 per day
First bus from Le Prarion: 9.15pm; last bus 11.30pm
First bus from Argentière: 9.15pm; last bus 11.30pm

Mont Blanc Express Train
(☎ 02-77 23 33 30, 💻 www.mont-blanc-express.com)
D Chamonix–Les Houches–Le Fayet
Daily 15-17 per day
First train from Le Fayet: 7.05am; last train 10.06pm
First train from Chamonix: 5.14am; last train 8.14pm

E Chamonix–Argentière
Daily 18-21 per day
First train from Chamonix: 7.54am; last train 7.54pm
First train from Argentière: 6.54am; last train 7.54pm

F Chamonix–Argentière–Martigny
Daily 13 per day

First train from Chamonix: 7.54am; last train 7.54pm
First train from Martigny: 6.53am; last train 6.46pm

Region Alps Train
(Switzerland ☎ 02-77 20 47 47, ▭ www.regionalps.ch)
G Martigny–Orsières
Daily 17 per day
First train from Martigny: 6.05am; last train 11.17pm
First train from Orsières: 6.10am; last train 10.41pm

TMR Bus
(Switzerland ☎ 02-77 21 68 40, ▭ www.tmrsa.ch)
H Orsières–Champex
Daily 8-9 per day
First bus from Orsières: 6.45am; last bus 8.50pm
First bus from Champex: 6.13am; last bus 9.18pm

J Orsières–Praz de Fort–La Fouly–Ferret
Daily 10 per day
First bus from Orsières: 6.45am; last bus 8.50pm.
First bus from Ferret: 7.15am; last bus 9.17pm.

SAT Bus
(France ☎ 04-50 78 05 33, ▭ www.sat-montblanc.com)
K Chamonix–Courmayeur (via Mont Blanc tunnel)
Daily 6 per day
First bus from Chamonix: 8.30am; last bus 6pm
First bus from Courmayeur: 9am; last bus 6pm

L Le Fayet–St-Gervais-Les-Bains–Les Contamines
Mon-Sat 8 per day
First bus from Le Fayet: 8.25am; last bus 7.10pm
First bus from Les Contamines: 6.50am; last bus 7pm

M Chamonix–Geneva–Geneva Airport (operated by Ouibus)
Daily 6 per day
First bus from Chamonix: 6am; last bus 6pm
First bus from Geneva Airport: 8.45am; last bus 8.45pm

SEPP Les Houches
(France ☎ 04-50 53 22 75, ▭ www.ski-leshouches.com)
N Les Houches–Bellevue
Daily every 15 mins
First cable car from Les Houches: 7.30am; last cable car 6pm
First cable car from Bellevue: 7.30am; last cable car 6pm

Mont Blanc Natural Resort
(France ☎ 04-50 53 22 75, ▭ www.montblancnaturalresort.fr)
In addition to the standard fares Mont Blanc Natural Resort offers a **Mont Blanc Multipass** which allows access to any of their cable cars. Passes available range from the day pass (€63) up to a 21-day pass (€291). For details contact the company or visit their website.

O Le Fayet–St Gervais–Col de Voza–Bellevue–Nid d'Aigle
Tramway (mountain railway) Daily 11 per day *(cont'd on p26)*

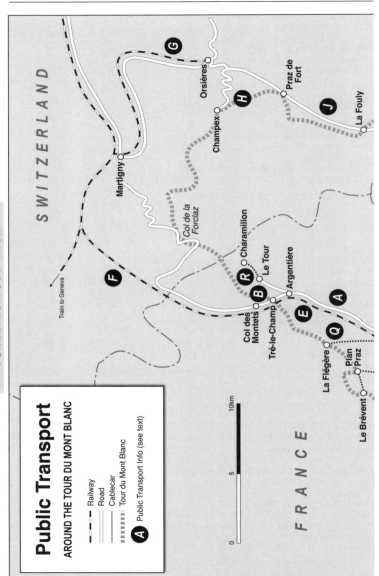

PLANNING YOUR TREK

Public Transport
AROUND THE TOUR DU MONT BLANC

- ━━━ Railway
- ──── Road
- ━━━━ Cablecar
- ▪▪▪▪ Tour du Mont Blanc
- Ⓐ Public Transport Info (see text)

0   5   10km

SWITZERLAND

FRANCE

Train to Geneva

Martigny
Orsières
Champex
Praz de Fort
La Fouly
Col de la Forclaz
Charamillon
Le Tour
Argentière
Col des Montets
Tré-le-Champ
La Flégère
Plan Praz
Le Brévent

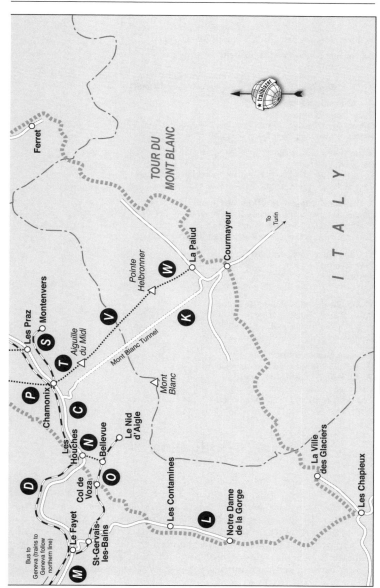

(cont'd from p23)
First train from Le Fayet: 7.20am; last train 5pm
First train from Nid d'Aigle: 8.35am; last train 6.30pm

P Chamonix–Plan Praz–Le Brévent
Daily every 15 mins
First cable car from Chamonix: 8.50am; last cable car 4pm
First cable car from Le Brévent: 9am; last cable car 4.45pm

Q Les Praz–La Flégère
Daily every 15 mins
First cable car from Les Praz: 8am; last cable car 5.15pm
First cable car from La Flégère: 8am; last cable car 5.30pm

R Le Tour–Charamillon
Daily every 15 mins
First cable car from Le Tour: 8.30am; last cable car 5.15pm
First cable car from Charamillon: 9am; last cable car 5.30pm

S Chamonix–Montenvers (Mer de Glace)
(Mountain railway) Daily every 20 to 30 mins
First train from Chamonix: 8am; last train 5pm
First train from Montenvers: 8.30am; last train 6.30pm

T Chamonix–Aiguille du Midi
Daily every 15 to 30 mins
First cable car from Chamonix: 7.10am; last cable car 4.30pm
Last cable car from Aiguille du Midi: 5.30pm

V Aiguille du Midi–Pointe Helbronner
(Mont Blanc Gondola) Daily
First gondola from Aiguille du Midi: 8am
Last gondola from Pointe Helbronner: 4pm

Skyway Monte Bianco
(Italy ☎ 01-658 9196, 🖥 www.montebianco.com)
W La Palud–Pointe Helbronner
First cable car from Pontal: 6.30am.
Last cable car from Pointe Helbronner: 4.35pm.

Budgeting

Prices in France and Italy are comparable to elsewhere in Western Europe. However, Switzerland can be a little more expensive. Your budget will depend on whether you camp, use *dortoirs* (dormitories) in refuges or have a room. Remember also to keep some cash for souvenirs, snacks and a night or two in the bar and to allow for the journey costs to and from Geneva airport/Chamonix.

Campers will find most sites charge around €10-15 (£9-13/US$12-17) per night (for a pitch plus one person). Sadly, official campsites (see p32) are few and far between and wild camping is generally frowned upon. Some refuges will allow camping outside the refuges if you ask nicely but not always. The animosity towards wild camping is particularly noticeable in Italy and Switzerland. Here you are better off sticking to official camp-sites. If you camp and cook your own food expect to need around €30-35 (£27-31/US$35-41) per day.

A bed in a dortoir costs €15-25 (UK£14-23/US$18-30) per night and a meal in a refuge costs around €15-25 (UK£14-23/US$18-30). Breakfast and packed lunch prices

❏ **Exchange rates**

	Euro	Swiss franc
Au$1	€0.63	CHF0.73
Can$1	€0.65	CHF0.76
Euro€1	–	CHF1.16
NZ$1	€0.58	CHF0.67
UK£1	€1.12	CHF1.30
US$1	€0.86	CHF0.99
CHF1	€0.86	–

For up-to-the-minute rates of exchange check 🖥 xe.com/ucc

vary wildly from refuge to refuge with the cheapest (and simplest) costing €6 (£5.40/US$7) and the priciest €12 (UK£11-US$14). If you choose to stay in dortoir accommodation most of the time and eat at the refuges you will need around €42-74 (UK£37-66/US$49-87) a day.

If you would prefer some peace get a room (*chambre*) for €20-40 (UK£18-36/US$24-48) per night. Add on the price of meals and drinks and you can count on a budget of €60-80 (UK£54-72/US$72-96) a day.

Be aware that many refuges, particularly the remote ones, do not have card machines so you will need plenty of cash to pay for a bed.

MONEY

The currency in France and Italy is the **euro** (€) which is divided into 100 cents. There are cash machines (ATMs) and banks in Chamonix, Les Contamines, Courmayeur, La Fouly, Champex and Argentière where you can withdraw money. The banks also have bureaux de change where you can exchange foreign cash for euros. Credit cards are widely accepted in most shops, restaurants and hotels and even in a few of the larger mountain huts (refuges/rifugios).

Switzerland, which the trail passes through for a few days between Grand Col de Ferret and Col de Balme, is not a member of the European Union and has a different currency, the **Swiss franc**. In practice, however, many business-es will accept euros.

PLANNING YOUR TREK

❏ **Phone and country codes** Phone numbers starting 06 and 04 are in France (+33); 01 and 03 are in Italy (+39); 026 and 027 are in Switzerland (+41)

What to take

THE PACK ON YOUR BACK

When you buy new shoes you try them out in the shop first. Do the same when buying a rucksack because you're going to be carrying the thing for 105 miles and you don't want to be cursing it when the straps start to chafe your hips and shoulders. Make sure all the straps are adjusted so that, when full, the rucksack sits comfortably. Many people forget to tighten up the hip and chest straps which can make a huge difference in the perceived weight of the burden on your back. The hip belt helps distribute the weight so that you are not carrying it all on your shoulders.

The size of rucksack depends on whether you are camping or not. Campers will need a rucksack that can accommodate all the paraphernalia that goes with outdoor living, such as a stove, cooking utensils, sleeping bag, sleeping mat and, of course, tent. A **65- to 75-litre rucksack** should do the job. The luxury of staying in places with a roof and walls is that you don't need to take all that extra kit so you should be fine with a **35-litre daypack**.

Be ruthless when deciding what to take with you: a heavy rucksack is a sure-fire way of making your trek a painful chore rather than a happy jaunt.

FOOTWEAR

Boots

Do not scrimp on footwear. This is probably the most important piece of equipment. There are two main styles of boots; **leather boots** and **fabric boots**.

Leather boots are better equipped to cope with rough terrain and sharp rocks so if you plan to go 'off-piste' in the Alps these could be the ones for you. Fabric boots, which should have a waterproof lining such as Gore-Tex, will just about cope with the Tour du Mont Blanc but be sure to get a strong pair with stiff soles because there are stretches of the route which throw up some tougher terrain, particularly on the high passes. See also p40.

Other footwear

You won't want to wear smelly, sweaty boots in the evening, so take some lightweight shoes for your après-trek moments. A pair of **sandals** or **trail shoes** will squeeze into a rucksack nicely.

Socks

Take two or three pairs of comfortable socks. A good pair will help prevent rubbing and blisters. There are all kinds on the market aimed at walkers but some of the best are the ones that have a high content of natural materials. Try socks made from merino wool which are comfortable, odourless and keep you warm when it's cold and cool when it's hot. Have you ever seen a sheep sweat or shiver?

Gaiters

These provide added protection for the lower part of your legs. They're not an essential piece of kit but if you are planning on trekking early in the summer you would be wise to take a pair because you are likely to encounter snow on the high passes and gaiters help keep the white stuff out of your boots. They are also helpful in wet grass, across boggy bits and on river crossings.

CLOTHES

Summer in the Alps is usually pretty warm and sunny but the Tour du Mont Blanc takes you high into the mountains where the weather is fickle. And when it's bad, it's really bad so **warm and waterproof clothing** is essential. Your waterproofs may sit in your rucksack for most of the trek but you will be grateful for them if the rain comes thundering down on a 2500-metre col. Good clothing is not just about comfort, it's about safety. Hypothermia is a killer and, when the temperature drops and the rain starts falling, it's a real and genuine threat so don't even think about walking in the Alps without the right kit.

Outdoor-equipment manufacturers have developed a whole range of clothing that corresponds to what they call a base layer, a mid-layer and an outer layer. Don't forget to pack some regular clothes for the evening.

Base layer

A **thermal top** that is tight-fitting and designed to wick moisture away from the skin is best; carry a spare one too. Avoid cotton garments which trap sweat and lead to shivering. Even on the coldest of days the body generates a lot of heat. Just five minutes after starting a walk most trekkers find themselves having to strip down to just the base layer. Try to avoid sweating too much because as soon as you stop walking to admire the view, damp clothes cool down very quickly. This is when it is time to put on the...

Mid-layer

A **fleecy mid-layer** will help keep the chill at bay on those cold cols. Take a spare in case the weather is harsher than expected and try to avoid getting it wet. Even if the rest of your clothing is damp with sweat at least you will have one warm and dry top to put on for those lunch breaks and photo stops.

Outer layer

Lightweight, windproof and shower-proof layers are useful in light showers but for real rain you need a real jacket. Afternoon thunderstorms are common in the Alps so even if the sky is blue in the morning you might need your jacket later in the day. Good **waterproof jackets** and **trousers** should be breathable, to allow moisture to escape, and windproof, to limit the effect of windchill on the body. An extendable hood is useful for when the rain gets really heavy.

Legwear

Thin, **lightweight trousers** that dry quickly and are not too tight are the most popular choice. Some now come with detachable calf sections, magically transforming them into a pair of shorts. Or you can just pack some **shorts**. **Thermal**

PLANNING YOUR TREK

leggings are useful for cold nights in tents and take a pair of **waterproof trousers** too. Never wear denim jeans which, once wet, take days to dry.

Headgear
A woollen **hat** should be enough to maintain a snug head. Consider taking a **balaclava** too for those really windy days and make sure your waterproof jacket has a **hood**. A **neck gaiter** or **baffle** is a good way of stopping cold draughts getting in but is not essential.

Gloves
In summer you are unlikely to need gloves other than on the highest parts of the trail. A lightweight pair of gloves will be enough. You won't need thick mitts unless you are walking outside the main summer season.

TOILETRIES

The essentials are all that are needed: **soap** (but don't use soap in mountain streams), **toothbrush** and **toothpaste**. Also worth considering are the following: a **razor**, **deodorant**, **shampoo** and **tampons/sanitary towels**. If you are spending any amount of time sleeping out rough you will also need to pack **toilet paper** and a **lighter** to burn it, but see pp71-2.

FIRST-AID KIT

A first-aid kit is one of those things that sits in a rucksack and, hopefully, collects dust. Never be tempted to do away with it on the grounds that it never gets used. It's there for an obvious reason. A trekker's first-aid kit should include **plasters**, **painkillers**, **sterile dressings**, **antiseptic wipes** and **antiseptic cream**, **porous adhesive tape**, **safety pins**, **tweezers**, **scissors** and a **blister kit**. The best blister kits are **Moleskin**, **Compeed** and **Second Skin**. Use them to prevent – rather than cure – blisters (see also p40) by putting one on at the first sign of any tenderness on the foot. Take a high-factor **suncream** (see p45) and **after-sun moisturiser** too, especially if you are not used to the prolonged exposure to the sun that comes with long days spent trekking in the mountains.

WATER BOTTLE

You will need a bottle that holds at least a litre, but preferably more. Even better are those plastic water **pouches** that hold two to four litres, fit snugly into a rucksack and come complete with a drinking tube that puts an end to rummaging for a bottle that has fallen to the bottom of the rucksack.

HARDWARE

Although navigation on the Tour is very easy thanks to the well-trodden trail and good signposting, it won't do any harm to pack a **compass**, especially if you plan to go off the route at all. A **GPS** device is also an excellent navigational tool but back it up with a compass in case the batteries die. Two good 1:25,000 **maps** cover the route (see p173). A **whistle** is a good way of summoning help (six blasts repeated at one-minute intervals is the international distress signal) as is a **headtorch** which also helps in navigating off the slopes after dark should a walk take longer than expected. A **bivvy bag** is a useful refuge, whether planned or unplanned, while **plastic bags** are worth having for taking out rubbish or keeping clothes dry. A **mobile phone** is useful but be aware that sometimes there is no signal in the mountains.

Trekking poles have become increasingly popular and while they may appear to be an unnecessary fashion item to some, there is no doubting that they do help ease the strain on over-worked knees and make carrying a heavy rucksack much easier. They are also useful for river crossings and even as an impromptu monopod for a camera.

Other items to consider include **sunglasses** (essential when snow is on the ground), a **penknife**, **flask** for hot drinks, **binoculars**, **notebook**, **camera** and **tripod** (see p179), a **watch** with **alarm** and a good **book** to pass the time on bus and train journeys. An **altimeter** is a good way of judging how much ascent is left to the next col and can aid navigation in poor visibility: Suunto and Silva both produce fancy watches that come with an altimeter. Some also include a **barometer** (for predicting what the overall weather is doing) and even an **anemometer** for measuring wind speed and windchill temperatures.

SLEEPING KIT

Refuges, particularly the *dortoir* accommodation, do not usually provide bedding so if you plan to stay in a *dortoir*, or if you plan to camp, you will need a good two-season **sleeping bag**. Campers will also need a **sleeping mat** or **inflatable mattress**. This is not just for comfort; it offers insulation from the cold ground. Inflatable mattresses, such as the ever-popular Thermarest, are much more comfortable than foam mats.

CAMPING GEAR

A lightweight dome or ridge **tent** is fine. In addition to sleeping kit (see above) campers will also need a **mug**, a couple of **cooking pots** with lids, **pan handle**, **spoon**, maybe a **scrubbing brush** and a **stove** and **fuel**. The very popular MSR stoves, which boil water in seconds, run best on petrol while the much slower Trangia stoves run on methylated spirits. These fuels are available in Chamonix and Courmayeur as are gas canisters for gas-based stoves.

BIVVY GEAR

Bivvy bags come in all shapes and sizes and some include a hoop over the head that offers a little more space than the simple 'sack' design. Make sure the bivvy bag is waterproof and breathable and ensure you have a good two-season **sleeping bag** and a **sleeping mat**. This can make for a surprisingly comfortable night's sleep if the weather is in your favour.

Waterproof, breathable bivvy bags cost around £150/US$300/€190 but are hardwearing and extremely light, making them a good alternative to a tent. As well as the bivvy bag you will need the same kit as you would for camping (except the tent of course). For more on bivvying see below.

Accommodation

At no point does the Tour stray far from accommodation but with the popularity of the route it is still wise to book a bed in advance. Booking a day or two ahead may be enough but in August it might be better to book further ahead.

All the accommodation that is available within striking distance of the trail is listed within the route guide (see Part 5). In the case of Chamonix, Les Contamines, Courmayeur and Champex there is too great a number of accommodation options for every one to be listed in this book so a selection has been offered instead.

CAMPING

Camping is a great way to immerse yourself in the outdoors. Rather than coop yourself up in a smelly dormitory with scores of others you can enjoy the night sky and the stars all to yourself.

There are campsites in Chamonix, Les Houches, near Les Contamines, at Les Chapieux, in the Val Veni (near Rifugio Monte Bianco), La Fouly, Champex, Col de la Forclaz, Le Peuty and Les Frasserands (near Tré le Champ). There are also simple permitted bivouac sites at La Rollaz and Le Balme.

Sadly, wild camping (see p72) is frowned upon and for much of the route is illegal. It is a much-flouted law and some people have had success in persuading the guardians of mountain huts (refuges/rifugios) to allow them to camp within the vicinity of the hut. If you do wild camp, be sure to leave no trace of your having been there to minimise your impact on the environment.

Be warned, however, that the police do check for illegal campers and will fine offenders. It is a shame that well-meaning campers are made to feel they are doing something wrong when camping is such a harmless activity if carried out in a responsible way; but that, unfortunately, is the reality of camping on the Tour.

BIVVYING

Another option is to bivvy. This is an even better way to feel part of the great

---

❏ **Mobile phone and wi-fi coverage**
Mobile phone coverage is patchy throughout the walk. The best signal tends to be in the larger towns and villages and on high, exposed ground. But it's best not to rely on a mobile phone on the TMB. Free wi-fi is generally available in most accommodation, although some refuges have limited access to it. Restaurants and bars in Chamonix and Courmayeur usually have free wi-fi as do tourist information centres.

❏ List of mountain refuges

Name	Map	Name	Map
Refuge du Fioux	2	Alpage de la Peule	24
Auberge de Bionnassay	2	Hôtel Col de la Fenêtre	24
Refuge de Miage	2b	Cabane Gîte de la Léchère	24
Auberge du Truc	2b	Le Dolent Gîte d'Étape	25
Chalet des Contamines	5	Auberge des Glaciers	25
Gîte d'étape du Pontet	5	Hôtel Edelweiss	25
Chalet Refuge Nant Borrant	6	Le Plein Air, Champex	29
Chalet la Balme	7	Gîte Bon Abri	29
Ref de la Croix du Bonhomme	8	Relais d'Arpette	29
Auberge de la Nova	9	Alp Bovine	31
Refuge des Mottets	11	Hôtel Col de la Forclaz	32
Rifugio Elisabetta	13	Refuge du Peuty	32
Cabane du Combal	14	Refuge Les Grands	33
Maison Vieille	16	Refuge du Col de Balme	34
Rifugio du Randonneur	16	L'Olympique Hôtel	35
Rifugio Monte Bianco	16a	Les Écuries de Charamillon	35
Rifugio Bertone	18	Auberge de La Boerne	36
Rifugio Bonatti	21	Refuge du Lac Blanc	37
Chalet Val Ferret	22	Refuge de la Flégère	38
Rifugio Elena	22	Refuge de Bellachat	40

outdoors. You can get away with sleeping in a Gore-Tex bivvy bag in the rain but it's not as much fun. The advantages of sleeping in such a minimalist way, aside from the obvious delight of sleeping rough beneath the stars and the night breeze, is that you don't have to carry as much as you would if you were camping and you can sleep just about anywhere; see also p72.

Bivvying in the Alps is a wonderful way of immersing yourself in this magnificent environment if the weather is good but consider staying in a refuge if a thunderstorm is forecast.

MOUNTAIN HUTS

Mountain huts, known as *refuges* in France and Switzerland and *rifugios* in Italy (and referred to as such in this guide), have been part of the mountain landscape of the Alps for a long time. They are popular places to stay, offering accommodation, sumptuous meals (see box p39 about Alpine food) – and sometimes a bar – in very remote and wild spots.

In a refuge there is the choice of a *chambre* (private room), usually a twin or double though singles are sometimes available for a supplement of around €10-15, or a *dortoir* (dormitory); the latter are cramped but far cheaper than a room. You can also choose to opt for bed only or for *demi-pension* (half board) which is usually worth plumping for since the meals are invariably excellent and very filling – just what you need after (and indeed before) a day's trek in the mountains.

(cont'd on p36)

Place name Places/distances in brackets refer to *variante* paths	Distance from previous place approx miles/km	ATM/ Bank	Post Office	**TOWN AND** Tourist Information Centre (TIC)
Les Houches		✔	✔	✔
Col de Voza	3/5			
(Chalets de Miage)	(4/6)			
(Auberge du Truc)	(1/1½)			
(Les Contamines)	(2/3½)	✔	✔	✔
Bionnassay	1/1½			
Le Champel	1½/2½			
Les Contamines	3½/5½	✔	✔	✔
Notre Dame de la Gorge	2/3			
Nant Borrant	1/1½			
Chalet la Balme	1½/2½			
Col de la Croix du Bonhomme	3/5			
(La Ville des G' via C des F)	(4/6)			
Les Chapieux	3/5			
La Ville des Glaciers	3/5			
Refuge des Mottets	1/1½			
Rifugio Elisabetta	4½/7			
Col Chécroui	6/10			
(Rifugio Monte Bianco)	(1/1½)			
(Courmayeur)	3½/5½ (3½/5½)	✔	✔	✔
(Rifugio Bonatti via Val Sapin)	(7/11)			
Rifugio Bertone	2/3½			
Rifugio Bonatti	6/10			
Val Ferret (Italy)	2½/4			
Rifugio Elena	1½/2½			
Alpage de la Peule	3/5			
Ferret	2/3½			
La Fouly	1½/2½	✔		✔
Les Arlaches	5.5 / 9			
Champex	3.5/5.5	✔	✔	✔
(Buvette du Glacier via F d'A)	(6/10)			
(Les Grands)	(1½/2½)			
(Col de Balme)	(2/3½)			
Alp Bovine	5/8			
Col de la Forclaz	3/5			
Le Peuty & Trient	1/1½			
Col de Balme	3/5			
(Le Tour)	(2/3½)			
(Tré le Champ & Les Frass'ds)	4½/7 (1½/2)			
(Argentière)	(1/1½)	✔		✔
(Col des Montets)	(½/1)			
(Lac Blanc)	(2½/4)			
La Flégère	5/8 (1½/2½)			
Le Brévent	6/10			
Refuge de Bellachat	1/1½			
Les Houches	4/6	✔	✔	✔

VILLAGE FACILITIES

Eating Place	Food Shop	Campsite	Mountain Hut	Gîte/hotel	Place name Places/distances in brackets refer to *variante* paths
✔	✔	✔		✔	Les Houches
✔				✔	Col de Voza
✔			✔		(Chalets de Miage)
			✔		(Auberge du Truc)
✔				✔	(Les Contamines)
✔				✔	Bionnassay
			✔		Le Champel
✔	✔		✔	✔	Les Contamines
✔		✔			Notre Dame de la Gorge
✔		✔	✔		Nant Borrant
✔		✔	✔		Chalet la Balme
✔			✔		Col de la Croix du B
					(Ville des G via C des F)
✔		✔		✔	Les Chapieux
					La Ville des Glaciers
✔			✔		Refuge des Mottets
✔		✔	✔		Rifugio Elisabetta
✔			✔		Col Chécroui
✔		✔(45 mins)	✔		(Rifugio Monte Bianco)
✔	✔			✔	(Courmayeur)
✔			✔		(Rifugio Bon'i via Val Sapin)
✔		✔	✔		Rifugio Bertone
✔			✔		Rifugio Bonatti
✔				✔	Val Ferret (Italy)
✔			✔		Rifugio Elena
✔			✔		Alpage de la Peule
✔			✔	✔	Ferret
✔	✔	✔		✔	La Fouly
				✔	Les Arlaches
✔	✔	✔		✔	Champex
✔					(Buvette du Glacier via F d'A)
		✔			(Les Grands)
✔			✔		(Col de Balme)
✔			✔		Alp Bovine
✔	✔	✔		✔	Col de la Forclaz
✔		✔	✔	✔	Le Peuty & Trient
✔			✔		Col de Balme
✔				✔	(Le Tour)
✔		✔	✔		(Tré le Champ & Les Frass's)
✔	✔	✔(15 mins)		✔	(Argentière)
✔					(Col des Montets)
✔			✔		(Lac Blanc)
✔			✔		La Flégère
✔					Le Brévent
✔			✔		Refuge de Bellachat
✔	✔			✔	Les Houches

PLANNING YOUR TREK

(cont'd from p33) When staying at mountain huts you should take your boots off at the door and use a pair of hut slippers, which should be provided. Book in at the reception and tell them whether you want any dinner or not. The hut custodian will tell you what time the evening meal is; it is usually a set meal at a set time for everyone. You can still book a seat for dinner even if you are camping outside.

Sleeping in a *dortoir* (dormitory) is a sociable experience in that, very often, the sleeping arrangements involve large sleeping platforms that accommodate large numbers of people. If you feel it is too early for this level of intimacy with strangers you've met on the trail opt for a *chambre*.

Most refuges will accept cash only (no cards) so be sure to have enough spare cash on you to cover accommodation costs.

GÎTES D'ÉTAPE

These are similar to mountain huts but, unlike the huts which are usually owned and run by a wider Alpine Club, these are privately operated affairs and can be found in small villages as well as remoter spots. *Gîtes d'étape* usually offer both *dortoir* and *chambre* accommodation with an evening meal and breakfast.

HOTELS

Hotels are the most luxurious choice but many are quite affordable. If you are on a budget but can afford a night or two in a hotel, choosing one in Courmayeur as a halfway-point treat and one in Chamonix at the end is a good way to spread out the luxury. You can also stay in hotels in Les Contamines and Champex if you really want to push the boat out.

Suggested itineraries

Part of the fun of walking the Tour is in the planning; the deciding on where to stay each night and how far to walk each day. The itineraries here are just suggestions so don't feel you have to stick to them. They are designed, simply, to help you with your own plans.

The table opposite is for those wishing to camp most of the time. Note that there is a dearth of official campsites and wild camping (see p72) is not looked upon kindly by the lawmakers. This makes it difficult to spend every night under canvas (although some do manage it) so be prepared to spend the occasional night in a hut.

Camping is not for everyone, though. The table opposite is for those who wouldn't dream of sleeping outside at night and would prefer a little comfort to finish off a hard day's trek.

However you decide to break up your days, always remember what happened to the best-laid plans of mice and men.

STAYING IN CAMPSITES AND/OR MOUNTAIN HUTS

	Relaxed pace		Steady pace	
Night	Place	Distance miles/km	Place	Distance miles/km
0	Les Houches		Les Houches	
1	Les Contamines	8½/14	Les Contamines	8½/14
2	Chalet la Balme	4½/7	Les Chapieux	10½/17
3	Les Chapieux	6/10	Rifugio Elisabetta	8½/13½
4	Rifugio Elisabetta	8½/13½	Rifugio Bertone	12/19
5	Rifugio Monte Bianco	7/11½	Rifugio Elena	10/16
6	Rifugio Bertone	5½/9	La Fouly	6½/11
7	Rifugio Bonatti	6/10	Champex	9/14
8	Rifugio Elena	4/6	Le Peuty	9/14½
9	La Fouly	6½/11	Tré le Champ	7½/12
10	Champex	9/14	Les Houches	16/25
11	Col de la Forclaz	8/13		
12	Tré le Champ	8½/13½		
13	La Flégère	5/8		
14	Refuge de Bellachat	7/11		
15	Les Houches	4/6		

In many places wild camping is frowned upon or illegal. In practice you can often camp outside mountain huts but be prepared to stay indoors if asked to do so.

STAYING IN MOUNTAIN HUTS, GÎTES AND HOTELS

	Relaxed pace		Steady pace	
Night	Place	Distance miles/km	Place	Distance miles/km
0	Les Houches		Les Houches	
1	Les Contamines	8½/14	Les Contamines	8½/14
2	Col d'Croix B'homme	7½/12	Les Chapieux	10½/17
3	Refuge des Mottets	7/11½	Rifugio Elisabetta	8½/13½
4	Rifugio Elisabetta	4½/7	Courmayeur	9½/15½
5	Courmayeur	9½/15½	Rifugio Elena	12/20½
6	Rifugio Bonatti	8½/13½	La Fouly	6½/11
7	Rifugio Elena	4/6	Champex	9/14
8	La Fouly	6½/11	Le Peuty	9/14½
9	Champex	9/14	Tré le Champ	7½/12
10	Col de la Forclaz	8/13	La Flégère	5/8
11	Tré le Champ	8½/13½	Les Houches	11/17
12	La Flégère	5/8		
13	Refuge de Bellachat	7/11		
14	Les Houches	4/6		

PLANNING YOUR TREK

Mountain safety and weather

Mountains can be dangerous but not if you are aware of the hazards, are willing to prepare for them and learn how to minimise their potential to happen. Start by wearing the right clothes (see p29) and follow this up by packing the extra clothing you may need to cope with any deterioration in the weather.

The next step is to learn about the mountains. If you are already an experienced mountain traveller you probably have an almost instinctive awareness of potential dangers. It is only with experience that you learn how to place your feet to avoid spraining an ankle, which rocks look unstable and what the weather is about to do.

KNOW YOUR LIMITS

The Tour du Mont Blanc is quite a demanding trek with some significant ascents and descents. It's always a good idea to build up a bit of stamina and fitness before you leave for the Alps and, once there, take the first two or three days steadily.

Don't try to do too much each day. The first few miles of the Tour offer quite a tough introduction with over 600 metres of ascent from Les Houches to Col de Voza. If you find this exhausting, don't let it dishearten you: it does get easier once you have a couple of days' trekking behind you.

It's worth keeping the first day as short as possible because of the tough ascent to Col de Voza. For this reason, it's wise to stick to the less strenuous main route via Bionnassay unless you have already done some trekking recently, in which case the variante route should prove more rewarding.

If you want to ease yourself into the first day and avoid that punishing ascent from Les Houches to Col de Voza you can jump on the Tramway du Mont Blanc from Le Fayet (accessible by train from Les Houches) and jump off at either Col de Voza or Bellevue.

MOUNTAIN SAFETY

Equipment

Effective pieces of equipment are the ingredients for enjoying the mountains. The essentials are strong boots, clothing that can cope with the worst the weather can serve up, a comfortable rucksack or daypack and a water bottle or pouch. There is a huge market for outdoor clothing and boots, so much so that manufacturers have gone to great lengths in researching and developing the best materials for walkers' needs.

Unfortunately a lot of outdoor clothing is expensive but don't be tempted to take shortcuts. While it is not necessary to buy the priciest jacket or boots, it is important to buy the *right* equipment that will last and will keep you safe in a potentially hostile environment.

The most important consideration when browsing for clothing is to ensure you have all the correct layers: a base layer that wicks moisture away from the body, a mid-layer that traps heat effectively and an outer layer that is waterproof, windproof and breathable (enabling moisture to escape easily). The big no-no is denim jeans, which trap moisture, stick to the skin and are very slow to dry out. For more detailed advice on clothing and other equipment, see p28-32.

Food and water

Choosing the right type and quantity of food and drinking enough water are both essential for getting the most out of a day. Doing so not only maintains energy levels and keeps morale high but also helps to minimise the risk of exhaustion and other ailments such as hypothermia and fatigue which can lead to clumsiness and accidents. The body burns up a lot of calories when walking up mountains so these need replenishing. As a rule, men need between 2500 and 3000 calories per day and women between 2000 and 2500 calories, depending on how strenuous the walk is.

Eat a good breakfast. Serviced accommodation will usually offer cereals, bread and orange juice. For lunch, some high-energy food such as tuna sand-

---

❑ ALPINE FOOD

Food-loving trekkers should prepare themselves for a treat when walking the Tour. The trail passes through three countries, each with its own particular culinary specialities. The Italians, of course, are famous for their pasta and pizza dishes but the cuisine of the Aosta region is very much based on potatoes and cheese, as it is in the French and Swiss Alpine regions. Potatoes grow well in the Alpine valleys and the cattle that graze the Alpine pastures have been the source of a variety of cheeses for generations of farmers. Little has changed today and you will find plenty of traditional dishes on restaurant menus all around Mont Blanc. The Swiss have their fondue and in the Savoyarde region of France, through which the Tour passes, there are a number of traditional cheese dishes. The following dishes are some of the most ubiquitous:

● *Carbonnade* A beef stew from the Aosta Valley. Look for it on menus in Courmayeur.
● *Fondue* This famous dish originates from Switzerland but there is also a Savoyarde version which you will find throughout the French section of the Tour. Fondue consists of melted cheese in a large pot into which food is dipped. The cheese ingredients vary from region to region; in Switzerland gruyère and emmental are the chief ingredients.
● *Gnocchi* Lovely Italian potato dumplings.
● *Raclette* This is a simple dish of boiled potatoes covered in melted raclette cheese.
● *La tartiflette* A very filling and tasty meal, *la tartiflette* is made with fried bacon, onion and potatoes which is then covered in reblochon cheese and baked in an oven.
● *Montebianco* A dessert named after Mont Blanc and designed to look like a mountain covered in snow. The ingredients include chestnut puree and lots of cream!
● *Omelette à la Savoyarde* An omelette made principally with potatoes and gruyère cheese.
● *Polenta* An Italian dish based on ground corn and cooked with cheese.
● *Salami frittata* Salami and onions fried in a pan. A common *antipasto* dish from the Aosta region of Italy.
● *Salsicce e pattate* A simple Italian dish of sausage and potatoes.

❏ **Drinking water out on the trail**

You will need to drink at least two litres of water a day, and much more than that if it is hot and sunny. There are streams and rivers along the way but many of them are full of silt from melting glaciers and there is also a small risk of contracting giardia. You can usually fill your water bottle up at refuges along the way and you will also find water fountains (marked on the trail maps) in many places. The water from these is not always treated and potable but I drank from them with no ill effects. Avoid buying water in disposable plastic bottles as these have a terrible and lasting impact on the environment. One section that is particularly bereft of running water is in the Aiguilles Rouges between Col des Montets and Les Houches, so be sure to have plenty of water with you before setting off.

wiches, bananas, nuts, raisins and chocolate will keep you going, and for dinner treat yourself to a good meal with lots of carbohydrates such as pasta or rice. Restaurants and serviced accommodation in the area offer a range of meals from local specialities such as *raclette* and *fondue* (see p39) to more international flavours including spaghetti bolognese and salmon.

Trekkers lose a lot of water through sweating so drink regularly. On average the body needs around two to four litres during the course of a day. On particularly hot, sunny days this amount may need doubling. Mountain streams are generally safe to drink from and the majority of trekkers happily do so but it is important to use a little commonsense when choosing a drinking spot. Choose tributaries rather than main rivers and avoid any water source that is downstream from buildings or farmland. The nearer to the source you are, the less probability there is of something dead lying in the water upstream.

If you are not happy with drinking directly from streams (there is a very small risk of contracting giardia or finding something smelly and organic in the water after having drunk from it) fill your bottle up with tap water at the start of the day or use water purification tablets or a couple of drops of iodine.

Blisters and other foot issues

It isn't the mountains ahead to climb that wear you out; it's the pebble in your shoe.

Muhammad Ali

Blisters occur with excessive friction on vulnerable spots like the heel and the ball of the foot. The chance of a blister developing is even higher with wet feet. Prevention is definitely better than cure when it comes to blisters. Make sure boots fit well and that there is not too much slippage. Orthotic insoles such as Superfeet are a worthy investment that help stabilise the foot. They also improve overall posture and therefore minimise stress on knees and other joints.

If you feel a blister may be developing, don't ignore it, hoping it will go away. Apply a dressing before it gets nasty and it becomes too painful to walk on. Blister kits such as Second Skin and Moleskin are excellent at protecting tender spots from further abrasion. If a blister does develop, try to avoid popping or tearing it. If it does burst, apply antiseptic cream to prevent infection and then put on a dressing.

Boots must also be waterproof. Use a boot wax on leather boots. It is also best to 'break in' new boots by wearing them round the house before setting off into the mountains.

Hypothermia

Hypothermia is the cooling of the core body temperature due to exposure to the elements. It is a potentially lethal condition but is totally avoidable. The wind, cold and rain are all elements that can lead to a case of hypothermia but their potential to cool the body's core (where all the vital organs such as heart, lungs and brain are located) can be minimised by preparing for them. Make sure the clothing you have insulates well, is breathable, effective in repelling water and windproof. And remember that it is just as important to take layers off to avoid sweating too much (which can lead to cooling of the body) as it is to keep layers on when it is cold.

Other factors that can increase the chances of hypothermia include exhaustion and dehydration. Combat these by eating high-energy food, drinking regularly throughout the day and ensuring you are fit enough for the planned walk. Spending some time training before a trip is very wise.

The early signs of hypothermia to look out for in a companion include occasional shivering and complaining of feeling cold. If nothing is done about this, the condition can worsen. A person can be considered hypothermic once the shivering becomes uncontrollable. Other obvious signs that may or may not be present in an individual with hypothermia include irrational behaviour, slurring of speech, irritability, clumsiness in walking and refusing to accept that anything is wrong. If you are alone it is essential to be aware of the early signs and to act accordingly since it becomes much harder to think straight and be rational once the condition progresses.

Anyone can and must treat an individual if they appear to have hypothermia. Find the nearest shelter or use a bivvy bag and make sure there is some insulation from the ground (a rucksack for example). Replace a patient's wet clothes with dry ones and give him or her food and a hot drink. Stay close to the patient to provide additional shelter and warmth and talk constantly in comforting and encouraging tones.

It may take some time for the patient to recover a sense of normality so it is also important to make sure you and anyone else in the group is warm and dry. When you are sure it is safe to continue, descend immediately by the quickest and safest route. If it becomes obvious that to continue would be too dangerous you may need to send someone to summon help. The best way of avoiding hypothermia is to not allow it to reach such a stage.

River crossings and snow bridges

Most streams and rivers on the Tour are bridged. There are a few exceptions, notably on the approach to and descent from Col de la Seigne, on the Val Sapin Variante Route at La Trappe and between Plan de l'Au and Alp Bovine. Even where streams are bridged you may find that some of them have been damaged or washed away. This was the case for me in updating this second edition when

---

❏ **Mountain rescue**

Calling the mountain rescue service is a very expensive operation and you will be left with a hefty bill if you are not adequately insured (see p45 and p46). The mountain rescue team that operates in the Mont Blanc area is the **Peloton Gendarmerie Haute Montagne** (🖥 www.pghm-chamonix.com). Their advice for dealing with an accident is to administer first aid and, as a last resort, call them on ☎ +33(0)4-50 53 16 89. They will need to know the following:

● the precise location of the casualty (give a description or, better still, a grid reference and your estimated altitude)
● how many people are in the group
● what each member of the group is wearing
● the names of everyone in the group
● a mobile phone number if you have one

To help the rescue team locate you, you should stand with your arms held aloft in a Y-shape. If the rescue is with a helicopter make sure nothing gets blown away by the rotors and do not move until the helicopter has come to a complete standstill.

The general emergency service number in France and Italy is ☎ 112.

	France	Switzerland	Italy
Police	☎ 112	117	112
Fire brigade	☎ 112	118	112
Ambulance	☎ 112	144 (not in all areas)	112

I found the bridge gone at the stream just below Rifugio Elena. None of these crossings is difficult and in good weather you won't even get your feet wet but in bad weather they may be impassable so be prepared to change plans.

If you have to cross a deep stream or river the best technique is to face upstream and cross with the aid of a strong stick or trekking pole which increases stability. Do not cross bare-footed since your boots will help grip on slippery rocks. Move steadily across the river, ensuring that every time you place a foot down you have a firm hold. When there is more than one person, cross in groups of two or three. With two people the partner stands behind the person holding the stick and holds on, moving in time with their partner. Three people can cross in a huddle with arms around each other's backs.

Another hazard you may encounter are snow bridges across the stream gullies, particularly in June. These melt gradually from the underside until they collapse. It is hard to judge which snow bridges are close to collapse so if you have to cross them proceed with caution and use a trekking pole to test stability.

DEALING WITH AN ACCIDENT

The Tour du Mont Blanc is a popular trail so finding help in the event of an accident should not be too difficult. If you or a companion has an accident, follow these steps:

● Use basic first aid to deal with any injuries but do not overstep your own knowledge or ability

● Work out your position and make a note of the grid reference on the map
● If you have a mobile phone, call for help (see box opposite)
● If you don't have a mobile phone try to attract attention by blowing a whistle, or flashing a headtorch if it's dark (six blasts or flashes repeated after a minute is the international distress call)
● In a group, leave at least one person with the casualty while others go for help. If there are two of you, you must decide if it is safe to leave the casualty alone. If you do, leave some spare warm clothing and food with the patient and remember to keep a note of the grid reference.

THE WEATHER

There is no such thing as bad weather, only bad clothing **Norwegian saying**

Along with the terrain, the weather is the most important factor affecting a trek in the mountains in terms of enjoyment, aesthetics, comfort, difficulty and, most pertinently, safety. Understanding the weather is so important and yet it is often overlooked. The weather in the valleys is usually very different from the weather at the top of a col and, more often than not, it is usually worse at the latter. However, bad weather does not necessarily mean that a day's trek has to be abandoned. While walking in extreme weather is quite foolish, walking in a bit of rain or a gusty wind can make for a most exhilarating day if you are prepared and properly clothed.

To know what weather to expect it is important to know how it works. During the summer, high-pressure systems, or anti-cyclones, usually bring settled weather, often with sunshine but not always. Low-pressure systems are bad news for the Tour du Mont Blanc trekker as these tend to bring rain, wind and thunderstorms.

Weather fronts, marking the boundary between warm and cold air masses, are usually quite benign when associated with high pressure, often leading to cloud and maybe a little light rain. Conversely, with low pressure, they are active affairs that produce prolonged precipitation. There are three types of weather front.

Cold fronts, where colder air replaces warmer air, bring intense rainfall that generally lasts for around six to twelve hours. Warm fronts, where warmer air replaces colder air, usually result in less intense rain but it lasts much longer. After the passage of a cold front the weather often turns showery but the visibility improves dramatically; a good time to enjoy wide-ranging views. Finally, occluded fronts mark the point where a warm and cold front have merged, often bringing prolonged spells of rain.

Understanding cloud

The weather, especially in the mountains, is extremely complex and difficult to forecast but there are some indicators that help us predict what is likely to happen. Reading the clouds is the best way of determining the likelihood of a breakdown in the weather. Weather fronts bring about the biggest changes and as they pass over they invariably bring precipitation.

In clear weather look out for high cirrus clouds (sometimes called mares' tails). These wispy clouds are over 10km high and signal the approach of a frontal system. In some cases a large area of high pressure may effectively block the weather front or divert it but more often than not expect the weather to deteriorate within the next 12 to 15 hours.

If the sky on the horizon looks milky and grey this is an even surer sign that the weather front is making progress as stratus clouds build up. If the cloud appears to be thicker and begins to lower to cut off the tops of the mountains precipitation is likely at any time.

After the passage of a front there is often a spell of sunshine and showers. However, in the mountains it is very hard to predict where the showers are most likely to occur. You can usually see them coming but how long they last depends on a number of factors, including wind direction and topography. As a general rule the lee sides of mountains are drier because of the rain shadow effect, in which most of the rain falls on the side of the mountain exposed to the approaching weather.

Wind

While winds do, in general, increase with altitude there are other factors to consider such as topography. Wind often gets forced through narrow passes, so a gentle breeze on the approach to a col can turn into a gale when you get there.

Once the wind speed starts gusting at around 40mph, walking becomes quite awkward. Above 50mph the wind can quite easily throw a walker from his or her feet. Add to this the risk of becoming exhausted by fighting against a strong headwind and the wisest course of action is to descend to a lower altitude.

Windchill

Everyone knows that it feels colder when the wind blows. This cooling effect caused by the wind is known as windchill. Windchill dramatically affects how cold it feels and can lead to exposure and hypothermia. For example, in winds of just 10mph a temperature of +5°C will feel more like -2°C and at speeds of 40mph it will feel more like -10°C. When you look at these figures, the case for a good windproof jacket and warm clothes becomes quite evident.

Rain, snow and ice

Just as the wind gets stronger with altitude and the temperature decreases so levels of precipitation increase. Roughly twice as much **rain** falls at 2000 metres than at 1000 metres. This is down to the cooling of moist air as it is forced over high ground, leading to condensation and eventually the formation of raindrops that can no longer be suspended in the air. Rainfall is only a problem if the clothing you have is not up to the job of repelling it. A wet walker first becomes an unhappy one and then potentially a hypothermic and dead one.

❑ **Weather forecasts**
General **weather forecasts** such as the national one at 🖳 meteofrance.com are better than nothing but you really want the mountain forecast which will give you information on freezing levels, altitudinal temperature variations, wind speeds and the likelihood of precipitation and thunderstorms. Detailed **mountain forecasts** in French and English are posted at TICs and some refuges and can be found online at 🖳 chamonix-meteo.com.

Snowfall occurs as the temperature approaches or drops below freezing point. It is unlikely to be a problem in summer although it can fall at any time of year on the high passes and is not at all uncommon in spring and autumn. When the ground temperature reaches freezing point, **ice** begins to form and any snow falling begins to settle. In such conditions it is wise to head down to a lower altitude and maybe wait a day before continuing your walk.

Snow that is already on the ground from winter snowfall can and does last on high ground well into the summer. Even in late August there will be some sizable patches on north-facing slopes above 2000 metres. Try to avoid large snow patches if you are not used to walking on them but if they are unavoidable kick some steps into them before putting all your weight upon them. The upside of so many people walking this trail is that plenty of feet have already stamped down good firm foot holes in these late snow patches, which makes crossing them much easier.

Sun and heat
Always apply **high-factor sun cream** to exposed skin when walking in the summer. The sun's rays are strong in the mountains and many people are not used to the long exposures to them that come with trekking all day.

Sunburn even occurs on cloudy days and if there is snow on the ground 99% of the sun's rays are reflected straight back from the surface directly onto vulnerable areas such as bare arms, legs, lips, ears and shaved chins.

Temperature lapse rate
As a rule of thumb the temperature drops at a rate of 1°C for every 100 to 150 metres of altitude. In one day on the Tour du Mont Blanc you may climb 1000 metres or more so while the temperature in the valley might be 25°C don't be surprised if it's a chilly 15°C at the pass.

Lightning
Summer thunderstorms are common in the Alps and they are violent. Hot weather invariably results in an afternoon or evening storm. This is not a time to be out and about and certainly not a good time to be on any exposed ridges or cols. Local weather forecasts are usually posted at refuges and will warn of

PLANNING YOUR TREK

❑ **British Mountaineering Council insurance**
For British travellers the BMC's travel insurance is a wise option because it is geared specifically to mountain travellers. It is also very good value for money and some of the cost of your insurance is invested in conservation work, access work and safety training.

Of the five options available there are two that are appropriate for those heading to the Mont Blanc massif. The **Trek** option is for those walking the Tour du Mont Blanc. The policy will cost around £42-46 for 10 to 17 days respectively. If you are not already a member of the BMC you will need to take out membership at a cost of £31.45pp.

If you plan to climb Mont Blanc you will need the **Alpine and Ski** option. The 3-day option costs £32.45. For more price options and full details on the insurance cover take a look at their website ❑ www.thebmc.co.uk.

Don't forget to pack your litter out

any storms (*orages* in French). If you don't know the forecast, keep an eye on the sky; the build up of towering anvil-headed cumulonimbus shower clouds are an obvious sign of a thunderstorm developing.

The best way to avoid a lightning strike is to stay indoors. If you do get caught out, keep well away from cols and ridges, which receive most direct strikes. Never shelter beneath trees, in caves or below cliffs, all of which act as channels for electrical currents. If a thunderstorm is building the only course of action that should be countenanced is to descend at the next safest opportunity.

Walkers who have been struck by lightning and survived report a tingling sensation prior to the strike. Should you start to get that prickling on the nape of your neck get as close to the ground as possible. Sit on your legs and tuck your head under yourself on the ground.

INSURANCE

You are strongly advised to get specialist insurance for travelling in the mountains. Mountain rescue is extremely expensive so having a tumble whilst trekking or climbing without insurance could cost you more than just an arm and a leg.

The British Mountaineering Council has an excellent range of insurance options for the adventurous traveller (see box, p45). Other insurance companies may also offer to insure you but be sure that they cover you for rescue from the mountains. Most of them specify the altitude up to which you are covered. If you are sticking to the Tour du Mont Blanc trail you will go no higher than 3000 metres. If you intend to climb Mont Blanc (4808m) you will probably need a more expensive option that covers Alpine mountaineering.

MONT BLANC

2

Flora and fauna

VEGETATION ZONES

It's not difficult to see the change in vegetation as one climbs a mountain. Down in the valley, below about 1200 metres, are the deciduous trees: **beech**, **oak** and **ash**. The Tour du Mont Blanc trekker will see little of this broad-leaved woodland, partly because most of the trail lies above its altitudinal limit and partly because much of it has been felled anyway. There are still some pockets remaining, however, particularly to the south of Les Contamines.

Above 1200 metres the forest cover is dominated by **mountain pine** and **European larch** whose thin needles are more resistant to the colder temperatures that occur at these heights. At the upper limit of this coniferous zone, around 2000 to 2200 metres, the trees are stunted and more sparsely distributed as the climate gets harsher.

Eventually, they give way to a shrub zone where **alpenrose** and ground-hugging **juniper** dominate. At altitudes of 2500 metres and higher plant life struggles to grow and the bare, frost-shattered rock is left to the **lichens**. Surprisingly, however, a few flowering plants, such as **Alpine rock jasmine** and the **glacier buttercup**, have adapted to live in this particular niche.

FLOWERING PLANTS

There are said to be 4500 species of plants in the Alps and nearly a tenth of those are endemic. This immense variety of plant life is quite evident throughout the summer when the high Alpine meadows, alive with dancing, hissing grasshoppers, burn with reds, blues and yellows.

● **Alpenrose** This native dwarf rhododendron grows between 1200 and 2200 metres and can form quite dense shrub layers. Its flimsy pink flowers are at their best in July and August. One good location for them is on the Aiguillette des Posettes, between Col de Balme and Tré le Champ and also on the high route between Rifugio Bonatti and Chalet La Ferret.
● **Alpine rock jasmine** Alpine rock jasmine is one of the few flowering plants to grow above 4000 metres. It forms small cushions of delicate white and pink flowers amongst broken rocks.

● **Alpine gentian** Of the many gentians that flourish in the Alps, this is one of the most beautiful. It has striking, deep-blue trumpet flowers.

● **Bavarian gentian** Rarer than the Alpine gentian but locally abundant in parts of the Alps, Bavarian gentian is quite distinct from the Alpine gentian in several ways: it grows closer to the ground, is smaller, grows in abundant clusters and each flower has five blue petals rather than a single trumpet. It has a wide altitudinal range from around 1600 to 3500 metres.

● **Edelweiss** The flower most commonly associated with the Alps, edelweiss is an extraordinary plant. It has very fine soft hairs on both the leaves and the petals, giving it a diffused frosted appearance. The flower heads are a pale yellow with a star-shaped corolla of pale off-white petals. It flowers from July to September at between 2000 and 3000 metres.

● **False aster** As is clearly evident from its appearance, the false aster is a member of the daisy family, with large thin white petals encircling a large yellow flower head. They are a common component in Alpine meadows and a welcome splash of emulsion amongst gaudier colours. The aster flowers from April to August up to an altitude of 2500 metres.

● **Glacier buttercup** Another flower that manages to eke out an existence above 4000 metres, the glacier buttercup has a pretty white corolla of petals emanating from a yellow flower head.

● **Glacier mouse-ear chickweed** The name of this scarce flower comes from the arrangement of the white petals around the small flower head. Each corolla is made up of five pairs of petals which are said to look like mouse ears. It flowers from July to August at between 2000 and 3000 metres.

● **Globe flower** In flower from April to July, this easily identified plant found in wet meadows and woodland is a distinctive globe-shaped yellow flower on a single stem. Present up to 2500 metres, it's said to have laxative qualities.

● **Mountain buttercup** Boasting large orange flowers on a long, single stem, the mountain buttercup prefers lower altitudes but can grow up to a height of 3000 metres. It's in flower from June to August.

● **Mountain houseleek** An unusual plant of the open mountainside, growing at an altitude of 3500 metres, the thick red stalk of the mountain houseleek rises to a cluster of star-shaped flower heads. As such it looks a bit like a vegetable – hence the name – and is in flower from June to August.

● **Mountain cornflower** Frequently found in Alpine meadows up to 2000 metres, this member of the daisy family has distinctive flowers made up of fragile purple petals arranged in a cup shape. It flowers in mid-summer.

● **Pyramidal bugle** A common flower in the valleys but only present up to an altitude of 2200 metres, the pyramidal bugle is in flower from May to September. In appearance it is a short, cone-shaped plant with purple flowers.

Alpenrose
Rhododendron ferrugineum

Western Marsh Orchid
Dactylorhiza majalis

Mountain Houseleek
Sempervivum montanum

Bird's eye Primrose
Primula farinosa

Herb-Robert
Geranium robertianum

Common Knapweed
Centauria nigra

Wild Pansy
Viola tricolor

Alpine Gentian
Gentiana alpina

Edelweiss
Leontopodium alpinum

Mountain Avens
Dryas octopetala

Germander Speedwell
Veronica chamaedrys

Spring Gentian
Gentiana verna

Globeflower
Trollius europaeus

St John's Wort
Hypericum perforatum

Meadow Clary
Salvia pratensis

Rock Jasmine
Androsace

Alpine Cinquefoil
Potentilla crantzii

Marsh Marigold
Caltha palustris

Alpine Poppy
Papaver alpinum

Common Dog Violet
Viola riviniana

Cottongrass
Eriophorum angustifolium

Tormentil
Potentilla erecta

Heather (Ling)
Calluna vulgaris

Honeysuckle
Lonicera periclymemum

Red Campion
Silene dioica

Foxglove
Digitalis purpurea

Rosebay Willowherb
Epilobium angustifolium

Rowan (tree)
Sorbus aucuparia

Alpine Rose
Rosa pendulina

Alpine Forget-me-not
Myosotis arvensis

Glacier Crowfoot/Buttercup
Ranunculus glacialis

False Aster
Aster belliastrum

Mossy Saxifrage
Saxifraga bryoides

Bellflower
Campanula persicifolia

Chamois Ragwort
Senecio doronicum

Purple Saxifrage
Saxifragia appositfolia

Top: Alpine ibex above the Glacier du Miage. **Above left**: Alpine chough searching for scraps from trekkers at the Fenêtre d'Arpette. **Right**: Alpine marmot.

MAMMALS AND REPTILES

● **Alpine marmot** If there is one mammal you are likely to see whilst walking the trail, it's the marmot. You will, at the very least, hear it. When danger approaches – and walkers are perceived as such – these rotund rodents, related to squirrels, sit up on their hind legs and whistle manically. It's an impressively loud and piercing noise which is unmistakable. Good marmot territory is on soft sloping ground with a few rocks scattered about on which they like to sit. By rodent standards they are quite big with a body over half a metre long.

Marmots are sociable animals, living in large colonies in burrows on the mountainsides. Look out for them in the Vallon de la Lée Blanche, on Mont de la Saxe near Courmayeur and in Aiguilles Rouges Natural Reserve.

● **Common lizard** With a body about the length of your index finger and a tail not much longer, this is hardly a monster reptile but they can be quite conspicuous. Look out for them basking in the sun, particularly in the mornings when they rely on energy from the sun to get them going. Rocks, stone walls and open sandy pathways are all popular sunbathing spots for a lizard.

● **Mountain hare** Rarely seen because of its excellent camouflage that hides it from predators, the mountain hare is greyish blue in summer to match the colour of the rocks but turns white in winter to match the snow. It's present above the tree line throughout the year.

● **Chamois** The chamois is like a small antelope, measuring 80cm at the shoulder. It is common throughout the Alps, particularly around the treeline at about 2000 metres. The females and young tend to hang out in small groups while the males are more solitary. Both sexes have a pair of short horns which hook backwards at the top. In summer they are a light brown colour with dark and pale markings across the face. In winter the coat becomes darker. It is not unusual to see chamois; the best place is probably in Aiguilles Rouges Natural Reserve.

● **Ibex** The ibex is something of an iconic Alpine species. Living constantly above the treeline, these beautiful animals are the very essence of the high mountain environment, appearing completely at ease traversing precipitous cliffs. Ibex are not as common as they once were so it is quite a privilege to see them – and see them you can. As with much of the wildlife described here, your best chances of spotting them are in Aiguilles Rouges Natural Reserve. I have seen scores of them browsing by the trailside at Tête aux Vents and also on Le Brévent. They are so used to trekkers walking by that they will happily watch you pass just metres away.

Both sexes have large horns but the ones belonging to the male are the most impressive. The horns are banded and you can tell the age of the beast by the number of ridges on them. Ibex are gregarious, with females and young forming small groups. The males wander alone in the mountains until August when they congregate to form large bachelor groups. Shortly after, the rut starts and the males compete for the attention of the females by fighting each other – which is when those horns come into their own.

● **Roe deer** This beautiful animal is diminutive compared to most species of deer, standing just 75cm at the shoulder. The roe deer is most active at dawn and dusk when it is more likely to venture from the dense woodland it inhabits to graze in open areas, often on the borders of woodland and pastureland or in woodland clearings and rides. Roe deer are mostly solitary but can sometimes be seen in pairs. The male has a small set of pointed antlers with two or three short tines on each. When disturbed they often bark to warn others of the approaching danger.

● **Fox** Foxes are elusive animals, probably because of the persecution they have suffered over centuries. They are usually nocturnal but it's possible to see them during the day, particularly at dawn and dusk. Forest edges are a good place to see them hunting for small mammals. They are also quite partial to a marmot or two but they're not above a spot of scavenging either. In summer, foxes have quite thin coats and appear sleek, possibly even scrawny, while their winter coats make them look fatter and furrier and, quite frankly, much more beautiful.

● **Badger** You are unlikely to see a badger. They tend to inhabit areas of woodland and farmland in equal measure. They are a rare sight at high altitude due to the lack of food and shelter. Badgers like good soft soil so are more likely to be found in the valleys. They are almost entirely nocturnal; you are most likely to see them running through the headlights whilst driving at night. Badgers live in large sociable groups in underground setts which can be well over a hundred years old. The earth, or 'spoil' at the entrances to some of their tunnels can be very large indeed, consisting of tonnes of earth excavated over the years. Although badgers do kill and eat small mammals and birds on occasion, the main bulk of their diet is made up of earthworms and, in the autumn, berries.

● **Pine marten** This sleek and athletic member of the weasel family (related to stoats, badgers and otters) is a beautiful creature equally at home on the ground or bounding through the treetops. It's about the size of a small cat but looks more like a large squirrel with a long bushy tail. Its chocolate brown coat is interrupted on the breast by a yellow bib. Despite its name pine martens can be found not only in pine forests but also in deciduous woodland and even quite open country.

● **Beech marten** Very similar to its cousin the pine marten, the beech marten differs in having a lighter coat and a white, rather than yellow, bib. It is also slightly smaller. The beech marten prefers deciduous woodland to pine forests but is also known to hole up in the roofs of houses and in outbuildings.

● **Stoat** The stoat, sometimes called ermine, is a slender little carnivore common in rocky areas where it brings up large litters of young. The stoat is much maligned because of its fondness for preying on songbirds and ground-nesting birds' eggs. It is an unfair criticism since they are just as important a part of the ecosystem as the birds on which they prey.

● **Wild boar** The wild boar is an intimidating coarse-haired pig that inhabits woodland areas in the valleys. Despite their formidable size – one metre at the shoulder – they are not often seen, preferring to hide away in dense vegetation during the day and waking at night. You are more likely to see signs of their presence in the shape of snuffle holes where they have been searching out roots and tubers.

● **Wolf** The wolf is making a remarkable comeback to large parts of Europe after a long history of persecution and extirpation. Although there has been no sighting of the wolf around the Mont Blanc massif, the growing population in the south-east of France is getting closer. A pair of wolves was spotted at Courchevel, about twenty miles south, as the crow flies, from the Tour du Mont Blanc's southern extreme.

BIRDS

● **Alpine chough** This is probably the most elegant member of the crow family with its glossy sheen, bright yellow bill and skilful flight patterns. The Alpine chough is a common sight above the tree line. Like most corvids it makes the most of filthy human habits and it's no coincidence that you'll see large flocks wherever people congregate and drop litter, such as at high-altitude refuges and cols. The refuge at Lac Blanc, in the Aiguilles Rouges, seems to be a favourite spot; scores of them gather on the rooftops and surrounding crags making this eerie place feel disturbingly like a scene from a particular Hitchcock film.

● **Raven** The raven is a huge bird with a wingspan of nearly 1.5m. It's the biggest member of the crow family and easily identified, not just by its size but by its deep guttural croak. Quite at home in the high mountains, it often nests on cliff ledges.

● **Nutcracker** The nutcracker is another member of the crow family and the most attractively patterned. Its plumage is soft brown with white spots and it has black wings and a white rump, making it quite easy to identify. It lives in open forests where it commonly perches at the tops of pine trees.

● **Black redstart** The black redstart is a pretty little bird that can be found in small flocks in the mountains, just above the tree line. The Aiguilles Rouges is a particularly good place to see them. They are almost entirely black except for a bright red rump and tail which catches the eye when the bird is in flight. The female is duller in colour.

● **Crested tit** A handsome member of the tit family, more commonly associated with northern pine forests but also present in mixed woodlands in central Europe, the crested tit is rarely seen and not present in the mountains but may be seen in forests at lower altitude.

● **Wallcreeper** A mountain specialist, present up to about 2000 metres, wallcreepers are distinctive birds with a striking plumage of grey, black and red feathers. Despite this eye-catching appearance they are seldom seen as they live in inaccessible spots on cliffs and rocky terrain where they feed on insects and moths.

● **Alpine accentor** A small bird with brown plumage, grey head, white and chestnut breast and distinctive black and white speckles on the chin, the Alpine accentor is not easily seen but they are present throughout the Alps. They tend to sing whilst perched on rocks above the tree line.

● **Alpine swift** With a wingspan of half a metre the Alpine swift is significantly bigger than the swift that visits the rest of Europe. Alpine swifts are dark brown with a white underbelly and chin. Their large pointed wings make them expert fliers.

● **Kestrel** A common falcon found throughout Europe, the kestrel is not a mountain species so the only place you are likely to see it whilst walking the Tour du Mont Blanc is in the valleys. Kestrels are brown with black primary feathers and a slate-grey head and tail. They are very skilled at hovering in the same spot, even in a strong wind, and will stoop down to pounce on voles and mice in rough grassland.

GOLDEN EAGLE

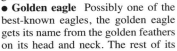

● **Golden eagle** Possibly one of the best-known eagles, the golden eagle gets its name from the golden feathers on its head and neck. The rest of its feathers are mostly brown with some white under the wings in immature birds. Golden eagles nest on cliff ledges and sometimes in tree tops. They are an impressive sight when seen soaring above the mountains. In French they are called the Aigle royale or Royal eagle.

● **Griffon vulture** This huge vulture, with a wingspan of nearly three metres, is not a common sight but you may be lucky to see one soaring on the thermals above the Val Veni in Italy. They have a wedge-shaped appearance when viewed from below.

● **Lammergeier** The lammergeier, or bearded vulture, is another huge raptor with a similar wing span to that of the griffon vulture. It's distinctive bearded appearance is only apparent if you are fortunate enough to see one up close. When seen in the sky they can be identified by their long, slender wings and long, fan-shaped tail. Lammergeier's specialise in feeding on bone marrow. They take bones from carcasses and drop them from a great height to break them open. In the early 20th century bearded vultures were persecuted to local extinction in the Alps but thanks to a reintroduction project they returned to former haunts from 1986 and there are now over 100 individuals in the Alps. I was lucky enough to see one at the Col du Bonhomme while researching this second edition.

Geology

'All the peaks are of wonderful beauty; their fretted, weather-beaten tops, like Gothic, time-worn spires, or stalactites reversed, are by no means the least delightful and striking item seen in this extraordinary journey; they are all of granite; and the incalculable number of years that have brought these mountain tops to what they are, strikes the mind with awe, and enlarges one's ideas to the verge of bewilderment as to what this earth must have gone through' **JD Gardner**, ***Ascent & Tour of Mont Blanc…***, describing Grandes Jorasses & Dent du Géant

It seems inconceivable that any mountain range is anything but a permanent fixture on the surface of the Earth. The Massif du Mont Blanc, with its black granite spires and towers, frozen under the grip of ice and snow, is no exception. But the Alps, of which the Massif du Mont Blanc is a part, is a young mountain range and it is still growing.

The story began 500 million years ago during a time that geologists call the Alpine Orogeny. During this period the African continental plate drifted northwards to collide with the Eurasian continental plate. Over millennia this grad-

View of Mont Blanc, showing the route taken by de Saussure in 1787.
(Edward Whymper, *A Guide to Chamonix and the Range of Mont Blanc*)

MONT BLANC

De Saussure descending from the Col du Géant.
(Edward Whymper, *A Guide to Chamonix and the Range of Mont Blanc*)

ual thrusting of Africa into Europe caused the disappearance of the Tethys Sea which once lay between the two continents. The sediments that had been laid down at the seabed were forced upwards and put under so much pressure that layers of rock were folded over one another.

It was about 100 million years ago that the process of mountain building began with these folds of rock forced ever higher to form not just the Alps but the Caucasus and Pyrenees too. These ranges have also been subjected to a series of ice ages. The most recent of these, which ended around 10,000 years ago, was responsible for much of the present mountain architecture: the valleys, arêtes and shattered peaks. The glaciers which still fill the high cirques and deep valleys are remnants of a once much greater and thicker ice sheet.

This dynamic landscape of granite, gneiss and schist is evidently far from permanent; its present-day appearance is a result of 500 million years of mountain building and the effects of ice ages. And the story hasn't finished; the Alps are still rising by a millimetre a year and while the glaciers may be retreating for now, who knows when the next ice age will come?

MONT BLANC

History

HISTORY OF THE TOUR DU MONT BLANC

'I heard nothing but the sounds of avalanches...this conversation of nature in the highest Alps ...impresses the mind with a terrible sublimity; for all else is icy stillness'
JD Gardner *Ascent and Tour of Mont Blanc ...* 1851

It wasn't until 1952 that the Tour du Mont Blanc was officially inaugurated as a *'grande-randonnée'* and the route waymarked but the history of the trail stretches back to 1758. It was in that year that Professor Horace-Bénédict de Saussure made the first full circuit of the Massif du Mont Blanc. His inspiration was not solely recreational: de Saussure was a scientist and a man driven by the allure of Mont Blanc so he used the journey to take notes on the botany and geology and, most importantly to him, to look for a potential route to the summit of the mountain (see 'History of mountaineering on Mont Blanc', p57).

De Saussure was not the only man who had been bewitched by the seductive snowy dome of Mont Blanc. His contemporary, Marc-Théodore Bourrit, followed in his footsteps in 1785 and in 1847 Francis Trench made the same

Dr Janssen ascending Mont Blanc.
(Edward Whymper, *A Guide to Chamonix and the Range of Mont Blanc*)

MONT BLANC

'Coming down!'
(From *A Handbook of Mr Albert Smith's Ascent of Mont Blanc*,
illustrated by William Beverley)

journey. His journal, *A Walk Round Mont Blanc*, is one of the most detailed
early accounts of the route. In it, he reveals as much about the beauty of the
mountains as he does about his ability to 'bear fatigue' and keep pace with the
ladies. It appears that the best way to hide one's own shortcomings at the time
was to disguise them as chivalrous concern for the well-being of the women in
your party:

*'It was between three and four o'clock before we reached Chamonix, after making this
interesting expedition. Such was the spirit and capacity to bear fatigue on the part of the
ladies in our party, that as we descended, to my great surprise, the proposition was made
to undertake another excursion in the evening ... I must confess that I personally felt that a
very good day's work had been already performed, and though I was perfectly willing to
undertake an evening walk if decided upon yet, on another consideration, could not with
sincerity give every cordial encouragement to the design. For I really considered it almost
a matter of certainty that such continued exertion must be too much for any female capacity, and accordingly, when referred to, ventured to use some dissuasive argument.'*

Since Francis Trench's noble concern for the capacity of his female friends,
the popularity of the Tour du Mont Blanc has grown to such an extent that it is
widely believed to be Europe's most well-trodden long-distance trail.
Consequently, it is easy to follow with clear paths and frequent waymarking. In
contrast, any attempt to circumambulate the massif in the 19th century would
have been a much more serious undertaking. Mr J D Gardner, in his account of
his Tour du Mont Blanc in 1850, talks of making a will before his journey 'as
many do' and his list of equipment and beverages, when compared with mod-

ern technologies and isotonic drinks, gives an indication of why this may have been necessary: 'wax candle lanterns, blankets, fur-lined boots, wine with sugar, cognac and brandy'.

While the equipment may have changed in the past 150 years, the mountains have changed little. The seven valleys that surround the massif may have been more wooded at the time of de Saussure's exploration but, just like today, there would have been small farmsteads, villages and sheep grazing in the alpine pastures. Shepherds would have crossed from one valley to the next using paths over the high mountain passes. Today the paths are wider and more heavily-eroded and, of course, the signposts, waymark paint splashed on rocks, bridges, roads and high-altitude mountain refuges are thoroughly modern additions to

Monument in Chamonix to Horace Bénédict de Saussure, with Balmat beside him.
(From *A Guide to Chamonix and the Range of Mont Blanc*, Edward Whymper).

the landscape that somewhat detract from the sense of wilderness that de Saussure would have felt as he wandered the valleys.

What has not changed are the extraordinary views of ice-shattered granite spires, echoing the shape of resinous mountain pines, that drew the likes of Gardner and Trench, and de Saussure before them. These are the same views that entice somewhere between 10,000 and 20,000 trekkers a year on a pilgrimage around this massif. It's a pilgrimage to admire the beauty of these mountains and for many it's a journey of contemplation and wonder.

HISTORY OF MOUNTAINEERING ON MONT BLANC

'As long as the stomach is able to resist vomiting, and to keep its tone, a strong, healthy, well-formed person is sure to ascend, if he puts himself under the regimen of good guides'
J D Gardner *Ascent and Tour of Mont Blanc...*1851

The name of Professor Horace Bénédict de Saussure will be associated indelibly with Mont Blanc. This well-to-do fellow from Geneva was obsessed with the mountain and made several visits to the Chamonix valley in the 1760s and 1770s to study the Alpine environment and try to work out a route to the summit. De Saussure was so determined to have the mountain conquered that if he

MONT BLANC

was not to be the one to do so, someone else should, so in 1760 he offered a reward to the first man to achieve the feat.

A number of half-hearted attempts on the mountain were made by the people who lived in the Chamonix valley. Most were poor farmers and cheese makers and had little interest in climbing the mountain until de Saussure's money was put on the table. So it was not until 1775 that any serious effort was made. In that year, on 14 July, Jean Nicolas Couteran, accompanied by François Paccard, Dr Michel Paccard and Victor Tissai, made a valiant effort, gaining the summit of the Dôme du Gouter – at 4303 metres, just 506 metres and about a mile short of the summit.

In 1783 another Mont Blanc fanatic, Marc-Théodore Bourrit, made an attempt on the mountain. Bourrit was a well-known Geneva socialite who had a genuine passion for the Alps which he explored and painted. His chief motivation for climbing Mont Blanc, however, appears to have been egotistical and competitive. While Bourrit certainly had a passion for the mountains, he did not have the physical or mental capability to endure a serious attempt on the high summits. In his book *Killing Dragons*, Fergus Fleming notes how Bourrit's repeated efforts to climb in the Alps were 'thwarted by three debilitations: he dreaded cold, he disliked rain and he suffered from vertigo'. Nevertheless Bourrit was talented when it came to self-glorification, praising himself for his noble assault, with Dr Michel Paccard, on Mont Blanc in 1783.

Dr Michel Paccard, however, found Bourrit to be nothing more than a coward who painted himself as a dashing hero of the mountains. While Bourrit wrote of their valiant travails on the mountain, Dr Paccard merely commented on how Bourrit 'did not dare go on the ice'. Unsurprisingly, Dr Paccard never climbed again with Bourrit. That's not to say that he never climbed again, however. Indeed, in 1786 Paccard decided to have another shot. He hired a porter, Jacques Balmat, to help him carry his food and equipment and, on 8 August 1786 at 6.23pm, the two men became the first to reach the summit of Mont Blanc, using what is now known as the Grands Mulets route (see p165).

The ascent was witnessed by Baron Adolf Traugott von Gersdorf who watched through his telescope as the men scaled the mountain. The day after the summiteers' successful climb he interviewed Paccard. This written account of what he saw remains an invaluable record of that day:

'He had a very extensive all round view [from the summit] *and parts were only occasionally concealed by deep clouds. The Herr Doctor lost his hat above. He tied a red handkerchief to a stick and planted it on the summit and we saw it both yesterday and today.'*
From Brown and de Beer, ***The First Ascent of Mont Blanc***, 1957

While von Gersdorf had the greatest admiration for Paccard, the hero of Mont Blanc was not without his detractors. Indeed, Marc-Théodore Bourrit, his climbing companion on that previous expedition, was more than a detractor of Paccard, he was a rival; and as such he found it hard to accept he had been beaten to the summit.

Bourrit wrote his own account of the first ascent in which he not only belittled the achievement but went so far as to doubt the account that Paccard had given to von Gersdorf, suggesting that it was the porter Balmat who had reached the summit first. In Bourrit's account there is no mistaking his contempt for Paccard:

'Dr Paccard begins to be breathless; his knees stiffen and the cold makes him stop: his companion, braver and more inured, encourages him ... Balmat, resolute to make certain [of the summit] *goes on alone; the difficulties lessen as he ascends; the snow is firm, and but a few steps remain to be taken to the summit of Mont Blanc: he reaches it. What joy, what triumph, what a reward for his labours! All nature is at his feet; all that is strangest before his eyes; he shouts his triumph to his companion: he does more, he descends to him, he rouses him, he helps him, and at thirty minutes past six they find themselves together on the famous Mont Blanc, at a height of 2,426 fathoms above the sea.'*
Brown and de Beer, ***The First Ascent of Mont Blanc***

The truth is that Paccard reached the summit without assistance from his porter. Indeed, Balmat is said to have talked of having 'to run to reach the summit nearly at the same time as Dr Paccard'.

In their book *The First Ascent of Mont Blanc*, the authors try to put the record straight, commenting that 'Bourrit makes Balmat the sole hero of the great adventure; but the story – that Dr Paccard collapsed, that Balmat reached the summit first and alone, and that he then helped the doctor to reach it late – is a lie without excuse or foundation.'

Despite its falsehood, Bourrit's brutal assessment of the day's events became so well known that it has become part of history. So much so that the statue that stands in the centre of Chamonix shows not Paccard but Balmat looking up at Mont Blanc with de Saussure, the man who offered the reward to the first summiteers and the man who made the third successful attempt on the mountain together with Balmat. A statue of Paccard, sitting alone and looking nowhere in particular, sits just down the road.

❏ **Ultra trail**

It takes about a week and a half to complete the 168km of length and 10,000m of ascent that constitute the Tour du Mont Blanc – unless you are a competitor in the Ultra Trail, an annual race around the massif, in which case it should take less than 46.5 hours. The Ultra Trail is one of a number of endurance marathons held in mountainous regions around the world. In truth, the route laid out for these athletes varies slightly from the trekkers' route described in this book. There are two alternatives to choose from. The first is the 'Full Tour' which starts and finishes in Chamonix and measures 163km with a combined ascent of 8900 metres. There's a time limit of an astonishing 46.5 hours with many competitors completing the circuit in under 24 hours. If that seems a little excessive the 'easier' option is the CCC (Courmayeur–Champex–Chamonix) event which is a mere 86km with 5000 metres of ascent and a time limit of just 24 hours.

So when you find yourself on that final stretch of the Tour du Mont Blanc, and you have nine or ten days' of trekking behind you, spare a thought for the guys and gals who ran the same route in under 24 hours.

The Ultra Trail takes place in the last week of August and causes little disruption to the more leisurely TMB trekker, not least because it's all over with so quickly. See 🖳 www.utmbmontblanc.com

MONT BLANC

❏ HIGHLIGHTS – DAY AND WEEKEND WALKS

Not everyone has the time or inclination to walk the whole trail so here are some day/weekend walks that take in some of the highlights. Access to the start and end of the walks is usually possible by public transport.

Les Houches to Les Contamines via Col de Tricot (see pp74-86)
This is the start of the trail and a fantastic introduction to the Alpine environment taking in a glacier, a high col, beautiful cattle pasture and a cool forest on the descent to Les Contamines. When you reach the town you can treat yourself to a good meal and a night in a hotel before catching the bus to Le Fayet and, from there, the train back to Les Houches.

At the start of the walk you can miss out the tough ascent to the Col de Voza either by hopping on the Les Houches to Bellevue cable car or by making use of the mountain railway from Le Fayet or St Gervais to Col de Voza or Bellevue.

Val Sapin and Mont de la Saxe
This is simply the best circular day walk on the Tour. From Courmayeur follow the *Variante Route* up the Val Sapin to Col Sapin (see pp115-6) and then follow the main trail (in the opposite direction to the route described on pp113-5) over the Tête de la Tranche and along the wide grassy ridge of Mont de la Saxe before descending via Rifugio Bertone back to Courmayeur.

This is wonderful walking country; the first half of the day is spent in the cool forest and wildflower meadows of the Val Sapin and is followed in the afternoon by a magnificent trek along Mont de la Saxe which offers unsurpassed views of the Grandes Jorasses and Mont Blanc. Sensational stuff.

Fenêtre d'Arpette and Alp Bovine
This two-day excursion begins and ends in Champex in Switzerland. Whether you go anti-clockwise or clockwise depends on a couple of things: fitness and weather. If you have just arrived in the Alps and want to ease yourself in, go anti-clockwise because the first day is less strenuous. Likewise, if the weather is bad on the first day, go anti-clockwise and pray the weather improves for the following day when the 2665m Fenêtre d'Arpette must be negotiated.

The anti-clockwise approach follows the 'Champex to Col de la Forclaz via Alp Bovine' route described on pp133-5. This follows a mostly level path through some gorgeous larch and pine forests, topped off by far-reaching views down the Rhône valley from Alp Bovine. Spend the night at Hôtel Col de la Forclaz (or camp there) and return to Champex via the Fenêtre d'Arpette (ie in the opposite direction to the route description on pp135-44).

The Aiguilles Rouges
The Aiguilles Rouges lends itself very well to short walks. Take a look at the IGN 1:25,000 map of the area and you will see a maze of paths crisscrossing the mountainsides. At any time you can drop back down via one of the many trails to the valley floor where you can catch the bus or train to wherever it is you are staying in the valley. The longest route begins at Col des Montets from where you can travel south along the Tour du Mont Blanc as it traverses the Grand Balcon Sud, with Mont Blanc a constant companion across the valley.

You can spend the night at the refuge at Lac Blanc or the one at La Flégère before continuing over Le Brévent to Les Houches. See p154 for a description of the route.

CHAMONIX

3

The town of Chamonix is small and, independent of its locality, would be quite devoid of interest. Its peculiar position, however, renders it one of the most interesting localities in the whole world. **Francis Trench**, *A Walk Round Mont Blanc* 1847

Chamonix has been a popular tourist resort for over a hundred years so it has plenty of experience in catering for visitors; and unlike some tourist destinations, it has just about learnt how to get it right. Certainly, some may find its unashamed drive on tourism a little off-putting but this is still a lively and friendly town with plenty of rustic tradition amongst the chintzy street cafés and knick-knack shops.

With Mont Blanc a metaphorical stone's throw away it was perhaps inevitable that Chamonix would mature from a sleepy little farming community in the 1800s into one of the world's most important mountain resorts. It is considered by many to be the birthplace of mountaineering. More recently it has opened itself up to the skiing fraternity making it a year-round destination. After the exertions of the Tour du Mont Blanc, Chamonix is a wonderful antidote to roughing it. Let yourself be a tourist and wander the streets, have plenty of long lunches at pavement cafés and enjoy the bustle of life passing by.

Of the sights to see around town one of the most interesting is the **Musée Alpin** (☎ 04-50 53 25 93; daily 2-6pm (closed Tue) plus 10am-noon in school holidays; Jul-Aug 10am-1pm, 2-7pm; €5.90), a good place to while away a rainy afternoon. It specialises in the history of mountaineering and skiing in the region. There are some interesting old paintings of the surrounding area from when Chamonix was just a tiny village and the glaciers used to spill into the main valley. The highlights, however, are the old wooden bobsleigh from the 1924 Winter Olympics and examples of early ice axes and crampons from the late 18th century.

Out on the bridge by Place Balmat is the famous **Monument Saussure** depicting Jacques Balmat pointing out a route up Mont Blanc to Horace-Bénédict de Saussure, alpine climber, Mont Blanc obsessive and widely presumed founder of alpinism. De Saussure offered a reward to the first person to conquer the mountain. On 8 August 1786 Jacques Balmat and Michel-Gabriel Paccard achieved just that, with de Saussure following in their footsteps a year later (see pp57-9).

CHAMONIX

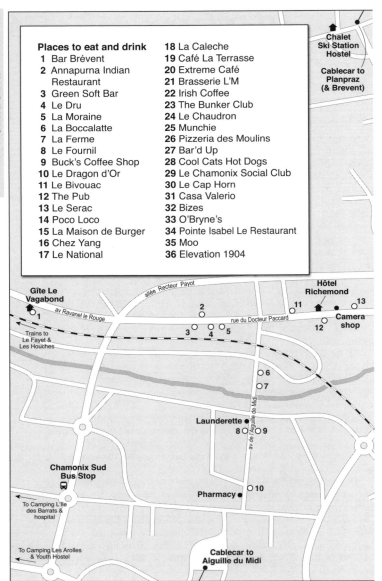

Places to eat and drink
1 Bar Brévent
2 Annapurna Indian Restaurant
3 Green Soft Bar
4 Le Dru
5 La Moraine
6 La Boccalatte
7 La Ferme
8 Le Fournil
9 Buck's Coffee Shop
10 Le Dragon d'Or
11 Le Bivouac
12 The Pub
13 Le Serac
14 Poco Loco
15 La Maison de Burger
16 Chez Yang
17 Le National
18 La Caleche
19 Café La Terrasse
20 Extreme Café
21 Brasserie L'M
22 Irish Coffee
23 The Bunker Club
24 Le Chaudron
25 Munchie
26 Pizzeria des Moulins
27 Bar'd Up
28 Cool Cats Hot Dogs
29 Le Chamonix Social Club
30 Le Cap Horn
31 Casa Valerio
32 Bizes
33 O'Bryne's
34 Pointe Isabel Le Restaurant
35 Moo
36 Elevation 1904

Chalet Ski Station Hostel

Cablecar to Planpraz (& Brevent)

Gîte Le Vagabond

av Ravanel le Rouge

allée Recteur Payot

Hôtel Richemond

Camera shop

rue du Docteur Paccard

Trains to Le Fayet & Les Houches

Launderette

av de l'Aiguille de Midi

Chamonix Sud Bus Stop

To Camping L'Ile des Barrats & hospital

Pharmacy

To Camping Les Arolles & Youth Hostel

Cablecar to Aiguille du Midi

CHAMONIX

Chamonix

0   50   100   150m

Tourist
Information
ⓘ

Toilets
☒

Chamonix
Centre
Bus Stop

Snell Sports
€ ATM

Maison de
la Presse

Grand Hôtel
des Alpes

Hôtel
Gourmets
et Italy

La Mollard

Maison
de la
Montagne
✝

Hôtel Le
Chamonix ♠

Bakery

Cinema

18

14 15 16 17

31

Pharmacy

Hôtel ♠
Croix Blanche

Supermarket

ATM €
place
Balmat

O 20

O 19

32

Intersport

O 22

33

Pharmacy

Musée Alpin
de Chamonix
🏛

rue Whymper

21 O

Post
Office
& ATM

Club Alpin
Français

Camera
shop

Supermarket

av. Michel Croz

rue Joseph Vallot

L'Arve

26 ● 27

25
23 24
rue des Moulins
30 29

28

Bus
stop

av. du Mont Blanc

place du
Mont Blanc

Hôtel ♠
Pointe Isabelle

O 34

€ ATM

O 35

O 36

Trains to
Argentière &
Switzerland

Main
railway
station

Gare du
Montenvers

Mountain train
to Mer de Glace

CHAMONIX

SERVICES

Chamonix has almost everything you could possibly need. The helpful staff at the **tourist information centre** (☎ 04-50 53 00 24; ⌨ www.chamonix.com; July-Aug daily 9am-7pm; rest of the year daily 9am-7pm & 2-6.30pm, but closed Sunday afternoon) can give advice on everything from accommodation and transport to walking routes and wildlife.

After a week or two of sweating around the Tour a **launderette** may be a priority. There's one (daily 8am-10pm) on Avenue de l'Aiguille de Midi. The biggest centrally located **supermarket** (Mon-Sat 8am-8pm, Sun 8.30am-12.30pm) is on rue Joseph Vallot. There are also smaller ones dotted about; the one on Michel Croz is handy if you are near the railway station. For the best fresh bread and pastries hunt down the **boulangerie** (bakery), not far from the tourist office on Place de l'Eglise.

There are two **pharmacies** on rue Joseph Vallot, both of which should be able to offer remedies for blisters, sunburn and other minor ailments. There is another pharmacy on Avenue de l'Aiguille de Midi. For more serious problems contact the **hospital** on ☎ 04-50 53 84 00, or one of the local **doctors** (the tourist information centre can provide a list).

There is a plethora of outdoor equipment stores where you can get last-minute **trekking supplies** (or replace what you've worn out on the trail!). Most central are Intersport, which has a good choice of equipment from boots and clothing to trekking poles, and the enormous Snell Sports on rue du Docteur Paccard. For photographic equipment try the **camera shop** on rue du Docteur Paccard or Photo Tairraz on avenue Michel Croz. Both sell SD cards, batteries and even old-school rolls of film. Also on rue du Docteur Paccard is an excellent **bookshop**, La Maison de la Presse, which stocks some English-language books.

Free **wi-fi** is available at most restaurants and bars and the tourist information centre. The **post office** (Mon-Fri 9am-noon and 2-5pm, Sat 9am-noon) is on Place Balmat.

The mountain **weather forecast** is posted in the window of **Club Alpin Français,** 136 Avenue Michel Croz, (Tue-Sat 4-6.45pm). This is also where you will find information on climbing and walking in the region along with details about mountain refuges. The **cinema** on rue du Docteur Paccard occasionally shows undubbed English-language films. Check the listings outside the door.

WHERE TO STAY

Unless you are camping it is imperative that you book well in advance if you are in Chamonix in the summer months (July and August).

The best **campsites** are out of town in Argentière (see p148) and Les Houches (see p74) which is right at the start of the Tour. There are sites closer to Chamonix if you can't be bothered with the bus ride. Down the valley from the centre is *Camping Les Arolles* (☎ 04-50 53 14 30, ⌨ www.lesarolles.com; mid-June to end Sep; 30 spaces) where a pitch costs €4 plus €6.40 per person. Closer to the river and a little more peaceful is **Camping L'Ile des Barrats** (☎ 04-50 53 51 44, 🖳 www.campingdesbarrats.com; Jun-mid Sep; 52 spaces), which has fantastic views of Mont Blanc and the Aiguilles Rouges. Prices here are €13.65pp. There is also a handful of campsites in Les Praz de Chamonix, one train stop away to the north.

Chamonix Mont Blanc Youth Hostel (☎ 04-50 53 14 52, 🖳 www.hifrance.org; mid-May to Sep; 120 beds; from €42pp inc breakfast) is a mile south of town at Les Pèlerins. It's a 20-minute walk or you can catch one of the seven daily buses or the more frequent train. If you have a lot of luggage, take the bus as it drops you almost at the door, while the train itself goes only as near as the village of Les Pèlerins from where it is a steep climb to the hostel. The hostel is big and a little soulless. In summer it is often crowded with school groups. Dormitories usually comprise a couple of bunks and a wash basin. There's a TV room, games room and a large dining area where you can get breakfast. There may be a lack of atmosphere but it does offer good value for money.

There are a couple of independent hostels closer to the centre. At the top of the steep La Mollard road is **Chalet Ski Station** (☎ 04-50 53 20 25, 🖳 www.hostel-skistation-chamonix.com; 45 beds; dortoir €18pp), managed by a delightful woman who set the place up while still a student. It's a very laid-back, no-frills hostel; don't expect luxury but do expect to be made welcome. The alternative is **Gîte Le Vagabond** (☎ 04-50 53 15 43, 🖳 www.gite-vagabond.com), an expats' retreat on ave Ravanel le Rouge, complete with late-night bar. Beds cost €21.36pp dortoir (€28.18pp demi-pension), €50.45 (dbl) demi-pension and €43.12 (sgl) demi-pension.

In the town centre there are countless affordable hotels. **Hôtel Le Chamonix** (☎ 04-50 53 11 07, 🖳 www.hotel-le-chamonix.com; 16 rooms) is one of the cheapest and most homely. You'll find it on a quiet street right in the centre, close to the tourist office. Prices range from €40-61pp; breakfast is €8.

Just a short stroll from the railway station is the **Hôtel Pointe Isabelle** (☎ 04-50 53 12 87, 🖳 www.pointeisabelle.com; 45 rooms) with balconies looking onto the busy street. The tariff is €70-94pp with breakfast an extra €13. The hotel's biggest attraction is their restaurant where you can get a filling lunch or dinner (see p66).

The large **Hôtel Croix Blanche** (☎ 04-50 53 00 11; 35 rooms) has rooms looking over the hustle and bustle of the town-centre plazas. Prices are from €50-75pp; breakfast is €12. **Hôtel Gourmets et Italy** (☎ 04-50 53 01 38; 🖳 www.hotelgourmets-chamonix.com), perched on the riverbank, is close to the town centre yet away from much of the noise associated with it. All rooms are en suite with prices at €45-85pp (from €73pp sgl occ); breakfast is an extra €14.50. The traditional **Hôtel Richemond** (☎ 04-50 53 08 85, 🖳 www.richemond.fr; 53 rooms) is a substantial hotel in a quiet location a few minutes' walk from the town centre. The tariff ranges from €45-75pp (€59.60 sgl occ); breakfast is €9.50.

Finally, if you have money to burn look no further than **Grand Hôtel des**

Alpes (☎ 04-50 53 37 80, 🖥 www.grandhoteldesalpes.com; 30 rooms) offering four-star opulence from €88-210pp. Breakfast is €20. It has everything you might expect from such an establishment including an indoor swimming pool, jacuzzi and a private garden.

WHERE TO EAT AND DRINK

Almost every building in the centre appears to offer food and drink. Most of it is of excellent quality. The following are particularly noteworthy. Near the station is *Elevation 1904 Café & Bar* (☎ 04-50 53 00 52) which does some simple snacks and lunches including burgers from €6.90, sandwiches from €4.50 and paninis from €5.50. For lovely hot bagels and imaginative smoothies, teas and coffees head down the road to the *Pointe Isabelle Restaurant* (see Hôtel Pointe Isabelle in Where to Stay; daily noon-2pm & 7-10pm). There is a myriad of dishes to choose from including gnocchi and burger & fries, both for €16.50. Nearby is the contemporary bar-restaurant *Moo* (04-50 55 33 42; noon-3pm and 7-11pm) which does beef and chorizo burgers for €14.70.

An excellent spot for light lunches, and a good place for people watching, is around Place Balmat. The *Extreme Café* (☎ 04-50 21 99 45; open daily 11am-2am) has all sorts of paninis and bagels (from €3.90). They also do rather expensive, albeit refreshing, smoothies from €3.90. Next door is *Café la Terrasse* (☎ 06-18 16 87 24; 9am-6pm) a popular place for breakfast and lunch with smoked salmon for €11. They also do a full cooked breakfast for €12.

The restaurants that look onto Place de Garmisch have so much outdoor seating that they threaten to engulf the square. The ostentatious and always busy *Irish Coffee* (☎ 04-50 53 05 19; daily from 11am to late) is a large and lively street café which does traditional local fare such as escalope Savoyarde for €18 as well as not-so-local dishes including burgers for €13.90 and pizzas from €9.50. Just as bustling is *Brasserie L'M* (☎ 04-50 53 58 30); food is served noon-2pm and 7-9.30pm. Here you can enjoy trout for €26.50 or tartiflette for €7.50 on their raised deck overlooking the square.

The nearby rue des Moulins is known for its bars and late-night clubs. Many of these do cheap food through the day (see 'Nightlife' p68) and there are some good restaurants too. At the cheap end of the scale is the tiny street café *Cool Cats Hot Dogs* (☎ 06-37 81 99 72; noon-1.30am) which is popular with late-night drinkers looking for something to soak up the beer. You can get a hot dog here for €9 and a bowl of nachos for €8. They also do takeaways.

Far classier is *Munchie Restaurant* (☎ 04-50 53 45 41), a contemporary establishment specialising in sushi, with fancy dishes like duck teriyaki for €25. For a more rustic look with candlelit dinners try *Le Chaudron* (☎ 04-50 53 40 34)). The food is expensive but of high quality; the ravioli is €17.50 and the Angus steak is €33.

Opposite this is *Le Cap Horn* (☎ 04-50 21 80 80; noon-3pm and 7-10.30pm) a smart, sophisticated joint with dishes ranging in price from the sushi at €26 to the pasta at €21. Pizza lovers should be satisfied with what's on offer at *Pizzeria des Moulins* (☎ 06-70 68 99 82; noon-11pm) where prices start from €7.50. You can sit in or take away.

A good hunting ground for traditional local food is on rue du Docteur Paccard which runs into avenue Ravanel le Rouge. At the north end is *Restaurant La Calèche* (☎ 04-50 55 94 68; 🖥 www.restaurant-caleche.com; noon-11pm) where you can indulge in grilled beef for €27 and fondue for €26. It's a cavernous place decorated in a traditional style but lacks a little authenticity. Opposite is *Le National* (☎ 04-50 53 02 23) on the edge of Place Balmat, which has a huge variety of pizzas priced from €9.50-16, as well as many other dishes; the half-duck breast is €29.

Head down the street to *Le Serac* (☎ 04-28 31 69 84; noon-5.30pm and 6.30-10pm) for a Savoyarde salad with bacon, nuts and cheese (€14.90). Next is *Le Bivouac* (☎ 04-50 53 34 08), small and rustic and a good place to try fondue (€17.40-21.40) or *escalope de veau* (veal) *Savoyarde* (€23.30).

Another fondue specialist is *Le Dru* (☎ 04-50 34 10 35) which has a small outside decking area. The fondue is €15.70 but they have other dishes too, including grilled lamb for €23.40. *Green Soft Bar* (☎ 04-56 12 30 83; 8.30am-10pm) is at the southern end of rue du Docteur Paccard. They have a long list of pizzas on their menu with prices starting around €10. They also do excellent coffee.

Another street to wander down if you have a rumbling tum is Avenue de l'Aiguille de Midi. The rustic *La Boccalatte* (☎ 04-50 53 52 14) with its covered terrace is a good place for pizzas and pastas (€9.50) and local specialities such as fondue (€16.50). *La Moraine* (☎ 04-50 21 18 13; noon-11pm) with its pretty hanging baskets does local fare as well as lasagne for €16. If you need something for lunch or breakfast to take away try *Le Fournil* bakery. They do sandwiches and paninis from €6 and there is a quiet terrace around the back. Don't be misled by the name; the very hip *Buck's Coffee Shop* (☎ 04-50 53 16 04) does more than just good coffee. You can get a burger, drink and cake for under €10 as well as mini pizzas for €3.30.

There are a number of crêperies around town. Try *Poco Loco* (☎ 04-50 53 43 03; 11am-10pm) on rue du Docteur Paccard. It is a claustrophobic little place with a bar and a long narrow seating area upstairs. You can choose from a variety of fillings for your crêpe, including chocolate and maple syrup, with prices around the €3-4 mark. They also do burgers from €5. Next door is *La Maison du Burger* (☎ 04-50 53 44 10; 10am-midnight), a tiny eatery with a street terrace. The burgers cost from €6. *La Ferme* also does good crêpes from €3.80-9.20 as well as pasta dishes from €11.20. You'll find it on Avenue de l'Aiguillette de Midi.

For those with a gluten-free diet head to *Bizes* (☎ 04-51 92 25 03; noon-2.30pm and 7-10pm) a peaceful and intimate restaurant with gazpacho for €9.50 and veggie curry for €19.50.

Finally, if you'd like a taste of some cuisine from other parts of the globe you could do worse than *Casa Valerio* (☎ 04-50 55 93 40), a smart Italian joint with pizza and pasta from €13. Chinese food can be found at *Chez Yang* (☎ 04-50 53

CHAMONIX

18 35) which does chicken dishes from €15 and fish from €19. Alternatively, *Le Dragon d'Or* (☎ 04-50 53 37 25; 10am-11pm) does noodle soup with vegetables (€9.50) and fried noodles with vegetables (€7.80). If these don't appeal – yet a curry does – you'll find **Annapurna Indian Restaurant** (☎ 04-50 55 81 39), on rue du Dr Paccard, has curries from €10-17.

NIGHTLIFE

Throughout the summer the town centre street cafés are chock full throughout the day, as well as into the evening when the late night bars also open their doors. The best of these are all crammed into one tiny cobbled street: rue des Moulins.

At the far end of the street is Anglocentric *Bar'd Up* which has a small outside seating area, pool table, computer games and lots of TV screens, with one embedded in the surfboard above the bar. The surfing theme is evident throughout, as you would expect from a pub in a mountainous region 200 miles from the sea. There is another English theme pub on rue du Docteur Paccard called, imaginatively, *The Pub*. Another popular spot for English speakers is *Bar Brévent*, part of Gîte Le Vagabond, a small bar with a lively atmosphere and sport on the TV. Finally, no town would be complete without a faux-Irish pub: Chamonix's is called *O'Byrne's* (11am-2am) and you'll find it by the red telephone box.

There are two popular nightclubs on Rue des Moulins; *Le Chamonix Social Club* (5pm-2am) is where most late-night revellers start, before moving on to *The Bunker Club* (Mon-Thur 1-6am, Fri-Sat 12.30-6am) which has a bizarre 1970s Russia theme. If you pine for the days of the Cold War you will feel very at home here.

LOCAL TRANSPORT

Chamonix Bus (see p22) runs up and down the valley regularly and daily from late April to early September. A one-way ticket to anywhere is €3. From the third week of June to early September there is also a night bus (€2 per journey). It's the most convenient way of getting to Les Houches, Argentière, Le Tour and Col des Montets. The main **bus station** is in Chamonix Sud but there are several places to catch the bus; the most convenient stops for the town centre are Chamonix Centre (near the tourist information centre) and north of Place du Mont Blanc.

For the **railway station**, for trains up and down the valley between St Gervais (Le Fayet) and Argentière (and beyond to Martigny in Switzerland) head to the end of avenue Michel Croz. There is a second railway station, Gare du Montenvers, for the tourist train to the Mer de Glace (see p152 and p168). You'll find it over the bridge beyond the main railway station.

For free rides around town hop on the **Mulet minibus** (the one with a picture of a mule on it) that circulates the town throughout the day. It passes by frequently but, to be honest, most of Chamonix is easy to reach on foot.

MINIMUM IMPACT TREKKING

Landscapes as beautiful as those found on the Tour inevitably attract hordes of visitors. From skiing to paragliding, mountain biking to trekking, people have found all sorts of ways of enjoying the fresh mountain air and exploring the wild valleys and peaks. With this wonderful opportunity to discover the mountains, however, comes a responsibility to tread lightly in a fragile environment that is home to a diverse range of species and also the home and workplace of many people.

THE LURE OF THE MOUNTAINS

The Mont Blanc massif is a big old beast but even a massif nearly five kilometres high can easily be missed if you're looking at the path in front of you all the time; and if it's possible to miss a mountain it's possible to miss the wildflowers, grasshoppers, butterflies and birds. You could walk through a beautiful Alpine meadow and feel nothing, hear nothing and see nothing but the path at your feet. But lie in that meadow and you'll feel the sun on your face, hear the incessant hiss of grasshoppers and see wildflower heads dancing around you. You can get as much or as little out of the mountains as you wish but so many people walk as if hurrying to catch a bus. Perhaps you really are. But perhaps it doesn't matter if you miss it. Take time to stop, look around and enjoy the sights and sounds.

It usually takes a few days to shake off the stresses and worries of everyday life. Your first day's trekking could feel like purgatory but stick with it. After a few days you get into the rhythm of walking through the landscape to a point where the mountains feel more like home than beautiful suburbia ever could. By the end of the trek you won't want to stop. (Well, possibly you might!)

Whether you are drawn to the mountains for the views or for the opportunity to explore, one thing is certain; the mountains have an ability to humble even the greatest of egos. Feeling in awe of the landscape helps us to think more broadly about ourselves and our place within the natural world. Some might call it going back to nature or reconnecting with nature. Whatever you call it, it's a valuable mindset, particularly in an age when so many of us are virtual slaves to urban living and consumerism. Perhaps the mountains help to put our lives and the way we lead them into perspective.

Ethics

The frog does not drink up the pond in which he lives **American Indian proverb**

In the past, the talk was of conquering mountains. Today, it is about appreciating and admiring them. More and more of us recognise the short-term satisfaction that comes from our gluttonous and materialistic lifestyles. In contrast, the wild places give us something much greater and lasting. Unfortunately, we have become so disconnected from the natural world we sometimes forget that we are part of it. With our love for the mountains comes a responsibility to protect them, for their sake and for ours.

MINIMISING YOUR ENVIRONMENTAL IMPACT

Trekkers are often among the most knowledgeable when it comes to environmental issues, particularly their own impact on the immediate surroundings but, sadly, it is still all too common to see thoughtless damage to the environment, be it litter dropped on the trail, human faeces and toilet tissue stuffed under a rock, or tree branches sawn off for a campfire that never gets cleaned up. It's likely that anyone reading this book will already have an innate respect for the mountains, forests and valleys they will venture through so, at the risk of preaching to the converted or patronising an entire readership, here are some commonly held rules that will minimise your 'footprint' on the mountain environment.

Litter

Litter, which is not just unsightly but also a danger to wildlife, is easily dealt with by not dropping it in the first place. The saintly trekker will even pick up litter that others have left behind. It's worth carrying a plastic bag, stuffed in a pocket or at the top of your rucksack, for this very purpose. Picking up other people's litter is a great way of giving something back and improving the environment for those who follow behind you. It's also a great way of feeling very good about yourself. Just don't get all self-righteous about it.

Everything that is taken on an expedition into the mountains must either be eaten or taken back out. It is worth considering just how long the life cycle of litter is. Orange peel, for example, lasts for six months and, unless someone picks it up, an aluminium can will still be rotting on the ground well after the person who threw it there has completed his or her own life cycle.

Erosion

It's hard to imagine how your own two feet can make much of a difference to the topsoil of something as big as a mountain. But consider that your two feet are part of a collective of up to 50,000 feet that pound the paths of the Tour du Mont Blanc every summer and the impact that trekkers have becomes clear. Soil erosion is a serious problem because it loosens the surrounding topsoil and can cause large landslips which scar the mountainside and destroy valuable habitats. Runoff water from heavy summer storms exacerbates the problem.

Trekkers can help by sticking to the main trail and not taking shortcuts. A path is, by its very nature, an eroded strip of land. If the erosion is kept in check it is hardly a problem and the path does its job in helping to guide us through the mountains. But when the path becomes a small ravine, that is when trekkers start taking new routes which leads to further erosion and a devastated mountainside.

Trekkers can help minimise the damage by sticking to the designated path to minimise pressure on the rest of the mountain and its associated habitats. This throws up the issue of freedom to roam. One of the attractions of the mountains is the sense of freedom they instil in us. Those great open spaces entice us and bring out the explorer in many of us. We go to the mountains to escape restrictions and not to be channelled along a set route.

But the Tour du Mont Blanc is a set route and as there are so many of us who want to walk it, surely in this instance we have a responsibility to minimise our collective impact by sticking to the designated route or routes. For those who want to wander there is plenty of scope to do so elsewhere, away from the crowds. Get a map of the region and see how many other paths there are to follow.

Wildlife disturbance
Wildlife is hard to see in the Alps. There is so much disturbance from trekkers, skiers, day-trippers and paragliders that most birds and mammals keep well hidden or come out only after dark. There are some exceptions: marmots are a common sight in some areas and in the Aiguilles Rouges there is a good chance of seeing ibex and chamois. If you are fortunate enough to see these beasts try to keep the disturbance down to a minimum. By all means take a photograph but do not linger and do not try to approach too closely. Animals that are frequently disturbed may desert a region or become more hostile to human presence which will make it less likely that others will enjoy an encounter. Never approach or touch young animals or birds. In many circumstances they are temporarily left alone by the parents and are not, as is often assumed, abandoned. Handling them may lead to abandonment by the parents.

Wildflower meadows
The Alps are blessed with some beautiful meadows which come alive in summer with the dancing reds, blues and yellows of the many wildflowers endemic to the region. These Alpine meadows are very sensitive to disturbance. If at all possible stay out of the meadows and certainly don't pick the flowers. The Tour passes through many of these meadows and the path is usually quite obvious so there is no excuse for trampling about all over the place. At higher altitudes where the ground cover is less thick it can be easier to stray from the path or take a shortcut. Try to avoid this, not just because you may end up flattening the wildflowers but also because you will be exacerbating the erosion.

Crouching behind bushes
It hardly needs saying that human waste is disturbing to our senses. It also contaminates mountain streams that act as a drinking water supply to both trekkers and local properties. The unwritten rule of defecating at least 30 metres away from any water source is there for a good reason. This distance should be increased to 200 metres anywhere near human habitation and overnight spots.

When it's time 'to go' use a public toilet if at all possible. Clearly this is not always practical as vast stretches of the Tour cross high mountain country, far from flushing toilets. When the distance to the next toilet is too great and things are getting uncomfortable, there's nothing for it but to go outdoors, which is actually the most enjoyable way to perform this act – so long as the sun is shining. Find yourself a quiet spot behind a bush or rock and well away from running water and dig a small hole. It's not such a daft idea to carry a small lightweight trowel or you can use a flat rock to make a scrape. After the business has been concluded, cover up the contents of the hole with loose soil. Toilet paper should not be buried since animals will quickly dig it up. Instead pack it out in a plastic bag and dispose at the next public toilet, or burn it, taking care not to set fire to the surrounding vegetation which can be highly flammable in hot weather.

Wild camping

Camping out in the forest or on a mountain top is an experience that few of us have enjoyed – which is a shame. Spending not just the day but the night in the great outdoors helps us reconnect with the real world of which we are an intrinsic part. Sadly, wild camping is frowned upon on much of the Tour du Mont Blanc and is illegal in Italy. This is understandable to a certain degree: this is a popular trek and if everyone started camping, the minority of bad campers would ruin the area for everyone else by littering, lighting fires and crapping everywhere.

For those responsible campers out there, all is not lost. You can usually get away with camping outside refuges so long as you ask permission from the guardian. There may be a small charge if you intend to use their facilities – and you will probably want to after trekking all day. If you do choose to camp outside a refuge, you can usually book a place at the dinner table if there is room. This has two benefits: you get well fed and the guardian of the refuge will be more likely to let you camp outside if you intend to spend at least some money there.

Camping out in the wilds is not allowed but people do it anyway. If you insist on doing so, always bear in mind that the land you are camping on is not only a fragile environment but it may also represent somebody's livelihood. Minimise your impact by following these simple rules:

- Pitch your tent out of sight of other trekkers and of any habitation
- Keep noise to a minimum
- Don't light fires (and take care not to accidentally light vegetation)
- Never leave any litter (this includes leftover food)
- Don't use soap or detergent in streams
- Don't disturb wildlife or domestic animals
- Follow the guidelines in this book when going to the toilet outdoors (see p71)
- Never keep your tent in the same position for more than one night
- Leave no trace of your having been there.

Bivvying

An often overlooked alternative to camping is bivvying (see p32). Whether bivvying is construed as camping by the authorities is unclear so the legality of sleeping in a bag in the woods is open for debate. If you decide to spend the night in a bivvy bag whilst walking the Tour – and this is a great way to appreciate the mountains – remember that the rules of camping also apply to bivvying.

Using this guide

ROUTE MAPS

Scale and walking times

The maps that correspond to the daily route descriptions are drawn at approximately 1:20,000 (1cm = 200m; 3¹/₈ inches = one mile) and represent one full day's trekking. It is important to remember that much of the walking is up- and down-hill and the mere length of a trail is no indication as to how long it will take you to complete the section. So in the margin of each map you'll see the approximate amount of time it takes to get from one point to another. Bear in mind that some people are going to walk faster than others, based on fitness, quantity of kit carried, the size of the group and the weather conditions encountered. As such, these times should be used as a rough guide only.

Note that the time given refers only to actual walking time and doesn't include time allowed for rest stops or food. Again, this obviously varies from person to person but as a rough guide add 20-30% to allow for stops. The arrows show in which direction the walking time refers. Finally, the trail map key is on p181.

Up or down?

The track is marked as a dotted line. Much of the Tour is up or down, as the track climbs in and out of Alpine valleys. An arrow across the

---

❏ **Getting to the start**
The unofficial start and finish of the Tour du Mont Blanc is at the point where the trail crosses the southern end of the Chamonix valley, at Les Houches, about 4 miles (6km) down valley from Chamonix. If staying in Chamonix, or anywhere along the Chamonix valley for that matter, you can get to Les Houches by bus or train quite easily. From the end of June to the end of August **Chamonix Bus** (see 'C'; p22) runs between Chamonix and Les Houches roughly every hour from 7am to 7pm (with a stop at Les Pélerins train station, useful for those staying at the youth hostel).

Alternatively, hop on the **Mont Blanc Express train** (see 'D'; p22) which runs roughly every hour and a half on a daily basis throughout the year.

To find the start of the trail once in Les Houches, see box p74.

trail indicates a slope and always points uphill. Two arrows placed close together mean that the gradient is steep. If, for example, you are walking from A (at 900m) to B (at 1200m) and the trail between the two is short and steep, it would be shown thus: A — — > > — — B.

The Tour du Mont Blanc

LES HOUCHES

Les Houches is a compact town with a village feel. Everything you might need before the trek – food, drink, money – can be found along a short stretch of the main street. There is also a great museum, **Musée Montagnard** (☎ 04-50 54 54 74; July to Aug Wed-Mon 2-6pm, late Dec to Apr Mon, Wed & Fri 2-6pm) which has reconstructions of what domestic life in the valley would have been like in the 19th century. The Tour du Mont Blanc starts about half a mile west of Les Houches near the Belleface cablecar.

Services

The **tourist information centre** which is right in the centre of the village, on the main road (TIC; ☎ 04-50 55 50 62, 💻 www.leshouches.com; daily 9am-noon & 2.30-6.30pm) has the usual pile of information on where to stay and eat. They can also give directions to the start of the trail though hopefully the box below is sufficient.

The Carrefour **supermarket** (Mon-Sat 8am-8pm, Sun 8am-1pm) is just behind the

tourist information centre. Across the road from the tourist information centre is a **post office** and almost next door to the TIC is a **bank** with ATM. The **bakery** (Thur-Sat & Mon-Tue 6am-12.30pm & 3-7pm, Sun 6am-12.30pm) is a good place to get a cheap lunch. At the start of the trek you may need the services of an **outdoor shop** for last minute supplies. There are three: one in Belleface near the start of the trek and two others about ten minutes' walk east of the centre of Les Houches. At the end of the trek you may require the services of the **laundrette** which is also ten minutes' walk east of the centre of Les Houches.

Where to stay

If you are sleeping under canvas the campsite that is closest to the start of the TMB is *Camping Bellevue* (☎ 06-33 50 34 12, 💻 camping-bellevue-leshouches.com) which has pitches for 20 tents. You'll find it a couple of minutes walk down Route des Trabets in Belleface. If you prefer a bed head for *Gîte Michel Fagot* (☎ 04-50 54 42 28, 💻 gite-fagot.com) a homely place right

❏ GETTING TO THE START FROM LES HOUCHES

By bus Arriving in Les Houches you'll alight near the tourist office on the main **rue de l'Essert**. Continue along the road for 10 mins to **Le Hôtel Slalom**, past Téléphérique (cable car) de Bellevue. The trail starts opposite on **Chemin du Bonnet**.

By train From the train station cross the road bridge over the river, then the dual carriageway, before climbing the steep road to reach **rue de l'Église**. Turn right along this road which soon becomes **rue de l'Essert**. Look out for the **tourist office** ahead on the left then follow the directions above to reach the start of the trail. The walk should take 20-25 minutes.

in the centre of Les Houches, by the museum, with 36 beds priced at €25pp. More upmarket is *Hôtel Chris-tal* (☎ 04-50 54 50 55, 🖳 www.chris-tal.com; 23 rooms; chambre €41-83pp; demi-pension €83-139) which comes complete with indoor swimming pool and satellite TV – perhaps a good place to go for a treat on finishing the trek. It is a ten-minute walk east of the main village but is only a few minutes from the train station. Even further east from the main village is the *Rocky Pop Hôtel* (☎ 04-85 30 00 00, 🖳 rockypop-chamonix.com) a recent addition to the local skyline, timber-clad on the outside and with an Eighties pop-art feel on the inside. Beds cost from €50pp. The best budget accommodation is at *Les Mélèzes* (☎ 04-50 54 40 09, 🖳 www.hotellesmelezes.com; 24 rooms; €39-55pp), ideally located on the main road and with good views from the room balconies.

For something special you could try *Tupilak les Méandres* (☎ 04-50 54 56 66, 🖳 tupilak.com/gite; 28 beds; €20pp, demi-pension €40pp), a gorgeous old timber-fronted farm building in the hamlet of Le Coupeau in the forest across the valley.

Ideally situated for those finishing the Tour, it's only five minutes from the trail near the Christ Roi statue (see Map 41, p160).

Where to eat

The wonderful *Kitsch Inn* (☎ (0) 450 344 174, 🖳 www.kitschinn.eu, food 9am-3pm & 6-9pm) is laid back in vibe and location, occupying a quiet spot behind the Bellevue cablecar station. There are plenty of outside tables where you can enjoy wholesome home-cooked food including burgers from €14.90 and pancakes from €8.50. There is usually live music at the weekends.

Another good place to get a meal before the walk is opposite the tourist office at *La Chavanne à Florent* (☎ 67-74 55 271, 🖳 www.lachavanneleshouches.com) which has a big outside terrace where you can enjoy tartiflette for €16 and burger Savoyarde for €19.

Also worth a look is *Le Délice Restaurant* (☎ 07-85 50 86 52; Tue-Sun noon-2.30pm & 7-9.30pm), which does steak and chips for €14.50. For takeaway pizza from around €8 try *Lou Vio Pizzas* (☎ 06-07 77 35 59; daily 6-9.30pm).

LES HOUCHES TO COL DE VOZA   [Map 1 p76, Map 2 p77]

Talk about throwing oneself in at the deep end – or rather, the steep end. From **Le Hôtel Slalom** it is a relentless and punishing ascent of 600 metres.

(cont'd on p78)

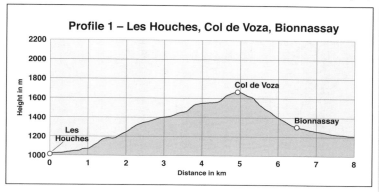

Profile 1 – Les Houches, Col de Voza, Bionnassay

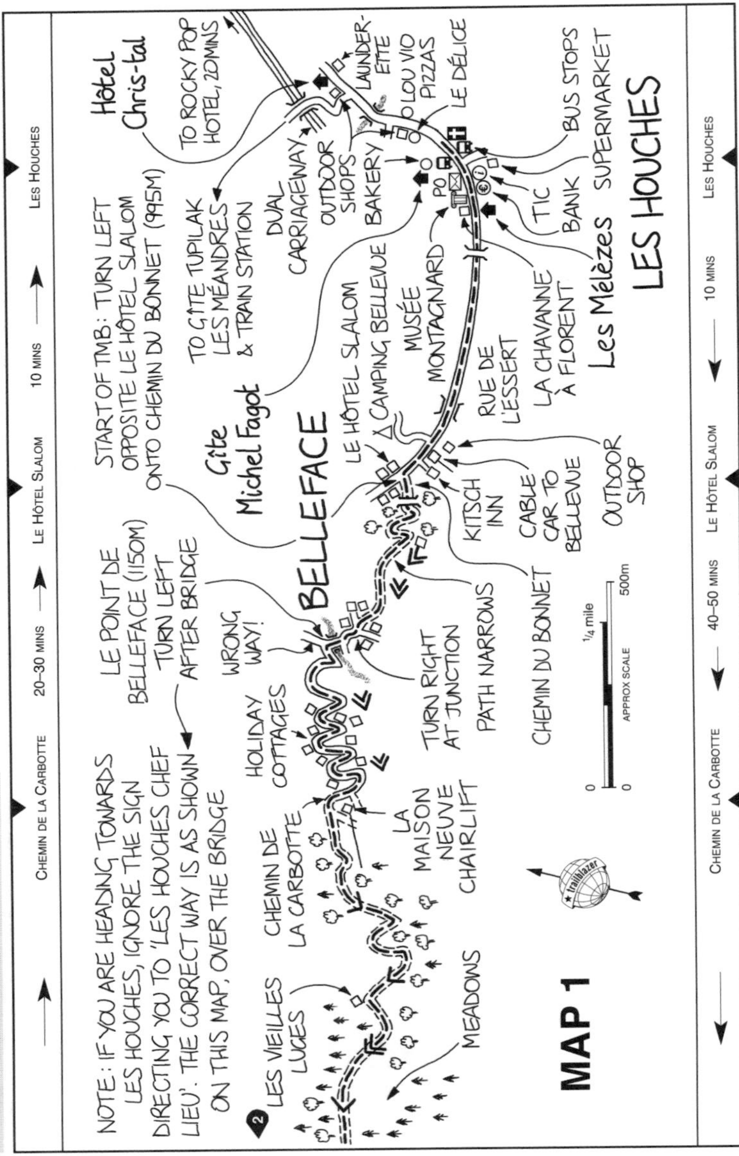

ROUTE GUIDE AND MAPS

MAP 1

CHEMIN DE LA CARBOTTE — 20–30 MINS — LE HÔTEL SLALOM — 10 MINS — LES HOUCHES

NOTE: IF YOU ARE HEADING TOWARDS LES HOUCHES, IGNORE THE SIGN DIRECTING YOU TO 'LES HOUCHES CHEF LIEU'. THE CORRECT WAY IS AS SHOWN ON THIS MAP, OVER THE BRIDGE

LE POINT DE BELLEFACE (1150M) TURN LEFT AFTER BRIDGE

WRONG WAY!

START OF TMB: TURN LEFT OPPOSITE LE HÔTEL SLALOM ONTO CHEMIN DU BONNET (995M)

Hôtel Chris-tal

TO ROCKY POP HOTEL, 2 MINS

LAUNDER-ETTE
O LOU VIO PIZZAS
LE DÉLICE
BUS STOPS

DUAL CARRIAGEWAY

TO GÎTE TUPILAK LES MÉANDRES & TRAIN STATION

OUTDOOR SHOPS
BAKERY
PO
TIC
BANK
SUPERMARKET

Gîte Michel Fagot

LE HÔTEL SLALOM
CAMPING BELLEVUE
MUSÉE MONTAGNARD
RUE DE L'ESSERT
LA CHAVANNE À FLORENT

LES HOUCHES

Les Mélèzes

BELLEFACE

KITSCH INN
CABLE CAR TO BELLEVUE
OUTDOOR SHOP

HOLIDAY COTTAGES

CHEMIN DE LA CARBOTTE

LA MAISON NEUVE CHAIRLIFT

TURN RIGHT AT JUNCTION

PATH NARROWS

CHEMIN DU BONNET

¼ mile
APPROX SCALE
0   500m
0

MEADOWS

2 LES VIEILLES LUCES

CHEMIN DE LA CARBOTTE — 40–50 MINS — LE HÔTEL SLALOM — 10 MINS — LES HOUCHES

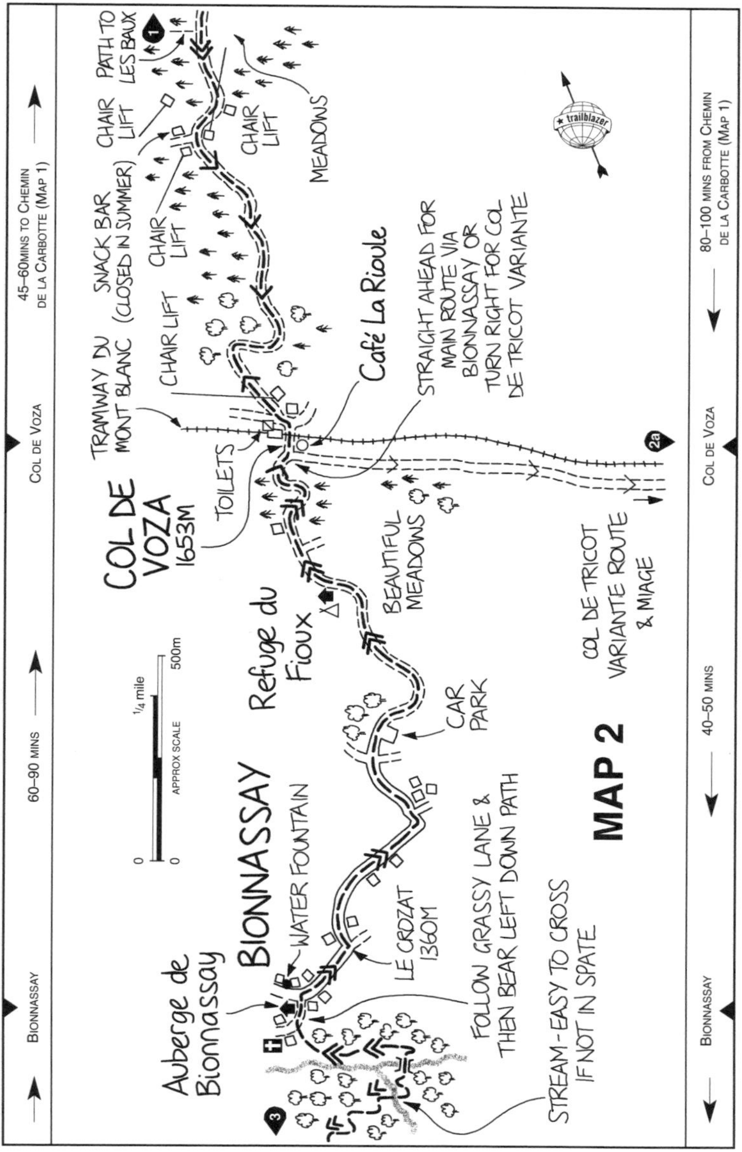

MAP 2

❏ **Tramway du Mont Blanc**
Tour du Mont Blanc trekkers wishing to cut out the big ascent from Les Houches may like to take this small mountain railway from Le Fayet, or St-Gervais-les-Bains. The railway crosses the Tour du Mont Blanc at both Col de Voza and Bellevue. It then goes up to 2372m and Nid d'Aigle for a fantastic view over the imposing Glacier de Bionnassay. A return ticket from St-Gervais to Bellevue costs €31.50. Trains operate between six and eleven times a day depending on the season: see 'N' on p23 and the map on pp24-5 for further details.

(cont'd from p75)   On a positive note, the view up the valley gets better and better with every step, following a wide track through a mixture of steep meadow, woodland and a ski area before arriving at the lovely viewpoint of **Col de Voza** (1653m).

The track begins in thick broadleaf woodland, eventually emerging at **Belleface**, a sort of alpine housing estate of holiday homes. Bear right at the junction following the sign to Col de Voza and then left after the bridge. Continue past more holiday homes on a zigzagging metalled road. At the La Maison Neuve chairlift follow **Chemin de la Carbotte**, a dirt track that climbs to *Les Vieilles Luges* (☎ 06-84 42 37 00, 🖥 lesvieillesluges.com), a lovely restaurant run by a local Les Houches man and his Australian wife. It's a bit early to stop but it's tempting: this is a genuine 250-year-old timber farmhouse with low ceilings. It's a beguiling spot with a large garden out front where you can sit and eat omelettes for €4-6 whilst enjoying the spectacular views of the Aiguilles Rouges across the valley.

Continue ever upwards past the grassy ski runs and through patches of woodland to **Col de Voza**. At the col there is an imposing hotel on the *alp* and a small station for the Tramway du Mont Blanc (see box above). *Café La Rioule*, just across the tramway tracks, is a welcome sight after such a relentless climb. Soft drinks, ice-creams and snacks are expensive (€4 for a Coke!) but you'll find it hard to resist. Take a seat outside and admire the view up the Chamonix valley.

COL DE VOZA TO LES CONTAMINES   [Maps 2 p77, 3 p80, 4 p86]

The route via Bionnassay is the easier of the two possibilities (see p81 for the Col de Tricot variante) for this section so if you found the first stretch to Col de Voza a little taxing this is the route for you. From the col continue along the main track, ignoring the turning to the left. The track drops sharply through the trees, passing a series of farm buildings and cottages. One of these is *Refuge du Fioux* (☎ 04-50 93 52 43, 🖥 www.montourdumontblanc.com; end May-end Sep; 24 beds; dortoir €25pp, demi-pension €40pp, full board €50) which must have one of the most enviable views in the region. If you are **camping** you can enjoy that view from their lawn where they have a few pitches for tents (€5pp). Meals include tartiflette for €20, repas du randonneur for €14 and omelettes for €6.50.

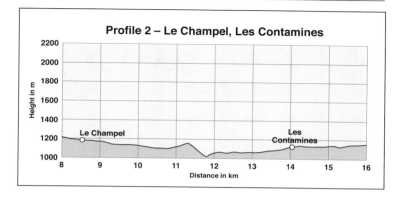

Profile 2 – Le Champel, Les Contamines

BIONNASSAY   [Map 2, p77]
This sleepy village, clinging to the lush
mountainside, is home to *Auberge de
Bionnassay* (☎ 04-50 93 45 23, 🖳 auberge-
bionnassay.com; June-Sep; 38 beds; dortoir
€14pp, dortoir with demi-pension €35pp,

chambre €21pp, chambre with demi-pension
€42pp). It's right in the centre of the village
and makes a good overnight stop for those
who are finding the first day a little punishing. They also do evening meals such as fondue Savoyarde (€18) and risotto (€14.50).

To continue on the path take a left as you enter the village, down the grassy
lane past the **church**. This leads through more cool, lush woodland and across
a crashing glacial river (fed by the Glacier de Bionnassay). The river is split into
two channels with one of them bridged but the other not. Fortunately it is not a
wide channel and, as long as it is not in spate, should be easy to skip over. A
short climb up the other side of the valley and the path meets a wide woodland
track that slowly loses height on its way to **Le Champel** (see Map 3, p80). Here
the grand **Val Montjoie** opens out before you. Aside from the peace and views
there is little here to keep you. If you wish to stay the night there is the wonderful *Gîte le Péclet* (☎ 06-84 18 45 55, 🖳 www.lepeclet.fr; mid June-mid Sep;
6 beds; B&B €30pp, demi-pension €45pp) on the left as you enter the village.

❑ **The Great Flood of 1892**
On 11th July 1892 a devastating flood hit the Bionnassay valley. The snout of the
Glacier de Bionnassay collapsed exposing a large chamber within the ice that held
200,000 cubic metres of meltwater. The resulting torrent of water, mud and other
debris that swept down the valley destroyed the village of Bionnay and flooded the
town of Saint Gervais, five miles away. Two hundred people lost their lives in the dis-
aster. The build up of water within the glacier still occurs today so the authorities have
established an early warning siren system and evacuation plan for the villages in the
valley. Thanks to these precautions and careful monitoring of the glacier, a repeat per-
formance of the 1892 tragedy seems less likely.

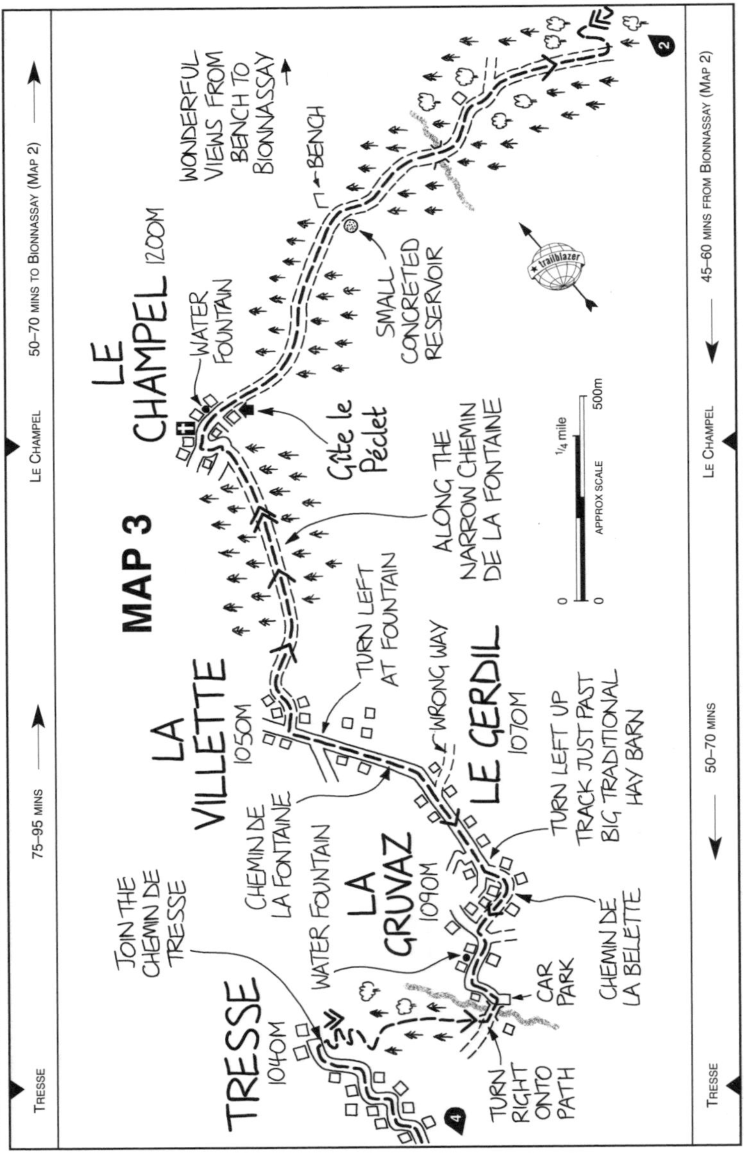

MAP 3

LE CHAMPEL 1200M

WONDERFUL VIEWS FROM BENCH TO BIONNASSAY

BENCH

WATER FOUNTAIN

Gîte le Péclet

SMALL CONCRETED RESERVOIR

trailblazer

ALONG THE NARROW CHEMIN DE LA FONTAINE

LA VILLETTE 1050M

TURN LEFT AT FOUNTAIN

CHEMIN DE LA FONTAINE

WRONG WAY

LE CERDIL 1070M

WATER FOUNTAIN

LA CRUVAZ 1090M

TURN LEFT UP TRACK JUST PAST BIG TRADITIONAL HAY BARN

CAR PARK

CHEMIN DE LA BELETTE

JOIN THE CHEMIN DE TRESSE

TRESSE 1040M

TURN RIGHT ONTO PATH

APPROX SCALE
¼ mile
0   500m
0

50–70 MINS TO BIONNASSAY (MAP 2)

45–60 MINS FROM BIONNASSAY (MAP 2)

75–95 MINS

50–70 MINS

TRESSE   LA VILLETTE   LE CHAMPEL

LE CHAMPEL

TRESSE

It's a well-kept traditional house with two rooms, one sleeping two and one sleeping four.

A path connects Le Champel to yet another delightful Alpine village, **La Villette**. Follow the road from here to **La Gruvaz** where another woodland path follows the river to **Tresse**. You are at the foot of the Val Montjoie – though it's still a fair trek to Les Contamines.

Cross the main road and river and follow the lane, then path, to the hamlet of **Les Meuniers** (see Map 4 p86). Look for an old hay barn on your left: inscribed on the wooden beam in French is: 'Birthplace of Alexis Bouvard 1767-1843, astronomer who discovered Neptune'. Cross the Pont du Nant de l'Ile and then the main river and then follow the riverside path through the woods to a junction. The Tour du Mont Blanc continues on the right but for **Les Contamines** (see p85) take a left up the hill.

Col de Tricot Variante
[Map 2 p77, Map 2a p82, Map 2b p83 & Map 2c p84]
This alternative route to Les Contamines may be too much to take on for a first day but if you feel fit enough go for it; you won't be disappointed. The route passes the snout of the Bionnassay glacier and then goes through delightful pastures below the icy Dômes de Miage before crossing over a ridge and descending through the forests of the Réserve Naturelle Contamines-Montjoie.

Begin by crossing the railway at Col de Voza and taking the left turn immediately after Café La Rioule. Follow the track to Bellevue and then continue on a narrower trail through the forest. After negotiating a couple of rocky outcrops, where fixed ropes offer some extra security, the trail opens out onto the beautiful high Alpine pasture of **L'Are**. The view from here of the 4052m Aiguille de Bionnassay is sensational. You can also see our next objective, the Col de Tricot, a perfect V-shaped notch in the ridge opposite.

To reach it, follow the trail over the forested banks of moraine and then drop steeply down to the barren rocky outwash plain of the glacier. Since the first edition of this book there has been a steady spread of bushes and trees (pioneer species) across the exposed moraine here; one of many indicators of a warming climate that are apparent in this landscape. The roar of the torrent tumbling from the glacier's snout gets more and more menacing as you approach it. Thankfully there is a small metal and wooden bridge, straight out of an Indiana Jones movie, strung across the water.

Col de Tricot is a 400m climb away but it is not a taxing ascent. At the top there are wonderful views across the Miage valley all the way to the Col du Bonhomme at the head of the Montjoie valley.

It's a knee-crunching descent to **Chalets de Miage**. This collection of pretty farm buildings surrounded by lush cattle pasture and in the icy shadow of the 3600m Dômes du Miage is a good spot to rest for the night. *Refuge de Miage* (☎ 04-50 93 22 91; June to mid Sep; 39 beds; dortoir €25pp, dortoir demi-pension €45, chambre demi-pension €65pp) is a relaxing place in a grand setting. Light meals are available during the day with sandwiches from €5.

Those with the bit between their teeth can continue for another 45mins-1hr to Auberge du Truc (see p84) which you will find by following the track across the river. *(cont'd on p84)*

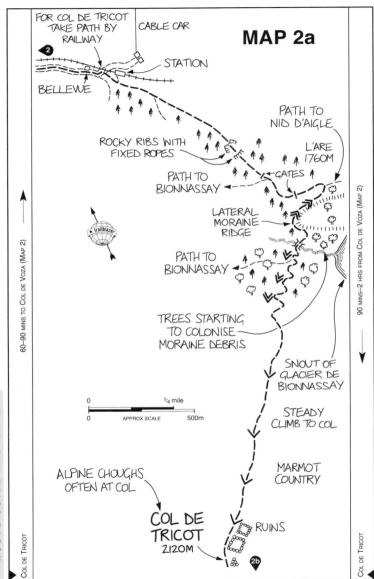

FOR COL DE TRICOT
TAKE PATH BY
RAILWAY

CABLE CAR

MAP 2a

STATION

BELLEVUE

PATH TO
NID D'AIGLE

ROCKY RIBS WITH
FIXED ROPES

L'ARE
1760M

PATH TO
BIONNASSAY

GATES

LATERAL
MORAINE
RIDGE

PATH TO
BIONNASSAY

TREES STARTING
TO COLONISE
MORAINE DEBRIS

SNOUT OF
GLACIER DE
BIONNASSAY

STEADY
CLIMB TO COL

MARMOT
COUNTRY

ALPINE CHOUGHS
OFTEN AT COL

COL DE
TRICOT
2120M

RUINS

trailblazer

0   ¼ mile
0   500m
APPROX SCALE

60–90 MINS TO COL DE VOZA (MAP 2)

90 MINS–2 HRS FROM COL DE VOZA (MAP 2)

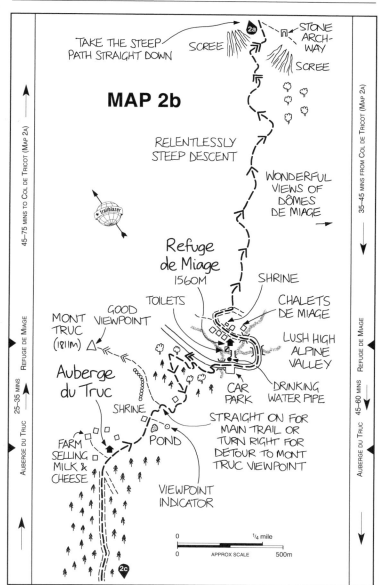

TAKE THE STEEP PATH STRAIGHT DOWN

SCREE

STONE ARCH-WAY

SCREE

MAP 2b

RELENTLESSLY STEEP DESCENT

WONDERFUL VIEWS OF DÔMES DE MIAGE

Refuge de Miage 1560M

SHRINE

TOILETS

GOOD VIEWPOINT

MONT TRUC (1811M) △

Auberge du Truc

CHALETS DE MIAGE

LUSH HIGH ALPINE VALLEY

SHRINE

POND

CAR PARK

DRINKING WATER PIPE

STRAIGHT ON FOR MAIN TRAIL OR TURN RIGHT FOR DETOUR TO MONT TRUC VIEWPOINT

FARM SELLING MILK & CHEESE

VIEWPOINT INDICATOR

* trailblazer

45-75 MINS TO COL DE TRICOT (MAP 2A)

REFUGE DE MIAGE

25-35 MINS

AUBERGE DU TRUC

35-45 MINS FROM COL DE TRICOT (MAP 2A)

REFUGE DE MIAGE

45-60 MINS

AUBERGE DU TRUC

0   ¼ mile
0   APPROX SCALE   500m

2a

2c

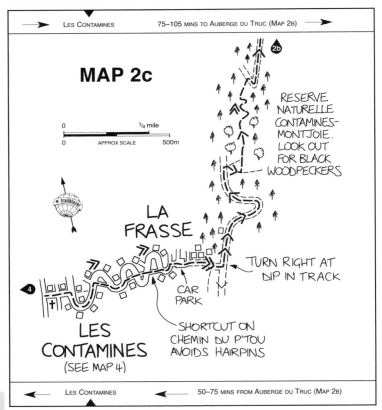

LES CONTAMINES   75–105 MINS TO AUBERGE DU TRUC (MAP 2B)

MAP 2c

RESERVE
NATURELLE
CONTAMINES-
MONTJOIE.
LOOK OUT
FOR BLACK
WOODPECKERS

LA
FRASSE

TURN RIGHT AT
DIP IN TRACK

CAR
PARK

LES
CONTAMINES
(SEE MAP 4)

SHORTCUT ON
CHEMIN DU P'TOU
AVOIDS HAIRPINS

LES CONTAMINES   50–75 MINS FROM AUBERGE DU TRUC (MAP 2B)

(cont'd from p81)
Just after a small car park and a bridge, pick up the path that climbs through bushes and trees to the top of the broad, flat-topped ridge that separates the Miage valley from that of Montjoie. As the path emerges from the trees onto the flat pastures look for the thin trail that climbs to the top of the little peak of **Mont Truc** (1811m). This is a very worthwhile diversion with cracking views in all directions. It only takes 20-30 mins there and back.

Back on the main trail an indicator dial shows the names of the peaks in the view in front of you. A couple of minutes further on is ***Auberge du Truc*** (☎ 04-50 93 12 48; mid Jun to mid Sep; 28 beds; dortoir €16pp, demi-pension €40pp) which is the last place to stay before Les Contamines. You can also eat here during the day; assiette Savoyarde is €15 and a cheese omelette is €5.80. Just around the corner, about 50 metres from the trail, is a pretty farm building where you can buy milk and cheese directly from the farmer. Look for the *Reblochon de Savoie* sign.

From the auberge head into the forest and after the first big hairpin (Map 2c) take the narrow trail left. This drops gradually to a wide forest track. Follow this south to a junction in a dip. Turn right to reach **La Frasse**, a residential area at the top of **Les Contamines**. It's a straightforward descent down Chemin du p'Tou (which cuts out the zigzags of the main road) to the church in the centre.

LES CONTAMINES   [Map 4, p86]

Les Contamines occupies the floor of the grand Val Montjoie. The older buildings complement the grand scenery with the spire of the old church reflecting the rocky mountain backdrop. This is the last settlement of any significance until Courmayeur, a few days' trek away, so make sure you enjoy the hospitality and stock up on any supplies you may need. A good rainy-day diversion is **Maison de la Réserve Naturelle des Contamines Montjoie** (Mon-Fri 10.30am-noon & 3-6.30pm), where you can learn about the wildlife of the area.

Services

The **tourist information centre** (TIC; ☎ 04-50 47 01 58, ☐ www.lescontamines .com; Mon-Sat 9am-noon & 2-7pm, Sun 9am-noon & 3-7pm) is well stocked with useful information. The helpful staff can help you find a bed and recommend things to do locally. There is also **wi-fi** here and a **weather forecast** is posted daily on the outside wall. There are three **supermarkets** on the main street: a Spar (Mon-Wed & Fri-Sat 8am-12.30pm & 3-7.30pm, Sun 8.30am-12.30pm), a Sherpa supermarket (daily 7.30am-1pm & 3-7.30pm, closed Sun afternoon) and a Carrefour Montagne. There is also a **post office**, a **bank**, a **pharmacy** (8.30am-12.15pm & 2.30-7.15pm) and a few **sport shops** (Sport 4807m and Intersport) with a range of hiking equipment.

Where to stay

The cheapest accommodation is about a 10-minute walk out of town on the other side of the river at *Chalet des Contamines* (☎ 04-50 47 00 88, ☐ www.chaletdescontamines.ffcam.fr; mid June to mid Sep; 26 beds; dortoir €16.20pp).

Of the more upmarket hotels, *Le Gai Soleil* (☎ 04-50 47 02 94, ☐ www.gaisoleil.com; B&B €65-75pp, demi-pension €85-95pp) is a good choice and not too far from the town centre.

Where to eat

For a quick dinner head to *La Fringale Pizzeria* (☎ 04-50 47 77 29; daily 9.30am-1.30pm & 4-10pm) which does excellent pizzas for €8.80-12. A few steps from here is *Le Husky* (☎ 04-50 47 03 13) which has more local dishes including fondue for €20 as well as fillet of bream for €23. There are also pizzas, and pasta and burgers, at *Au Bistro Gourmand*. Prices are around the €10 mark.

On the southern edge of town is the contemporary *Le Glacier Restaurant* with a large outside terrace. It's a more peaceful place to eat, away from the bustle of the town centre. Dishes include pork (€15) and lasagne (€16). They also do tasty crêpes from €3.50-8.

For lunch the cheapest option is the *bakery* on the main street. For a sit-down lunch try *La Bérangère*, a bar that does burgers with reblochon cheese for €16 and pasta dishes for around €10. Head to *Les Airelles Crêperie* (☎ 04-50 47 10 49, ☐ www.creperielesairelles.fr; open from 4pm) to sample their mind-boggling array of filled crêpes.

❏ **Important note – walking times**
All times in this book refer only to the time spent walking. You will need to add 20-30% to allow for rests, photography, checking the map, drinking water etc.

ROUTE GUIDE AND MAPS

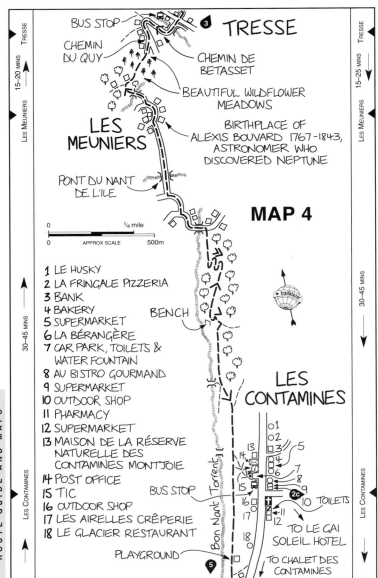

BUS STOP
CHEMIN DU QUY
3 TRESSE
CHEMIN DE BETASSET
BEAUTIFUL WILDFLOWER MEADOWS
LES MEUNIERS
BIRTHPLACE OF ALEXIS BOUVARD 1767-1843, ASTRONOMER WHO DISCOVERED NEPTUNE
PONT DU NANT DE L'ILE

MAP 4

0   1/4 mile
0   500m
APPROX SCALE

BENCH

★ trailblazer

LES CONTAMINES

1 LE HUSKY
2 LA FRINGALE PIZZERIA
3 BANK
4 BAKERY
5 SUPERMARKET
6 LA BÉRANGÈRE
7 CAR PARK, TOILETS & WATER FOUNTAIN
8 AU BISTRO GOURMAND
9 SUPERMARKET
10 OUTDOOR SHOP
11 PHARMACY
12 SUPERMARKET
13 MAISON DE LA RÉSERVE NATURELLE DES CONTAMINES MONTJOIE
14 POST OFFICE
15 TIC
16 OUTDOOR SHOP
17 LES AIRELLES CRÊPERIE
18 LE GLACIER RESTAURANT

BUS STOP

1
2
3   5
4
6   7
8
9
2c   10 TOILETS
11
12   TO LE GAI SOLEIL HOTEL

Bon Nant Torrent

PLAYGROUND

5

TO CHALET DES CONTAMINES

15-20 MINS TRESSE
LES MEUNIERS
30-45 MINS LES CONTAMINES

15-25 MINS TRESSE
LES MEUNIERS
30-45 MINS
LES CONTAMINES

LES CONTAMINES TO COL DE LA CROIX DU BONHOMME
[Map 4, Map 5 p88, Map 6 p89, Map 7 p91, Map 8 p92]

The first half of this stretch involves gentle walking along the mostly flat valley floor, at first following the east bank of the river before crossing via a bridge to follow the opposite bank briefly along a pleasant path that flirts with woodland and fields as far as another road bridge.

From here we stick to the east side of the river, initially along the road and then a lovely path, past some tennis courts, a ski jump and a football pitch, all set amongst fields and woodland. *Camping et Gîte d'étape du Pontet* (☎ 04-50 47 04 04; 🖳 www.campinglepontet.fr; July-Sep; 60 camp pitches €4.20 per tent plus €5.80pp; dortoir 32 beds €14, breakfast €6.80, picnic lunch €8, dinner €16, self-catering kitchen access €2.50) is just past the tennis courts. It has a restaurant with an extensive menu, as well as a laundry and a small shop. It's a further 20 minutes of easy walking to **Notre Dame de la Gorge** (see box below), a good spot for a mid-morning break or even lunch.

The walk really gets interesting from here as the path begins to climb into the upper valley through sweet-smelling pine forest. The track beneath you is an old **Roman road**, hence the local name, Chemin Romain. At one point the track crosses an old Roman bridge by a waterfall. Look out too for the **natural bridge**, a rocky arch spanning the tumbling river just west of the track.

A short distance on from the Roman bridge is the *Chalet-Refuge Nant Borrant* (☎ 04-50 47 03 57, 🖳 www.refuge-nantborrant.com; June-Sep; 32 beds; dortoir €20pp, demi-pension €41.50). This is the last place to get food before the col. They do very tasty local dishes including assiette de jambon fumé (smoked ham) and tartiflette, both priced at €12.

Leaving the chalet behind the track now climbs sharply into more woodland before the gradient eases on reaching a beautiful flat area of meadows and cattle pasture in the upper valley.

Ten minutes beyond Nant Borrant, at Rollaz, there is a wonderful, informal **campsite** just a couple of minutes off the path in a beautiful spot by the tumbling river. Despite the unceasing crash of the river and the probable clanging of cow bells from the nearby meadow, this is a peaceful spot to spend the night.

❑ **Notre Dame de la Gorge**
This beautiful Baroque chapel dates from the 13th century, although it was rebuilt in 1699 by Jean de la Vougniaz. It at once served as the parish church for everyone who lived in Val Montjoie and to this day is still used as a place of worship and pilgrimage; it is the final destination for the many pilgrims who come here on the Feast of the Assumption (15 August) every year. For the TMB walker it marks the point where the road through the valley ends and the trail to the Col du Bonhomme begins. In the past, travellers crossing the pass visited the chapel, either to pray for a safe journey over the col or, if coming from the other side, to thank the Lord that they made it across. No doubt some people still do.

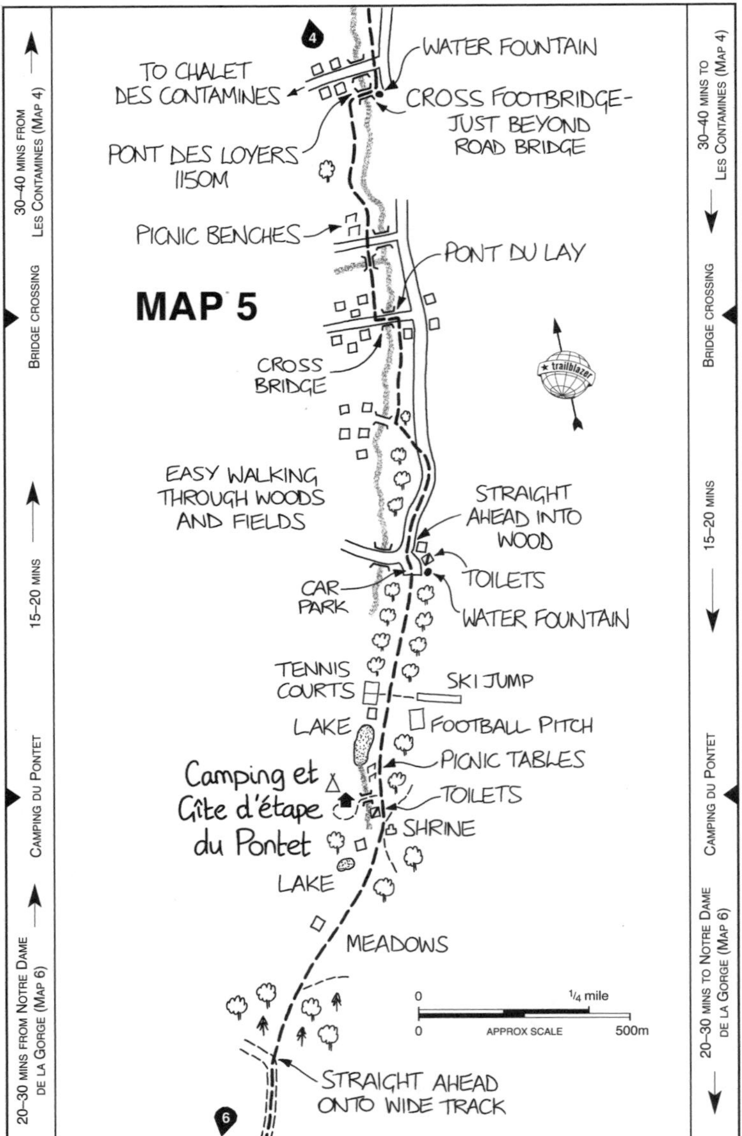
MAP 5
30–40 MINS FROM LES CONTAMINES (MAP 4)
BRIDGE CROSSING
15–20 MINS
CAMPING DU PONTET
20–30 MINS FROM NOTRE DAME DE LA GORGE (MAP 6)
30–40 MINS TO LES CONTAMINES (MAP 4)
BRIDGE CROSSING
15–20 MINS
CAMPING DU PONTET
20–30 MINS TO NOTRE DAME DE LA GORGE (MAP 6)
4
WATER FOUNTAIN
TO CHALET DES CONTAMINES
CROSS FOOTBRIDGE- JUST BEYOND ROAD BRIDGE
PONT DES LOYERS 1150M
PICNIC BENCHES
PONT DU LAY
CROSS BRIDGE
trailblazer
EASY WALKING THROUGH WOODS AND FIELDS
STRAIGHT AHEAD INTO WOOD
TOILETS
CAR PARK
WATER FOUNTAIN
TENNIS COURTS
SKI JUMP
LAKE
FOOTBALL PITCH
PICNIC TABLES
Camping et Gîte d'étape du Pontet
TOILETS
SHRINE
LAKE
MEADOWS
0
1/4 mile
0
APPROX SCALE
500m
STRAIGHT AHEAD ONTO WIDE TRACK
6

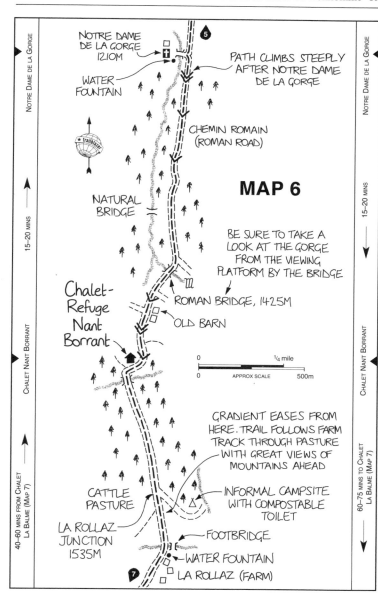

NOTRE DAME DE LA GORGE 1210M

5

PATH CLIMBS STEEPLY AFTER NOTRE DAME DE LA GORGE

WATER FOUNTAIN

★ trailblazer

CHEMIN ROMAIN (ROMAN ROAD)

MAP 6

NATURAL BRIDGE

BE SURE TO TAKE A LOOK AT THE GORGE FROM THE VIEWING PLATFORM BY THE BRIDGE

Chalet-Refuge Nant Borrant

ROMAN BRIDGE, 1425M

OLD BARN

0   ¼ mile

0   APPROX SCALE   500m

GRADIENT EASES FROM HERE. TRAIL FOLLOWS FARM TRACK THROUGH PASTURE WITH GREAT VIEWS OF MOUNTAINS AHEAD

CATTLE PASTURE

INFORMAL CAMPSITE WITH COMPOSTABLE TOILET

LA ROLLAZ JUNCTION 1535M

FOOTBRIDGE

WATER FOUNTAIN

7

LA ROLLAZ (FARM)

NOTRE DAME DE LA GORGE

NOTRE DAME DE LA GORGE

15-20 MINS

15-20 MINS

CHALET NANT BORRANT

CHALET NANT BORRANT

40-60 MINS FROM CHALET LA BALME (MAP 7)

60-75 MINS TO CHALET LA BALME (MAP 7)

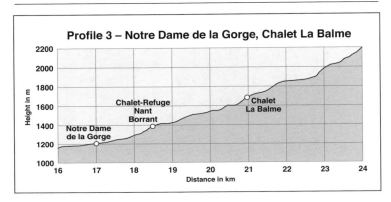

Profile 3 – Notre Dame de la Gorge, Chalet La Balme

Take the track on the left signposted 'bivouac'. There is room for half a dozen tents in among the trees. There are no facilities other than a compost toilet.

Back on the main trail, and beyond La Rollaz, the mountain wall ahead really begins to show its grandeur. Enjoy this easy gradient while it lasts because it soon gets steep again on its way up to **Chalet La Balme** (☎ 04-50 47 03 54, 🖳 www.montourdumontblanc.com; mid June to mid Sep; 62 beds; demi-pension dortoir €40pp, demi-pension chambre €50pp, lunch from noon-2.30pm €8) located spectacularly at the foot of some grassy terminal moraine and with magnificent views back down the valley. There is a **permitted bivvy site** opposite the refuge.

The track now deteriorates into a thin trail, at first following the ridge of an old bank of lateral moraine and then past the crashing **Cascade de la Balme** to climb steeply to a wider track. We are now well above the treeline. All around are wild flowers amongst the erratic boulders. Follow the track past some small hydroelectric pipes and into the upper reaches of the valley. The landscape is more savage now as the serrated ridges of the mountains begin to bare their teeth. Early in the season there may still be large semi-permanent snow patches across the path from here to the col.

At **Col du Bonhomme** there is a tiny doorless shelter which provides nothing more than brief respite from any rain or snow. Col de la Croix du Bonhomme is still 40-60 minutes away across a rough stretch of rocky ribs and bluffs. Cross these and climb up to the wide col, marked by a large rotund cairn. Those who wish to take the high route (see pp96-8) to La Ville des Glaciers need to take the trail north-east to the 2665m Col des Fours – but not yet! It's been a long day's trek and you'd be wise to bed down for the night. You'll find **Refuge de la Croix du Bonhomme** (☎ 04-79 07 05 28, 🖳 www.montourdu-montblanc.com; mid June to mid Sep; 113 beds; dortoir €22.80pp, demi-pension €49, picnic lunch €10) a few paces downhill to the south. Those taking the low route through the Vallée des Glaciers have the option of staying here or continuing down to Les Chapieux.

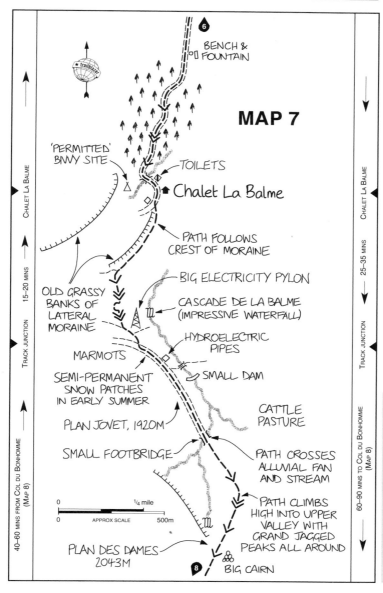

MAP 7

6

BENCH & FOUNTAIN

'PERMITTED' BIVVY SITE

TOILETS

Chalet La Balme

PATH FOLLOWS CREST OF MORAINE

BIG ELECTRICITY PYLON

OLD GRASSY BANKS OF LATERAL MORAINE

CASCADE DE LA BALME (IMPRESSIVE WATERFALL)

HYDROELECTRIC PIPES

MARMOTS

SMALL DAM

SEMI-PERMANENT SNOW PATCHES IN EARLY SUMMER

CATTLE PASTURE

PLAN JOVET, 1920M

SMALL FOOTBRIDGE

PATH CROSSES ALLUVIAL FAN AND STREAM

0   ¼ mile
0   APPROX SCALE   500m

PATH CLIMBS HIGH INTO UPPER VALLEY WITH GRAND JAGGED PEAKS ALL AROUND

PLAN DES DAMES 2043M

8   BIG CAIRN

CHALET LA BALME

15-20 MINS

TRACK JUNCTION

40-60 MINS FROM COL DU BONHOMME (MAP 8)

CHALET LA BALME

25-35 MINS

TRACK JUNCTION

60-90 MINS TO COL DU BONHOMME (MAP 8)

ROUTE GUIDE AND MAPS

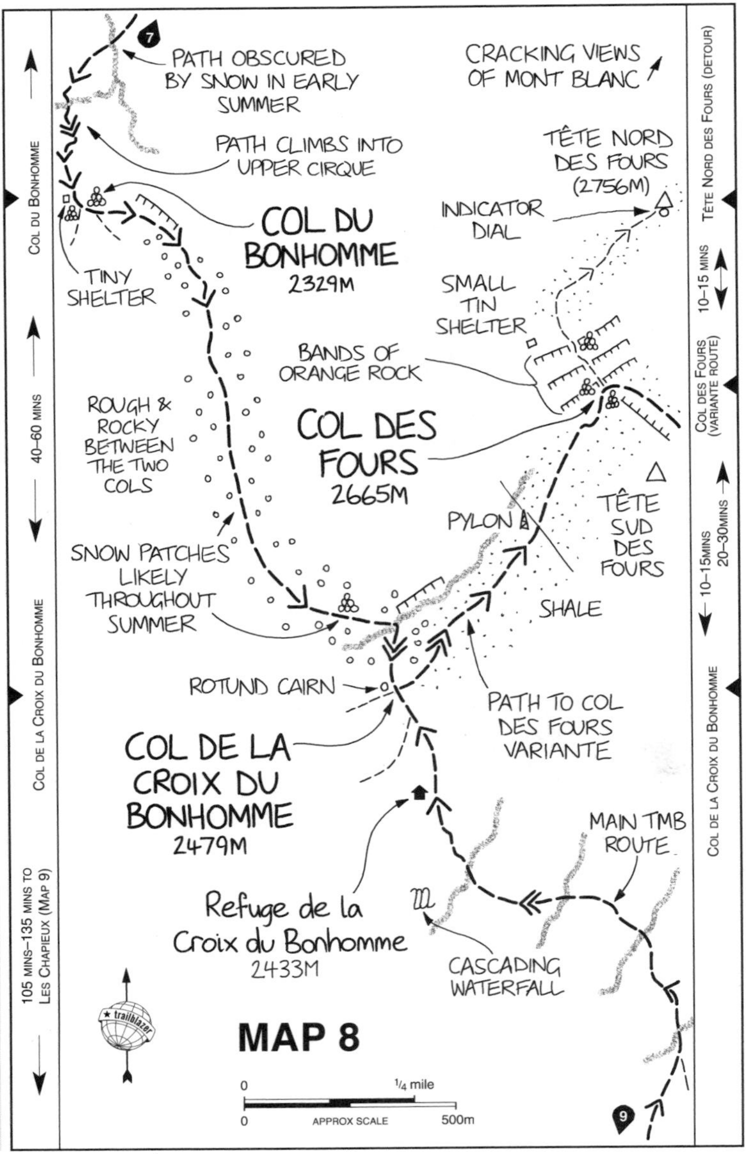

MAP 8

Path obscured by snow in early summer

Cracking views of Mont Blanc

Path climbs into upper cirque

Tête Nord des Fours (2756M)

Indicator dial

COL DU BONHOMME 2329M

Small tin shelter

Tiny shelter

Bands of orange rock

COL DES FOURS 2665M

Rough & rocky between the two cols

Tête Sud des Fours

Pylon

Snow patches likely throughout summer

Shale

Rotund cairn

Path to Col des Fours Variante

COL DE LA CROIX DU BONHOMME 2479M

Main TMB route

Refuge de la Croix du Bonhomme 2433M

Cascading waterfall

Col du Bonhomme — 40-60 mins — Col de la Croix du Bonhomme

105 mins-135 mins to Les Chapieux (Map 9)

Tête Nord des Fours (detour) — 10-15 mins — Col des Fours (variante route) — 20-30mins — 10-15mins — Col de la Croix du Bonhomme

0   ¼ mile
0   APPROX SCALE   500m

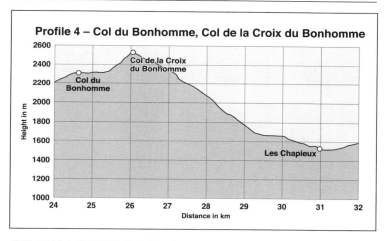

Profile 4 – Col du Bonhomme, Col de la Croix du Bonhomme

COL DE LA CROIX DU BONHOMME TO REFUGE DES MOTTETS
[Map 8, Map 9 p94, Map 10 p95, Map 11 p99]

The main route between Col de la Croix du Bonhomme and Refuge des Mottets goes via Les Chapieux; see p96 for the variante route via Col des Fours.

Step out of the refuge to find yourself high among brooding peaks. It's a long way down to Les Chapieux so prepare your knees for a relentless descent. The harsh, barren scenery of these upper slopes gives way to lush verdant pastures below. Fifteen minutes beyond the col there is a particularly steep stretch of path. At the foot of this be sure to look at the cascading waterfall behind you.

The path continues down the valley to a bridge where it joins a track through beautiful meadows full of wild flowers in summer. Leave the track by an indistinct path on the left (if you come to a road you have missed it). The path zigzags down through fields to the village of **Les Chapieux**, hidden behind a screen of trees in the bottom of the valley.

❏ **Tête Nord des Fours**
It takes only 10-15 minutes from Col des Fours [Map 8] to reach this 2756m summit. Follow a trail of small cairns across the orange ribs of rock and then across easier ground which brings you onto the summit ridge. There is a less than inviting shelter here. It's quite hard to find – hidden behind a rock wall – and is good only for sheltering from the rain as it has no door and a muddy floor. The summit is obvious ahead, marked by a big indicator dial which points out all the mountains you can see on a clear day. The rollcall includes Mont Pouri, Monte Rosa, the Matterhorn and, of course, the beautiful white dome of Mont Blanc looming right there in front of you. Retrace your steps to return to the col. The return trip from the col, not including time spent to admire the view, takes about 20-30 minutes.

ROUTE GUIDE AND MAPS

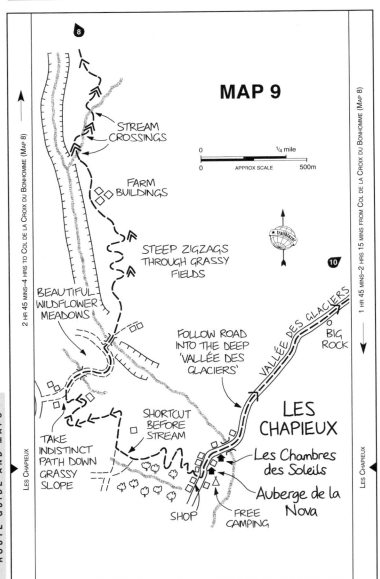

MAP 9

8

STREAM CROSSINGS

FARM BUILDINGS

STEEP ZIGZAGS THROUGH GRASSY FIELDS

BEAUTIFUL WILDFLOWER MEADOWS

FOLLOW ROAD INTO THE DEEP 'VALLÉE DES GLACIERS'

VALLÉE DES GLACIERS

BIG ROCK

10

LES CHAPIEUX

SHORTCUT BEFORE STREAM

TAKE INDISTINCT PATH DOWN GRASSY SLOPE

Les Chambres des Soleils

Auberge de la Nova

SHOP

FREE CAMPING

0   1/4 mile
0   APPROX SCALE   500m

★ trailblazer

2 HR 45 MINS–4 HRS TO COL DE LA CROIX DU BONHOMME (MAP 8)

1 HR 45 MINS–2 HRS 15 MINS FROM COL DE LA CROIX DU BONHOMME (MAP 8)

LES CHAPIEUX

LES CHAPIEUX

ROUTE GUIDE AND MAPS

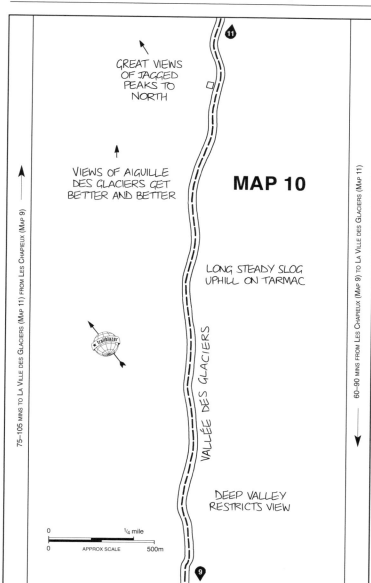

GREAT VIEWS
OF JAGGED
PEAKS TO
NORTH

VIEWS OF AIGUILLE
DES GLACIERS GET
BETTER AND BETTER

MAP 10

LONG STEADY SLOG
UPHILL ON TARMAC

VALLÉE DES GLACIERS

DEEP VALLEY
RESTRICTS VIEW

★ trailblazer

75–105 MINS TO LA VILLE DES GLACIERS (MAP 11) FROM LES CHAPIEUX (MAP 9)

60–90 MINS FROM LES CHAPIEUX (MAP 9) TO LA VILLE DES GLACIERS (MAP 11)

0   ¼ mile
0   APPROX SCALE   500m

ROUTE GUIDE AND MAPS

LES CHAPIEUX

The tiny little hamlet of Les Chapieux is a pretty spot tucked deep in the valley. It has a world-away-from-anywhere feel to it and yet it is often busy with hikers as it sits on the crossroads of the GR5 long-distance trail and the Tour du Mont Blanc. There are two places to stay here, both offering a warm, friendly welcome and good food. The *Auberge de la Nova* (☎ 04-79 89 07 15, 🖳 www.refugelanova.com; mid May-Oct; 70 beds) is over 100 years old and was once a refuge for French resistance fighters during the Second World War. It has dortoir beds for €52pp or rooms for two to four people for €62-65pp (both demi-pension). Breakfast is €5.50 and they do picnic lunches for €11. Evening meals are typically local Savoyarde specialities such as tartiflette or Diot sausages in white wine sauce (prices are around €22). You can also camp for free by the river. There are free toilets and a water fountain on site. The olde worlde **shop** is useful for bread, cheese and chocolate and they do a good line in locally produced honey.

The other place to stay is *Les Chambres des Soleils* (☎ 04-79 31 30 22, 🖳 leschambresdusoleil-montblanc.com; mid May-Sep) a few steps further along the street. Like its neighbour there has been a hotel here for well over 100 years, although it has only recently been resuscitated as a place to stay. It is smaller and more homely than Auberge de la Nova with three rooms sleeping one (B&B €61pp, demi-pension €85pp), two (B&B €48pp, demi-pension €72pp) and three (B&B €44pp, demi-pension €68pp). If you are aching after the climb over the Col du Bonhomme you might want to indulge in one of their massages for €40-60.

The route is easy to navigate to La Ville des Glaciers; simply follow the quiet road on its gradual climb up the **Vallée des Glaciers**. If the sun is beating down this can be a fairly excruciating slog along sticky tarmac but at least the views get better with every step. Ahead is the **Aiguille des Glaciers** and the glacier that seems to lend its name to every feature in the area – the **Glacier des Glaciers**.

La Ville des Glaciers has little to offer aside from a charming little chapel and a toilet block. In high summer it's under siege from motoring tourists in search of a remote roadhead. Turn right at the chapel, crossing the raging river for the track to the converted farm buildings of *Refuge des Mottets* (☎ 04-79 07 01 70, 🖳 www.lesmottets.com; mid June to mid Sep; 50 beds). To sleep here is more than affordable at €17pp in the dortoir, €46pp demi-pension. Breakfast is €8. For an evening meal try the beef Bourguignon with polenta for €17.

The refuge is the last feature of any significance before we cross the pass into Italy. Even if you don't plan to stay the night, you'll want to take a break before climbing to the Col de la Seigne. Refreshments are available from the refuge and you can sit at the picnic tables outside and turn your back on the steep climb to come and admire, instead, the views down valley.

Variante route via Col des Fours
[Map 8 p92, Map 8a, Map 11 p99]

If the weather is good, this high route proves to be a magnificent day's walk and is far more spectacular than anything the official route via Les Chapieux can offer. It also presents the opportunity for a short detour to the Tête Nord des Fours summit, from where the views of Mont Blanc are the finest you can expect anywhere on the trail. If, on the other hand, the weather looks iffy this

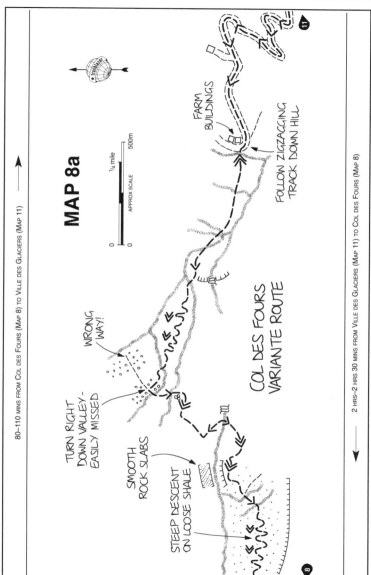

80–110 MINS FROM COL DES FOURS (MAP 8) TO VILLE DES GLACIERS (MAP 11)

MAP 8a

¼ mile

500m

0

0

APPROX SCALE

FARM BUILDINGS

FOLLOW ZIGZAGGING TRACK DOWN HILL

WRONG WAY!

TURN RIGHT DOWN VALLEY - EASILY MISSED

SMOOTH ROCK SLABS

STEEP DESCENT ON LOOSE SHALE

COL DES FOURS VARIANTE ROUTE

2 HRS–2 HRS 30 MINS FROM VILLE DES GLACIERS (MAP 11) TO COL DES FOURS (MAP 8)

ROUTE GUIDE AND MAPS

would be an unwise route choice and the path to Les Chapieux would be the only option.

From the large rotund cairn at the Col de la Croix du Bonhomme, follow the path that rises steadily over the shale towards the line of pylons above: if there is any snow around it may be tricky to locate the faint trail. Keep the shallow stream gully to your left and pass beneath the pylons. The trail continues for another 5-10 minutes to Col des Fours where the loose shale ends abruptly against a wide band of tilted orange rock ribs. From here the way descends ahead but having come this far it would be madness, if weather allows, not to take the short detour to the summit of **Tête Nord des Fours** (see box on p93 and Map 8, p92).

To continue on the trail, descend beyond the col on a path over more loose shale. Eventually the gradient eases as it reaches an area of fine alluvium. Here the path crosses a stream before contouring across the mountainside and dropping again to a junction. Turn right here and descend steeply by the banks of another stream.

At the bottom of the path there is a wide track that zigzags relentlessly to the valley floor and the small collection of buildings at **La Ville des Glaciers**. Next to the chapel follow the track down to the bridge and continue along it to **Refuge des Mottets** (see p96).

REFUGE DES MOTTETS TO COL CHÉCROUI   [Map 11, Map 12 p100, Map 13 p102, Map 14 p103, Map 15 p105, Map 16 p107]

From the refuge it is 750m of ascent to the 2516m **Col de la Seigne** on the France–Italy border. This may sound arduous but the gradient is never too steep – and just wait till you see the view on the far side of the col! The hardest part of the climb is the first section, following a steep zigzag track behind the refuge. Once this is over, a narrower trail contours the grassy mountainside, negotiates

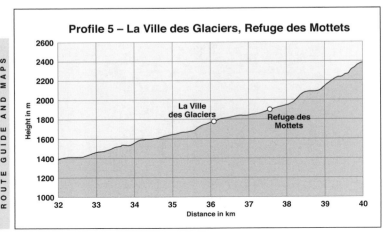

ROUTE GUIDE AND MAPS

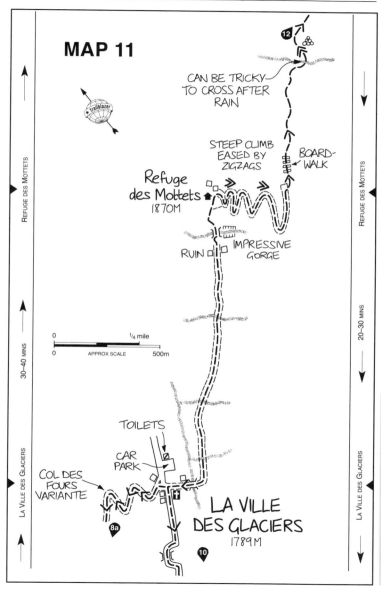

MAP 11

trailblazer

CAN BE TRICKY TO CROSS AFTER RAIN

STEEP CLIMB EASED BY ZIGZAGS

BOARD-WALK

Refuge des Mottets 1870M

IMPRESSIVE GORGE

RUIN

0   ¼ mile
0   APPROX SCALE   500m

TOILETS

CAR PARK

COL DES FOURS VARIANTE

8a

LA VILLE DES GLACIERS 1789M

10

REFUGE DES MOTTETS

REFUGE DES MOTTETS

30–40 MINS

20–30 MINS

LA VILLE DES GLACIERS

LA VILLE DES GLACIERS

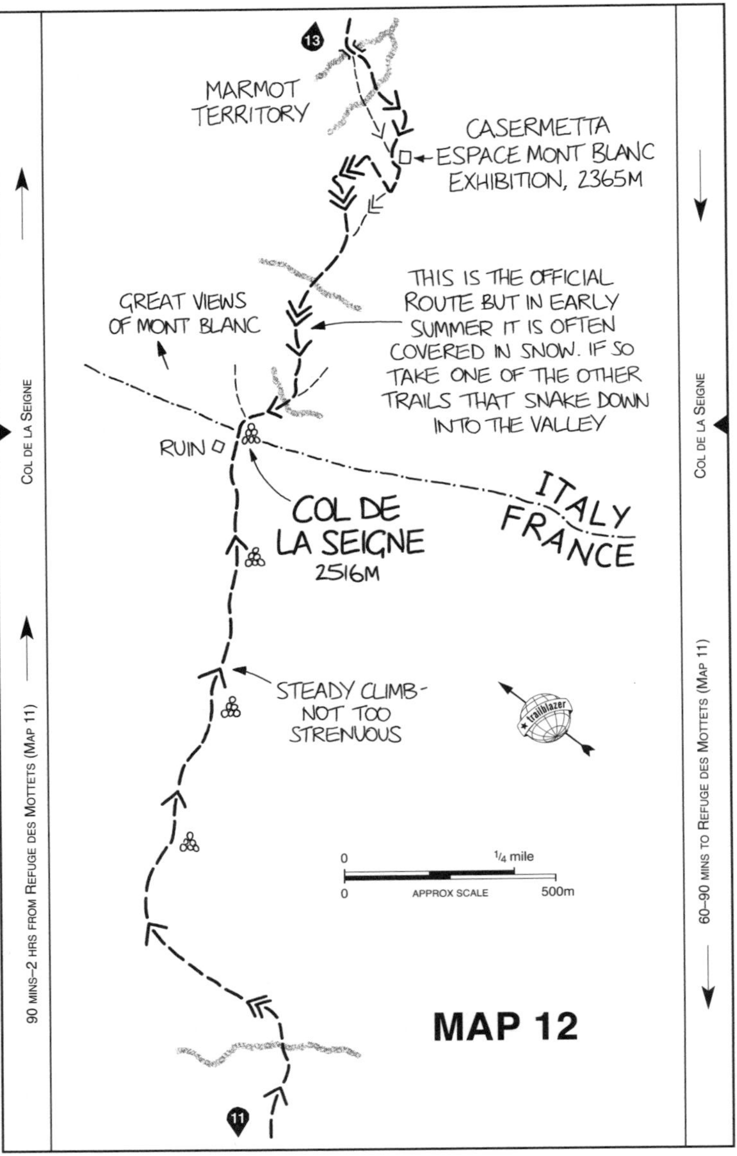

MARMOT TERRITORY

13

CASERMETTA
ESPACE MONT BLANC
EXHIBITION, 2365M

GREAT VIEWS
OF MONT BLANC

THIS IS THE OFFICIAL
ROUTE BUT IN EARLY
SUMMER IT IS OFTEN
COVERED IN SNOW. IF SO
TAKE ONE OF THE OTHER
TRAILS THAT SNAKE DOWN
INTO THE VALLEY

RUIN

ITALY
FRANCE

COL DE
LA SEIGNE
2516M

STEADY CLIMB -
NOT TOO
STRENUOUS

trailblazer

0   1/4 mile
0   APPROX SCALE   500m

MAP 12

11

COL DE LA SEIGNE

COL DE LA SEIGNE

90 MINS–2 HRS FROM REFUGE DES MOTTETS (MAP 11)

60–90 MINS TO REFUGE DES MOTTETS (MAP 11)

ROUTE GUIDE AND MAPS

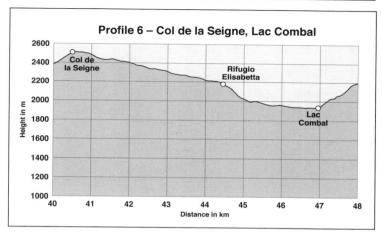

Profile 6 – Col de la Seigne, Lac Combal

a couple of streams and then follows a line of cairns across a sparsely vegetated slope of false summits to the col.

If the view back down the Vallée des Glaciers is breathtaking the view in the opposite direction into Italy may leave you on a respirator. Immediately below is **Vallon de la Lée Blanche** which leads in turn to the Val Veni and the Val Ferret. In the far distance is a later objective of ours: the Grand Col Ferret on the Swiss border. On the south side of the Val Veni is the relatively gentle, grassy mountainside that carries the trail, and on the north side the spectacular shattered peaks of the massif. Most eye-catching of all is the savage spire of **Aiguille Noire de Peuterey** and above everything the crystalline summit of Mont Blanc.

The dips and hollows on the north side of the col hold snow for longer, creating a beautiful pattern reminiscent of an Icelandic mountainside. In places it can be hard to follow the exact route of the trail as it negotiates some of these semi-permanent snow patches but there should be plenty of bootprints to suggest the way.

At 2365 metres there is a lonely stone building on the mountainside, the **Casermetta Espace Mont Blanc** (see Map 12, end Jun-Sep, free) which houses a relief model of the Mont Blanc massif and has interpretive displays about the flora, fauna, geology and history of the mountains. It is part of a cross-border environmental education initiative run by the Secure Mountain Foundation.

The trail descends to a clearer track on the floor of the Vallon de la Lée Blanche. Marmots and marigolds abound in the loose grassy moraine and pastures of the valley bottom. Soon, Rifugio Elisabetta appears above, to your left. The ruins of **Alpe Inferieur de la Lée Blanche** below are a former army post from the days when crossing European borders was less straightforward.

It's a short sharp climb to *Rifugio Elisabetta* (☎ 01-65 84 40 80, 🖳 www.rifugioelisabetta.com; mid Jun to mid Sep; 73 beds; dortoir demi-pension

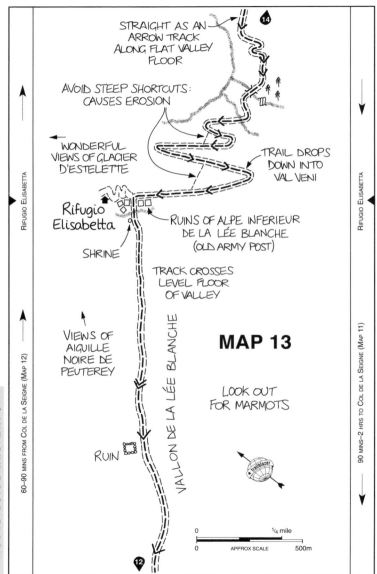

STRAIGHT AS AN
ARROW TRACK
ALONG FLAT VALLEY
FLOOR

14

AVOID STEEP SHORTCUTS:
CAUSES EROSION

WONDERFUL
VIEWS OF GLACIER
D'ESTELETTE

TRAIL DROPS
DOWN INTO
VAL VENI

RIFUGIO ELISABETTA

Rifugio
Elisabetta

RUINS OF ALPE INFERIEUR
DE LA LÉE BLANCHE
(OLD ARMY POST)

SHRINE

TRACK CROSSES
LEVEL FLOOR
OF VALLEY

RIFUGIO ELISABETTA

60–90 MINS FROM COL DE LA SEIGNE (MAP 12)

VIEWS OF
AIGUILLE
NOIRE DE
PEUTEREY

MAP 13

90 MINS–2 HRS TO COL DE LA SEIGNE (MAP 11)

LOOK OUT
FOR MARMOTS

VALLON DE LA LÉE BLANCHE

RUIN

trailblazer

12

0   ¼ mile

0   APPROX SCALE   500m

ROUTE GUIDE AND MAPS

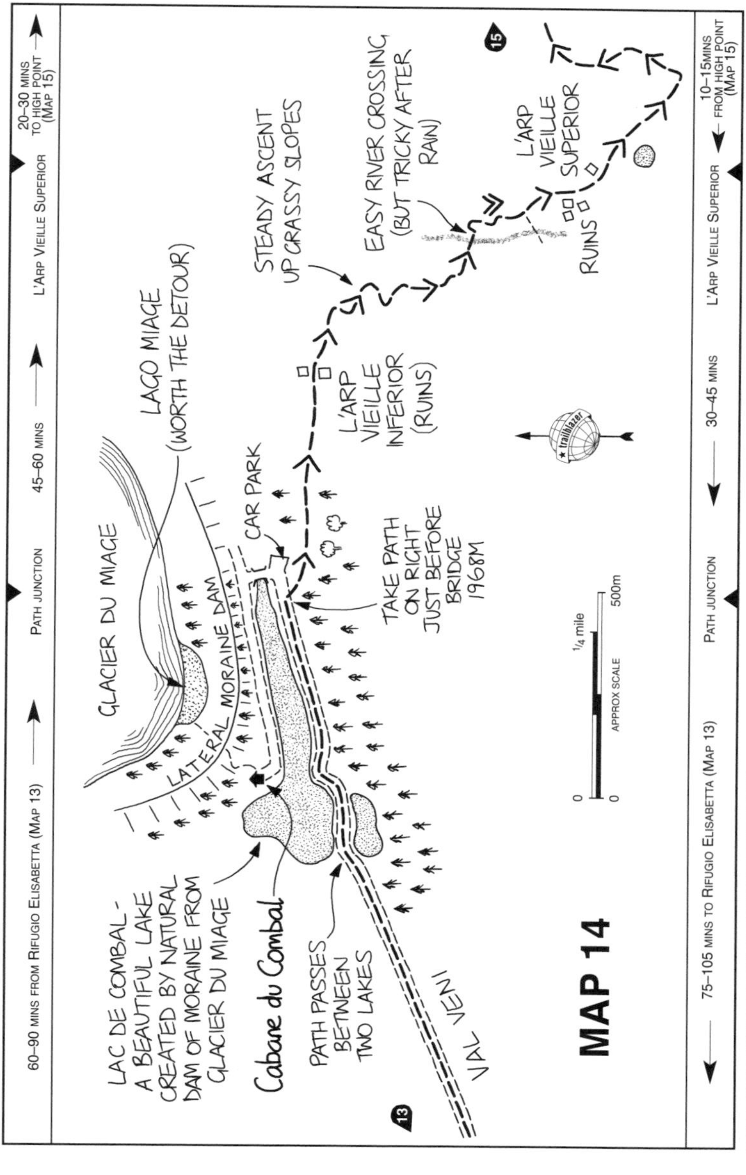

MAP 14

60-90 MINS FROM RIFUGIO ELISABETTA (MAP 13) → PATH JUNCTION → 45-60 MINS → L'ARP VIEILLE SUPERIOR → 20-30 MINS TO HIGH POINT (MAP 15)

75-105 MINS TO RIFUGIO ELISABETTA (MAP 13) → PATH JUNCTION → 30-45 MINS → L'ARP VIEILLE SUPERIOR → 10-15MINS FROM HIGH POINT (MAP 15)

LAC DE COMBAL - A BEAUTIFUL LAKE CREATED BY NATURAL DAM OF MORAINE FROM GLACIER DU MIAGE

Cabane du Combal

PATH PASSES BETWEEN TWO LAKES

VAL VENI

GLACIER DU MIAGE

LATERAL MORAINE DAM

LACO MIAGE (WORTH THE DETOUR)

CAR PARK

TAKE PATH ON RIGHT JUST BEFORE BRIDGE 1968M

L'ARP VIEILLE INFERIOR (RUINS)

STEADY ASCENT UP GRASSY SLOPES

EASY RIVER CROSSING (BUT TRICKY AFTER RAIN)

L'ARP VIEILLE SUPERIOR

RUINS

APPROX SCALE

¼ mile

0   500m

ROUTE GUIDE AND MAPS

€37pp, chambre demi-pension €42) perched spectacularly below the crevassed surface of Glacier de la Lée Blanche and the craggy sides of Aiguille de Tré la Tête beyond. The dinners here are excellent (pasta bolognese €11). They will also sort out a picnic lunch for you for €9.

Beyond the rifugio the track takes a wide zigzag to negotiate the steep drop into the **Val Veni**. Strong-kneed folk can bypass this zigzag by taking the steep shortcut path, although this does cause extra erosion so is perhaps best avoided. Another zigzag takes you down to a long flat alluvial plain. Cross the plain via a dead-straight track to the minty-blue **Lac de Combal**, naturally dammed by a massive moraine wall spilling across the width of the main valley. Ten minutes from the trail is the *Cabane du Combal* (☎ 01-65 17 56 421, 🖥 www.cabane-ducombal.com; 23 beds), a fairly recent addition to the accommodation choices on the trail. It's tucked below the huge piles of forested moraine between Lac de Combal and the Glacier du Miage. Find it by continuing along the track and crossing the bridge at the end of the lake. Then switchback along the track on the far side of the lake to reach the new cabin. During the day you can get paninis and sandwiches (€6) and more substantial dishes in the evening such as polenta e salsiccia (€12). Demi-pension is €70.

If you have come as far as the cabin it is well worth continuing on the path that climbs to **Lago Miage**, a beautiful pool of glacial water tucked beside the crumbling moraine. You can also climb onto the moraine to get a grandstand view of the **Glacier du Miage** but beware of falling rocks; this is not a static environment!

If you do not wish to go to the Cabane du Combal or visit the Glacier du Miage, continue on the TMB by taking the path on the right, about 50 metres before the road bridge. The narrow trail climbs past pine trees to some ruins and from there continues to climb for a further 300 metres to a second set of ruins on the open hillside. One of these buildings still has a roof and a stove inside and could be used as an emergency shelter. The wonderful views of the Massif du Mont Blanc across the valley will convince you to take a rest here.

Whoever was responsible for designing the route here deserves a big pat on the back: for the next hour it contours the mountainside with minimal effort allowing trekkers time to admire the grandstand views. Nowhere on the Tour are the views so delightfully uninterrupted as on this section. Things go downhill in every sense at the chairlifts and ski-run scars of **Col Chécroui** (1956m). Once past these eyesores you come to the delightfully rustic *Maison Vieille* (☎ 03-37 23 09 79, 🖥 www.maisonvieille.com; mid Jun to Sep; 60 beds; dortoir €25pp, demi-pension €50pp). This rambling stone rifugio sits on a sward of grass with a spectacular mountain backdrop. Evening meals are €25 and include dishes such as sausages and polenta. You can also get sandwiches through the day for €8. Breakfast is €10.

❑ **Phone and country codes**
Phone numbers starting 06 and 04 are in France (+33); 01 and 03 are in Italy (+39); 026 and 027 are in Switzerland (+41).

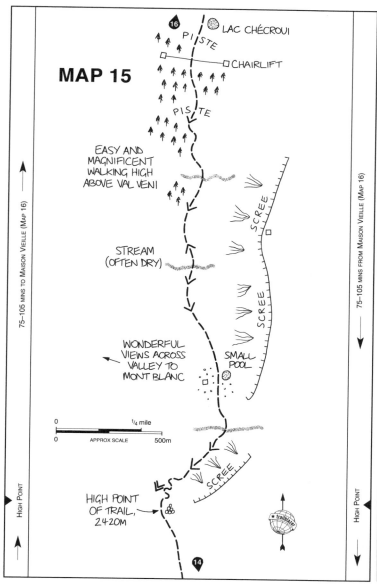

MAP 15

16 · LAC CHÉCROUI

PISTE

CHAIRLIFT

PISTE

EASY AND
MAGNIFICENT
WALKING HIGH
ABOVE VAL VENI

STREAM
(OFTEN DRY)

SCREE

SCREE

WONDERFUL
VIEWS ACROSS
VALLEY TO
MONT BLANC

SMALL
POOL

0   ¼ mile

0
APPROX SCALE   500m

SCREE

HIGH POINT
OF TRAIL,
2420M

14

75–105 MINS TO MAISON VIELLE (MAP 16)

75–105 MINS FROM MAISON VIELLE (MAP 16)

HIGH POINT

HIGH POINT

★ trailblazer

ROUTE GUIDE AND MAPS

COL CHÉCROUI TO COURMAYEUR   [Map 16, Map 17 p109]

The main route, described here, goes via Dolonne; see p110 for the variante route via Rifugio Monte Bianco. From Maison Vieille Rifugio head east on the path towards the hamlet of Pra Neyron, a recent development that acts as a winter base for the skiing fraternity. There is a confusing maze of paths and tracks around here. Keep a look out for the signs pointing the way to Pra Neyron and the ***Rifugio du Randonneur du Mont Blanc*** (☎ 03-49 53 68 898, 🖥 www.ran-donneurmb.com; dortoir B&B €35pp, dortoir demi-pension €50, chambre B&B €42pp, chambre demi-pension €70pp). Their ***Chez Ollier*** restaurant does pizzas for around €15. From Pra Neyron look for a path on the right, just before the snack bar (closed in summer). This drops steeply below the chairlift wires and on into the shady forest, running parallel to a dusty vehicle track beside more ski tows and chairlifts. The route starts off steeply and then gets even steeper. The path passes a ruin deep in the forest and then drops precipitously in a series of tight switchbacks. The gradient eases slightly once you are beyond the switchbacks but not by much.

The view into the deep Courmayeur valley is obscured for the most part by the thick forest but on a positive note your eyes are shielded from the ugly ski installations that scar the mountainside around here. By the time you reach the pretty stone village of **Dolonne** you may be cursing the gradient as the steep descent is punishing and relentless.

As you enter the village you will spot the ***Bar du Skilift*** on the left with tables and chairs on the lawn outside. You may be tempted, as I was, to stop for an ice-cream or cool drink. Take a right at the end of **Strada Chécrouit** onto **Via della Vittoria** and then left down **Strada della Vittoria**. Turn right again onto **Strada Dollone**. This takes you across the river and under the main road to the centre of **Courmayeur** (p111).

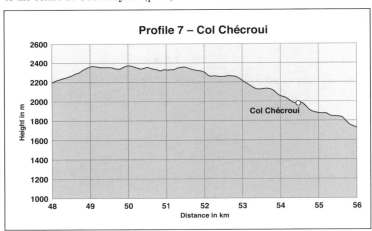

Profile 7 – Col Chécroui

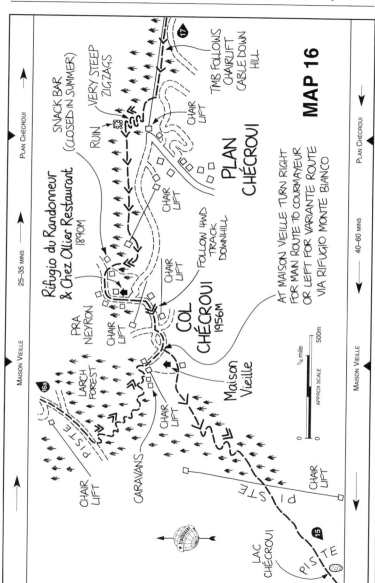

MAP 16

PLAN CHÉCROUI

TMB FOLLOWS CHAIRLIFT CABLE DOWN HILL

SNACK BAR (CLOSED IN SUMMER)

VERY STEEP ZIGZAGS

RUIN

CHAIR LIFT

Rifugio du Randonneur & Chez Olivier Restaurant 1890M

PRA NEYRON

CHAIR LIFT

CHAIR LIFT

FOLLOW 4WD TRACK DOWNHILL

COL CHÉCROUI 1956M

AT MAISON VIEILLE TURN RIGHT FOR MAIN ROUTE TO COURMAYEUR OR LEFT FOR VARIANTE ROUTE VIA RIFUGIO MONTE BIANCO

Maison Vieille

CHAIR LIFT

LARCH FOREST

PISTE

CARAVANS

CHAIR LIFT

¼ mile   500m
APPROX SCALE
0   0

CHAIR LIFT

PISTE

CHAIR LIFT

LAC CHÉCROUI

PISTE

PLAN CHÉCROUI →

25–35 MINS

MAISON VIEILLE ►

PLAN CHÉCROUI →

40–60 MINS

MAISON VIEILLE ►

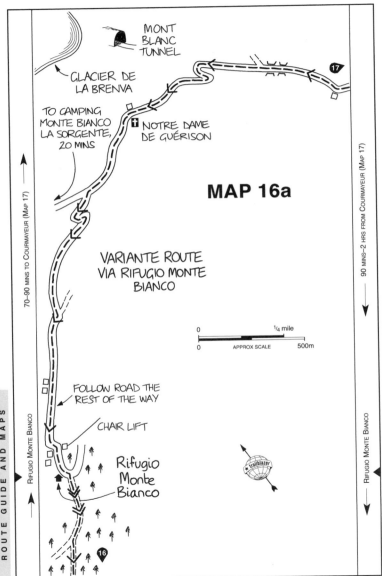

MONT BLANC TUNNEL

GLACIER DE LA BRENVA

TO CAMPING MONTE BIANCO LA SORGENTE, 20 MINS

NOTRE DAME DE GUÉRISON

MAP 16a

VARIANTE ROUTE VIA RIFUGIO MONTE BIANCO

70-90 MINS TO COURMAYEUR (MAP 17)

90 MINS–2 HRS FROM COURMAYEUR (MAP 17)

0   ¼ mile
0   APPROX SCALE   500m

FOLLOW ROAD THE REST OF THE WAY

CHAIR LIFT

Rifugio Monte Bianco

trailblazer

ROUTE GUIDE AND MAPS

RIFUGIO MONTE BIANCO

RIFUGIO MONTE BIANCO

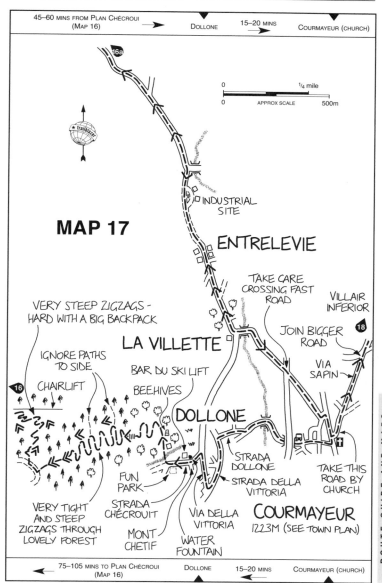

45–60 MINS FROM PLAN CHÉCROUI (MAP 16) → DOLLONE 15–20 → COURMAYEUR (CHURCH)

16a

★ trailblazer

1/4 mile

0 APPROX SCALE 500m

MAP 17

INDUSTRIAL SITE

ENTRELEVIE

TAKE CARE CROSSING FAST ROAD

VILLAIR INFERIOR

18

JOIN BIGGER ROAD

VERY STEEP ZIGZAGS – HARD WITH A BIG BACKPACK

LA VILLETTE

VIA SAPIN

IGNORE PATHS TO SIDE

BAR DU SKI LIFT

16

CHAIRLIFT

BEEHIVES

DOLLONE

VERY TIGHT AND STEEP ZIGZAGS THROUGH LOVELY FOREST

FUN PARK

STRADA CHÉCROUIT

MONT CHETIF

STRADA DOLLONE

STRADA DELLA VITTORIA

VIA DELLA VITTORIA

WATER FOUNTAIN

TAKE THIS ROAD BY CHURCH

COURMAYEUR 1223M (SEE TOWN PLAN)

← 75–105 MINS TO PLAN CHÉCROUI (MAP 16) DOLLONE 15–20 MINS COURMAYEUR (CHURCH) ←

❏ **Notre Dame de Guérison**
An oratory has stood at the site of this chapel since 1753. Following a number of miracles that occurred there, a chapel was built in 1781. The chapel has since been rebuilt twice, in 1821 and 1868, because of the advancement of the Brenva Glacier. Looking at the mass of ice now, far below the chapel, it is incredible to think that it has advanced and receded so much in such a short space of time.

Variante route via Rifugio Monte Bianco
[Map 16 p107, Map 16a p108, Map 17 p109]

The advantage of this route over the official route is the chance for an aerial view of the Brenva Glacier on its charge into the mouth of the Val Veni. The disadvantage is having to endure a bit of tarmac trekking at the end.

Begin by locating the caravans by the chairlift on Col Chécroui. It's just a stone's throw north-west from **Maison Vieille**. A path zigzags tightly down through a beautiful larch forest to a wide track by a **grassy ski piste**.

Head downhill along this track which gets steeper on its approach to the road and *Rifugio Monte Bianco* (☎ 01-65 86 90 97, 🖳 www.rifugiomonte bianco.com; mid Jun to mid Sep; 56 beds; dortoir €16pp, dortoir demi-pension €48pp, chambre €20-24pp, chambre demi-pension €52-55pp). From here to Courmayeur the trail follows the road. Distract yourself from the pounding road by admiring the Brenva Glacier, the snout of which noses into the main valley creating a mess of loose moraine.

At the foot of the slope is a road junction. Turn left for *Camping Monte Bianco La Sorgente* (☎ 01-389-9020772, 🖳 www.campinglasorgente.net; June to mid Sep; 30 beds; dortoir €16pp, chambre €25-40pp) in Peuterey in the Val Veni which has rooms as well as camping pitches.

The route to Courmayeur, however, is to the right. Follow the road down the valley, past **Notre Dame de Guérison** (see box above) and on round the foot of Mont Chétif.

The road soon drops to the bank of the river. Ignore the first bridge that crosses the torrent and continue downhill to the pretty village of **Entrelevie**.

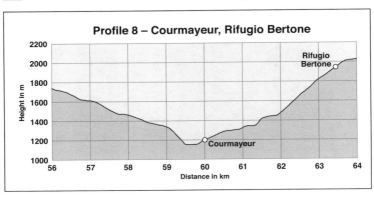

Profile 8 – Courmayeur, Rifugio Bertone

A few minutes further along this road is a road junction at **La Villette**. Cross the bridge here and climb up the steep road. After crossing the main road continue uphill to the centre of **Courmayeur**.

COURMAYEUR [map p112]

Stark black mountains weighed down by snow and ice tower above Courmayeur, sometimes like a protective hand and sometimes like a menacing giant. Courmayeur is Italy's answer to Chamonix – a skiing and mountaineering hub right on the doorstep of Mont Blanc. It grew from a small village into a thriving winter resort and has now become an all-year destination with crowds of Italians and foreigners arriving here to spend their summer holidays. The pedestrianised main street creates a relaxed village atmosphere and there is plenty to do here with sophisticated bars and street cafés.

The **Mountaineering Centre and Alpine Museum** (Thur-Tue 9am-12.30pm, 4-7pm) is the best spot to spend a rainy afternoon. This is the home of the Alpine Guides Society of Courmayeur and has been since 1929. Displays include historical photos, old log books from now-deceased mountain guides and artefacts from other mountain ranges including the Himalaya.

Services

At the **tourist information centre** (☎ 01-65 84 20 60, 🖳 www.lovevda.it) you can book accommodation and bus tickets to Chamonix and beyond. There are several **banks**, the **post office** is just behind the tourist office, while at the top of Via Croux you will find a **pharmacy**. There is another pharmacy further south on Via Roma. On the main street – Via Roma – there is a **fruit and veg shop** which is the best place to stock up for the trek ahead, though there's another at the southern end of town. Also on Via Roma there are countless **outdoor equipment shops**, one of the best being 4810 Sport (☎ 01-65 84 46 31). The **library** (Tue & Fri-Sat 10am-noon and 2.30-6.30pm, Wed-Thur 2.30-6.30pm, closed Mon & Sun) at the northern end of town, has free **wi-fi**.

Where to stay

As you might expect for an alpine town that thrives on tourism, there's plenty of accommodation but much of it is expensive.

The cheapest options are *Pensione Venezia* (☎ 01-65 84 24 61; €30pp), which is quite simple but very affordable, and *Hôtel Crampon* (☎ 01-65 84 23 85, 🖳 www.crampon.it; 23 en suite rooms; €55-65pp) which is smarter. Both are a short walk from the town centre.

Hôtel Croux (☎ 01-65 84 67 35, 🖳 www.hotelcroux.it; from €108-124pp) is reasonably priced, especially as it has a sauna/Turkish bath. Just as comfortable and affordable, *Hôtel Edelweiss* (☎ 01-65 84 15 90, 🖳 www.albergoedelweiss.it; €43-70pp) is on Via Marconi. *Hôtel Centrale* (☎ 01-65 84 66 44; €50-80pp) is where the name suggests, so convenient if you want to explore the town.

Trekkers on a budget can stay at *Camping Monte Bianco La Sorgente* campsite (see opposite) in Peuterey or continue to *Rifugio Bertone* (see p113) at the top of the hill. If on the other hand you would like a treat try one of the following: *Hôtel Berthod* (☎ 01-65 84 28 35, 🖳 www.hotelberthod.com; €47-100pp) is an intimate hotel with lots of hanging baskets; they've been in the hotel business since 1882 so should know what they're doing. *Hôtel Cristallo* (☎ 01-65 84 67 32, 🖳 www.hotelcourmayeur.it/hotel_cristallo; €55-110pp) is one of the plusher places to bed down, so some trekkers may feel a little out of place here. If they are full try their sister hotel, *Hôtel Courmayeur* (☎ 01-65 84 67 32, 🖳 www.hotelcourmayeur.it; €55-110pp).

Where to eat

You can't pass through Italy without having some genuine Italian pizza. There is no shortage of pizza outlets here and most are open through the day and on into the evening. None of them will disappoint. Try

ROUTE GUIDE AND MAPS

La Piazetta (☎ 01-65 84 41 50), a large and lively restaurant halfway down Via Roma. Pizzas and pastas are priced from €10. At the far end of Via Roma is *Mont Frety Pizzeria* (☎ 01-65 84 17 86) which does excellent pizzas from €12 which you can enjoy in their leafy garden. Other pizzerias to try include the large *Pizzeria du Parc* (☎ 01-65 84 25 90) with its shaded terrace (pizzas from €7-12), the small and rustic *Pizzeria du Tunnel* (☎ 01-65 84 17 05) with pizzas from €7-12 and *La Terrazza*

(☎ 01-65 84 33 30) which has pizzas from €12 and does other dishes too. The polenta with snails is €8.

It doesn't have to be a pizza for lunch. If you are after something different head for *Restaurant Pierre Alexis 1877* (☎ 01-65 84 67 00), a beautiful old restaurant on a quiet cobbled street away from the bustle of Via Roma. They do lots of interesting pasta dishes including egg tagliatelle with mushrooms for €15 and trout fillet for €20. The restaurant itself is beautiful with

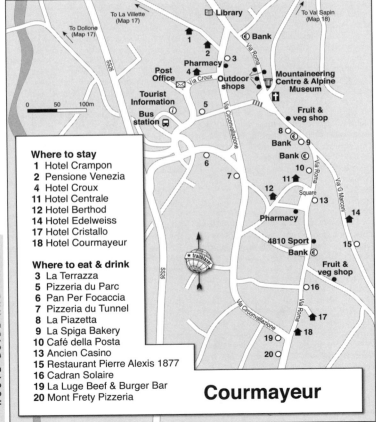

Where to stay
1 Hotel Crampon
2 Pensione Venezia
4 Hotel Croux
11 Hotel Centrale
12 Hotel Berthod
14 Hotel Edelweiss
17 Hotel Cristallo
18 Hotel Courmayeur

Where to eat & drink
3 La Terrazza
5 Pizzeria du Parc
6 Pan Per Focaccia
7 Pizzeria du Tunnel
8 La Piazetta
9 La Spiga Bakery
10 Café della Posta
13 Ancien Casino
15 Restaurant Pierre Alexis 1877
16 Cadran Solaire
19 La Luge Beef & Burger Bar
20 Mont Frety Pizzeria

Courmayeur

ROUTE GUIDE AND MAPS

vaulted brick ceilings and a tiled floor.

Back on Via Roma is *Café della Posta* (☎ 01-65 84 22 72), which has a big open frontage when the weather is hot and sunny (which is most of the time) and which is always a good place to sit with a coffee and people watch. For lunch they do some tasty salads, pastas and pastries. Nearby is *Ancien Casino* (☎ 01-65 84 22 49) with a wide choice of pizzas, pastas and fondues for around €14. Continuing along the street we reach *Cadran Solaire* (☎ 01-65 84 46

09), a rustic restaurant where you can try taglione with wild boar for €12 and guinea hen breast for €22.

For cheap breakfasts try *La Spiga bakery* (closed Wed) or for a quick lunch head for *La Luge Beef and Burger Bar* (☎ 01-65 84 3671) at the southern end of Via Roma. Another good find is *Pan per Focaccia* (☎ 01-65 84 23 03), near the bus station, with fantastic crêpes and pizzas to take away or you can perch on a bar stool and eat there.

COURMAYEUR TO RIFUGIO BONATTI [Map 17 p109, Map 18 p114, Map 19 p117, Map 20 p118, Map 21 p119]

The route described here goes via Rifugio Bertone; see p115 for the variante route via Val Sapin.

The route via Rifugio Bertone involves one of the steepest climbs on the Tour (see Profile 8, p110) but those who take it are rewarded with a great viewpoint at the top by Rifugio Bertone. Begin on the main pedestrianised street in the centre of town and take the road by the church and **Alpine Museum**. The road climbs through **Villair Inferior** and on to **Villair Superior** where it deteriorates into a track, eventually reaching a car park by a bridge. Cross the bridge and bear left to begin the steep climb up the wooded mountainside. I lost count of how many zigs and zags were on this path – the climb seems interminable. Keep straight on after the bridge if you prefer to take the variante (see p115) route. Finally, the trees begin to thin and you come to *Rifugio Bertone* (☎ 01-65 84 46 12, 🖳 www.rifugiobertone.it; mid June to Sep; 62 beds; dortoir €24pp, demi-pension €48-75pp), which looks down on Courmayeur far below, making you appreciate just how high you've climbed over such a short distance. Strictly speaking, wild **camping** is not allowed in Italy and the police do check. There is a beautiful grassy plateau just above the rifugio for anyone who wants to risk a run-in with the carabinieri. The views from here of the **Grandes Jorasses** across the valley are quite something. The **Dent du Géant** is particularly striking.

There's a real sense of elevation as you traverse the grassy ridge above the **Val Ferret**. Across the valley the shattered peaks and glaciers of the Grandes Jorasses keep neck muscles active by tempting you to look to your left almost constantly. These high cattle pastures offer some of the best opportunities on the walk for spotting wildflowers, butterflies and marmots.

Be sure to take a rest at the top of **Tête de la Tranche** (2584m) before descending to **Col Sapin** (2436m); take care on the descent as there's a lot of loose gravel and rock. The variante route rejoins the path here. The mountains ahead are green and eroded with scree fans spilling across the path. High above to the right is a waterfall cascading from the lip of a high cirque. After crossing the outflow from these falls the trail climbs a short distance to a high col, **Pas**

ROUTE GUIDE AND MAPS

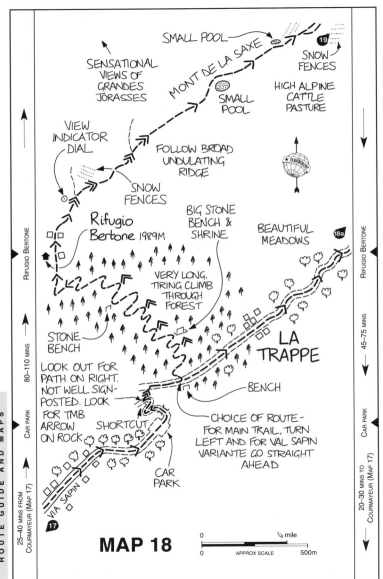

SMALL POOL

MONT DE LA SAXE

SENSATIONAL VIEWS OF GRANDES JORASSES

SMALL POOL

SNOW FENCES

19

HIGH ALPINE CATTLE PASTURE

VIEW INDICATOR DIAL

FOLLOW BROAD UNDULATING RIDGE

SNOW FENCES

★ trailblazer

Rifugio Bertone 1989M

BIG STONE BENCH & SHRINE

BEAUTIFUL MEADOWS

18a

VERY LONG, TIRING CLIMB THROUGH FOREST

STONE BENCH

LA TRAPPE

LOOK OUT FOR PATH ON RIGHT. NOT WELL SIGN-POSTED. LOOK FOR TMB ARROW ON ROCK

SHORTCUT

BENCH

CHOICE OF ROUTE— FOR MAIN TRAIL, TURN LEFT AND FOR VAL SAPIN VARIANTE GO STRAIGHT AHEAD

CAR PARK

VIA SAPIN

17

MAP 18

0   ¼ mile

0   APPROX SCALE   500m

RIFUGIO BERTONE ↑

RIFUGIO BERTONE ↓

80–110 MINS ↑

45–75 MINS ↓

CAR PARK ↑

CAR PARK ↓

25–40 MINS FROM COURMAYEUR (MAP 17) ↑

20–30 MINS TO COURMAYEUR (MAP 17) ↓

ROUTE GUIDE AND MAPS

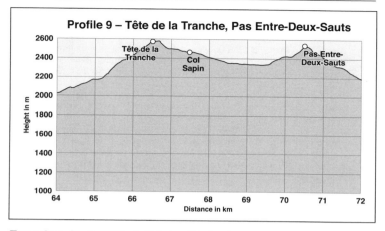

Profile 9 – Tête de la Tranche, Pas Entre-Deux-Sauts

Entre-deux-Sauts (2524m). This is wild, desolate country, strewn with erratic boulders and rough grassland.

It's a steady, gradual descent to **Rifugio Bonatti** (☎ 01-65 86 90 55, 🖥 www.rifugiobonatti.com; Mar-Oct; 90 beds; dortoir €27.50-39.50pp, demi-pension €45.50-68pp). On approaching the rifugio the vegetation becomes lusher and in high summer the wildflowers here are something else. The rifugio is named after the famous Italian climber Walter Bonatti, who was renowned for his pioneering climbs, not only here in the Alps but in the Himalaya and Patagonia too. Bonatti is perhaps most famous for soloing the north face of the Matterhorn under full winter conditions in 1965. The rifugio that bears his name overlooks the Val Ferret – the terrace out front is a great place for a lunch stop (polenta with cheese €12) and, of course, it's also a good spot to get a night's rest.

Variante route via Val Sapin
[Map 18, Map 18a p116, Map 19 p117]
It's hard to decide which is the better route; this one or the main trail via Rifugio Bertone. Certainly, the latter has the grander views and the sensation of being on top of the world but this alternative shouldn't be sniffed at, for it leads the walker through a beautiful wooded valley with spectacular views of its own. If you are not doing the whole Tour and are looking for a good circular walk, combining both routes will give you quite an outing.

From Courmayeur as far as the foot of the zigzag path the route is the same as that described previously for the route via Rifugio Bertone. This alternative route does not climb the zigzags to Rifugio Bertone but continues up the wide track along the floor of Val Sapin. Your track continues through the pretty hamlet of **La Trappe** and on through a mix of wildflower meadows and open woodland to **Chapy di Val Sapin**, a dilapidated mountain village hugging the foot of the mountain slope. Turn right here and cross the river. This should be straightforward unless it is in spate, in which case it may be impassable and you will have to return to take the main trail via Rifugio Bertone. On the other side of the river a narrow trail climbs through a lovely pine forest. Just before a shepherd's hut (hidden in the woods) there's a junction where an almost indiscernible path branches right and the main trail, the one to follow, veers left. The shepherd's hut is down to your right. Shortly after, the path breaks out of the forest to climb a steep gully alive with flowers, butterflies and crickets. It's a long climb to the junction at the top of the gully. Bear left and follow the path over the top of the wooded spur. There are wonderful views here across the valley to the mountains beyond.

The path roughly contours the mountainside, crosses a stream and passes a couple of ruined stone huts before climbing again up the open slopes to the Col Sapin. The mountains here are full of character; a dark cliff to the east and a scree slope interspersed with hardy pines to the west. At Col Sapin we rejoin the main trail; see p113.

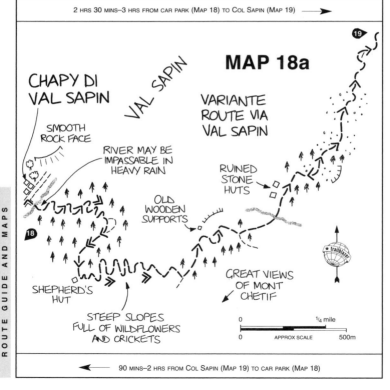

2 HRS 30 MINS–3 HRS FROM CAR PARK (MAP 18) TO COL SAPIN (MAP 19) ⟶

MAP 18a

CHAPY DI
VAL SAPIN

VAL SAPIN

VARIANTE
ROUTE VIA
VAL SAPIN

SMOOTH
ROCK FACE

RIVER MAY BE
IMPASSABLE IN
HEAVY RAIN

RUINED
STONE
HUTS

OLD
WOODEN
SUPPORTS

★ trailblazer

18

SHEPHERD'S
HUT

STEEP SLOPES
FULL OF WILDFLOWERS
AND CRICKETS

GREAT VIEWS
OF MONT
CHETIF

0   ¼ mile
0   APPROX SCALE   500m

⟵ 90 MINS–2 HRS FROM COL SAPIN (MAP 19) TO CAR PARK (MAP 18)

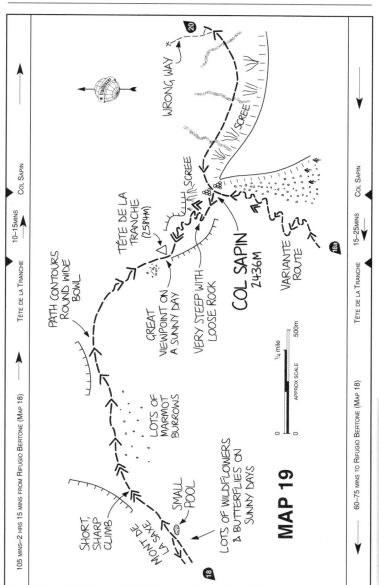

COL SAPIN

PATH CONTOURS ROUND WIDE BOWL

TÊTE DE LA TRANCHE (2584M)

GREAT VIEWPOINT ON A SUNNY DAY

VERY STEEP WITH LOOSE ROCK

SCREE

SCREE

WRONG WAY

20

COL SAPIN 2436M

VARIANTE ROUTE

18a

LOTS OF MARMOT BURROWS

SHORT, SHARP CLIMB

MONT DE LA SAXE

SMALL POOL

LOTS OF WILDFLOWERS & BUTTERFLIES ON SUNNY DAYS

18

MAP 19

APPROX SCALE

0   ¼ mile
0   500m

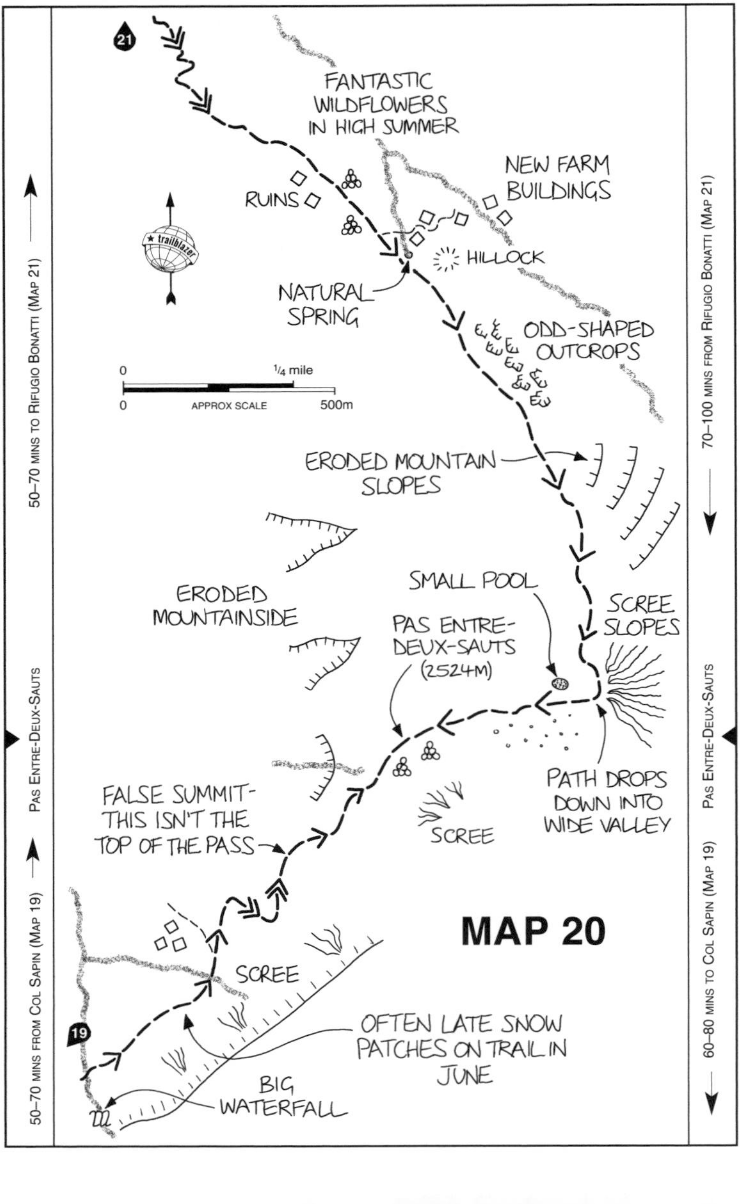

50–70 MINS TO RIFUGIO BONATTI (MAP 21)

PAS ENTRE-DEUX-SAUTS

50–70 MINS FROM COL SAPIN (MAP 19)

70–100 MINS FROM RIFUGIO BONATTI (MAP 21)

PAS ENTRE-DEUX-SAUTS

60–80 MINS TO COL SAPIN (MAP 19)

ROUTE GUIDE AND MAPS

21

FANTASTIC WILDFLOWERS IN HIGH SUMMER

NEW FARM BUILDINGS

RUINS

NATURAL SPRING

HILLOCK

ODD-SHAPED OUTCROPS

trailblazer

0   1/4 mile
0   APPROX SCALE   500m

ERODED MOUNTAIN SLOPES

ERODED MOUNTAINSIDE

SMALL POOL

PAS ENTRE-DEUX-SAUTS (2524M)

SCREE SLOPES

FALSE SUMMIT – THIS ISN'T THE TOP OF THE PASS

SCREE

PATH DROPS DOWN INTO WIDE VALLEY

MAP 20

SCREE

19

OFTEN LATE SNOW PATCHES ON TRAIL IN JUNE

BIG WATERFALL

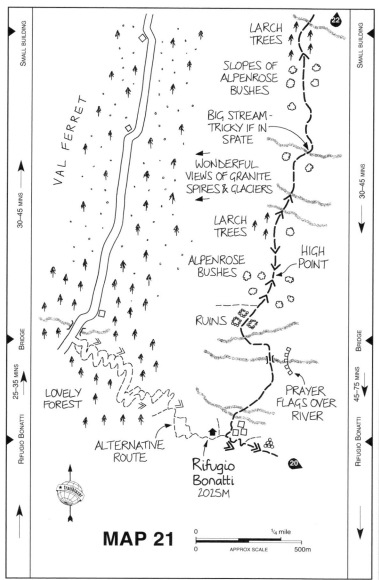

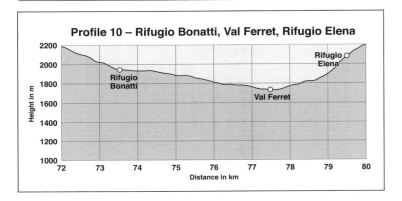

Profile 10 – Rifugio Bonatti, Val Ferret, Rifugio Elena

RIFUGIO BONATTI TO RIFUGIO ELENA [Map 21 p119, Map 22 opp]

Make the most of the next few miles because they are spectacular. The path contours high above the valley, traversing steep slopes of bright pink alpenrose with the icy Grandes Jorasses looming over the other side of the valley. And remember to look behind you for the wonderful view all the way back to the Col de la Seigne.

To pick up the path go behind the refuge and look for the trail that crosses the streams to the north. The path climbs a little after some ruins but is otherwise fairly level until the steep descent to the *Chalet Val Ferret* (☎ 01-65 84 49 59, 🖳 www.chaletvalferret.com; B&B €80pp, demi-pension €85). The lawn outside this old cattle byre is a perfect place to sit and rest your weary feet on a sunny day. The huge menu features polenta dishes from €9, spaghetti for €13 and gnocchi for €12.

Cross the bridge and leave the main track to join the path to the right. The path climbs steadily to contour the hillside. After crossing a stream it's just a short climb to *Rifugio Elena* (☎ 01-65 84 46 88, 🖳 www.rifugioelena.it; mid Jun to mid Sep; 127 beds; dortoir €25pp, chambre €38pp, demi-pension €45-61pp). The whole place is sparkling new, the original building having been destroyed by an avalanche. The terrace out front offers fantastic views of the Glacier Pré de Bar. Dinner is €21 and there's a bar open till late; breakfast costs €11 and a picnic lunch €9.50.

RIFUGIO ELENA TO LA FOULY [Map 22 opp, Maps 23-5 pp123-5]

Your brief sojourn into Italy ends on the ridge above you. Switzerland is over the crest. Take the obvious path behind the rifugio and follow its winding route up the steep grassy mountainside.

It's exactly 475 metres of ascent to the **Grand Col Ferret** on the Switzerland–Italy border. It's worth getting there early before the clouds bubble

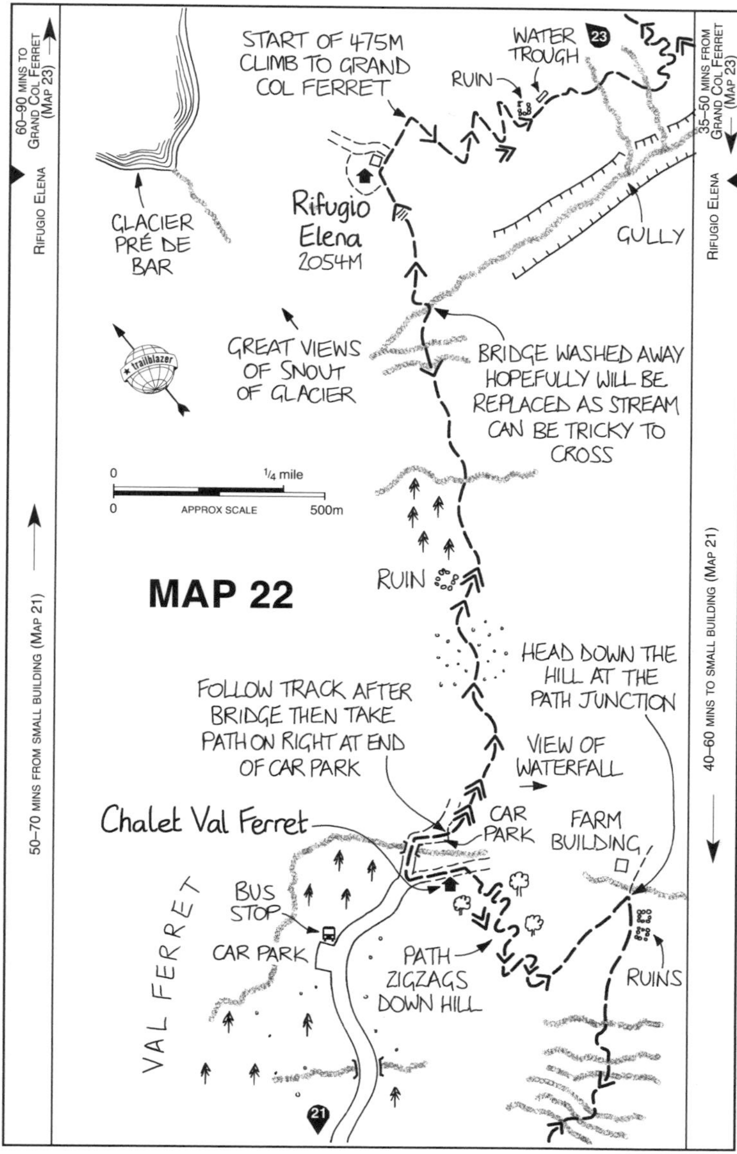

MAP 22
60–90 MINS TO GRAND COL FERRET (MAP 23)
RIFUGIO ELENA
50–70 MINS FROM SMALL BUILDING (MAP 21)
35–50 MINS FROM GRAND COL FERRET (MAP 23)
RIFUGIO ELENA
40–60 MINS TO SMALL BUILDING (MAP 21)
START OF 475M CLIMB TO GRAND COL FERRET
WATER TROUGH
RUIN
23
GLACIER PRÉ DE BAR
Rifugio Elena 2054M
GULLY
GREAT VIEWS OF SNOUT OF GLACIER
BRIDGE WASHED AWAY HOPEFULLY WILL BE REPLACED AS STREAM CAN BE TRICKY TO CROSS
trailblazer
0
1/4 mile
0
APPROX SCALE
500m
RUIN
HEAD DOWN THE HILL AT THE PATH JUNCTION
FOLLOW TRACK AFTER BRIDGE THEN TAKE PATH ON RIGHT AT END OF CAR PARK
VIEW OF WATERFALL
Chalet Val Ferret
CAR PARK
FARM BUILDING
BUS STOP
CAR PARK
VAL FERRET
PATH ZIGZAGS DOWN HILL
RUINS
21

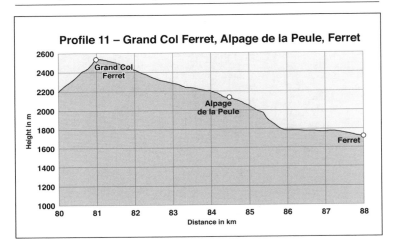

Profile 11 – Grand Col Ferret, Alpage de la Peule, Ferret

up because there are some tasty views. The indicator dial points out the imposing hulk of **Monte Rosa** to the east.

The trail descends gently into **La Peule**, a side valley leading to the upper reaches of Swiss Val Ferret.

Halfway down the mountainside is *Alpage de la Peule* (☎ 027 783 1041, 🖳 www.montourdumontblanc.com; mid Jun-mid Sep), a working farm offering simple demi-pension dortoir accommodation for around CHF62pp. They also do refreshments including very filling omelettes, made from, not one, not two, but three eggs. Beyond is a wide track that takes us down to the valley floor. This is Switzerland as you know it from children's books: goats with rattling bells, wildflower meadows, tidy timber huts, log piles so neat it seems a shame to disturb them – and all with a backdrop of icy peaks.

When the path reaches the valley floor we cross a bridge over the river and join the road. Near the head of the road is *Buvette des Ars* (🖳 www.alpagedesars.ch; daily from 9am Jun-Oct) which does food with ingredients directly from the farm. The fondue is €18 and the soup is €8. Fifteen minutes down this road is Ferret.

❏ Swiss francs or euros?

Switzerland is not a member of the European Union or Eurozone and has its own currency – the Swiss franc. You would be wise to carry a credit card to pay for transactions or use a debit card to withdraw Swiss francs from ATMs or cash machines; there is a bank in Champex and an ATM in La Fouly. Nevertheless, you will find that many hotels and restaurants do accept euros, although most prices will be given in Swiss francs. The prices in this Swiss section of the trail guide are given in Swiss francs (except where prices were available only in euros). At the time of writing the exchange rate was roughly CHF1 to €0.85 or €1 to CHF1.18.

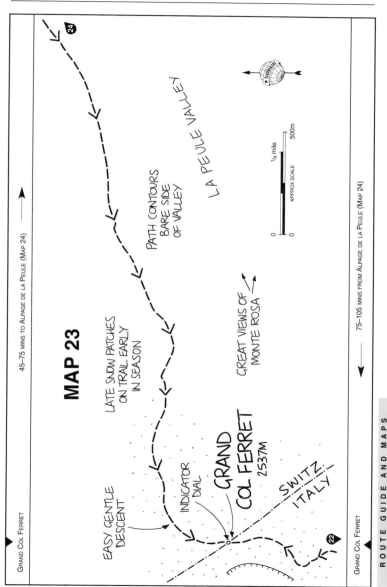

45–75 MINS TO ALPAGE DE LA PEULE (MAP 24)

MAP 23

LATE SNOW PATCHES
ON TRAIL EARLY
IN SEASON

EASY GENTLE
DESCENT

INDICATOR
DIAL

GRAND
COL FERRET
2537M

SWITZ.
ITALY

PATH CONTOURS
BARE SIDE
OF VALLEY

LA PEULE VALLEY

GREAT VIEWS OF
MONTE ROSA

¼ mile
APPROX SCALE
500m

75–105 MINS FROM ALPAGE DE LA PEULE (MAP 24)

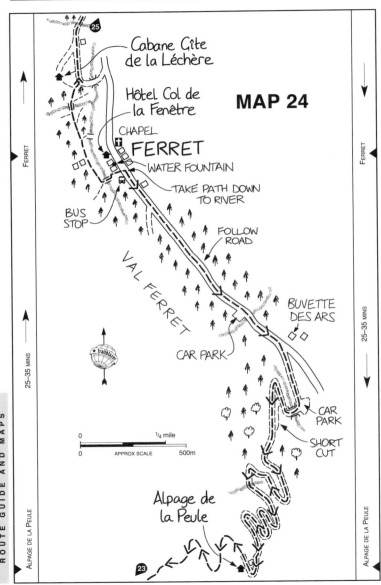

Cabane Gîte de la Léchère

Hôtel Col de la Fenêtre

MAP 24

CHAPEL

FERRET

WATER FOUNTAIN

TAKE PATH DOWN TO RIVER

BUS STOP

FOLLOW ROAD

VAL FERRET

BUVETTE DES ARS

CAR PARK

CAR PARK

SHORT CUT

0   ¼ mile

0   APPROX SCALE   500m

Alpage de la Peule

25

23

25-35 MINS

25-35 MINS

ALPAGE DE LA PEULE

ALPAGE DE LA PEULE

ROUTE GUIDE AND MAPS

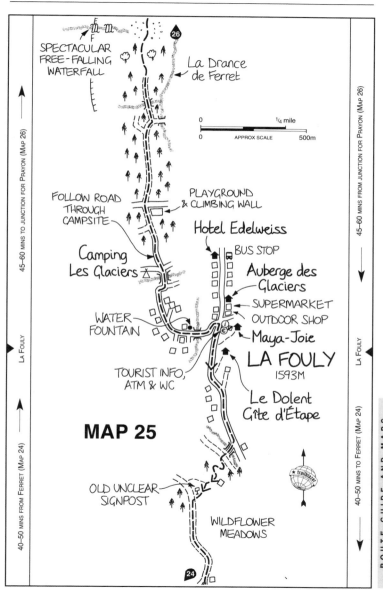

SPECTACULAR
FREE-FALLING
WATERFALL

26

La Drance
de Ferret

0   1/4 mile
APPROX SCALE
0   500m

FOLLOW ROAD
THROUGH
CAMPSITE

PLAYGROUND
& CLIMBING WALL

Hotel Edelweiss

BUS STOP

Camping
Les Glaciers

Auberge des
Glaciers

SUPERMARKET

OUTDOOR SHOP

WATER
FOUNTAIN

Maya-Joie

LA FOULY
1593M

TOURIST INFO,
ATM & WC

Le Dolent
Gîte d'Étape

MAP 25

OLD UNCLEAR
SIGNPOST

WILDFLOWER
MEADOWS

trailblazer

24

← 45-60 MINS TO JUNCTION FOR PRAYON (MAP 26)

LA FOULY

40-50 MINS FROM FERRET (MAP 24) →

45-60 MINS FROM JUNCTION FOR PRAYON (MAP 26)

LA FOULY

40-50 MINS TO FERRET (MAP 24)

ROUTE GUIDE AND MAPS

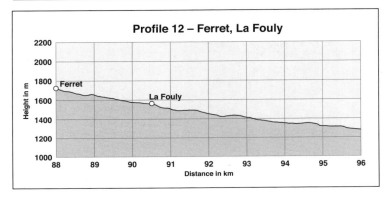

Profile 12 – Ferret, La Fouly

FERRET [Map 24, p124]

This attractive village with its tiny chapel is a good place to stop for the night; try *Hôtel Col de la Fenêtre* (☎ 027-783 1188, 🖥 www.montourdumontblanc.com; mid June-Oct; 31 beds; demi-pension dortoir CHF70pp, chambre demi-pension CHF100pp) at the northern end of the village. On the menu you will find tagliatelle Bolognese for CHF19.50 and polenta with mushrooms for CHF21.50.

Those who have the energy to continue to La Fouly need to take the path on the left just before entering the village. This crosses the river below and continues through some beautiful open pine forest to *Cabane Gîte de La Léchère* (☎ 79-891 50 20, 🖥 www.lalechere.ch; June-Sep; 35 beds; demi-pension dortoir CHF65pp). About 500 metres beyond Léchère take a right down to the river, cross the bridge and follow the road into La Fouly.

LA FOULY [Map 25, p125]

This ski resort is quite sleepy in summer but still offers a choice of food and accommodation. Just before entering the village is *Le Dolent Gîte d'Étape* (☎ 027-783 2931, 🖥 www.dolent.ch). *Camping Les Glaciers* (☎ 027-783 1826, 🖥 www.camping-glaciers.ch) is in a beautiful spot by the river. A pitch here costs CHF8pp plus CHF16 for the pitch. For more comfort try *Auberge des Glaciers* (☎ 027-783 1171, 🖥 www.aubergedesglaciers.ch; dortoir CHF32pp, dortoir and breakfast CHF44pp, demi-pension dortoir CHF69pp, chambre CHF62-67pp, chambre with breakfast CHF74-79pp, demi-pension chambre CHF99-104pp). They also do evening meals which you can enjoy on the rooftop terrace and the bar is open till late. There are fondues from CHF25 and omelettes from CHF11. The smartest place in town is the *Hôtel Edelweiss* (☎ 027-783 2621, 🖥 www.ledelweiss.ch) which has been constructed in an authentic Swiss log cabin style. Their evening meals include beef filet for CHF40 and pasta tortellini for CHF19. *Maya-Joie* (☎ 027-780 1166, 🖥 www.mayajoie.ch; dortoir with breakfast CHF30-40, chambre with breakfast CHF50) in a peaceful spot on the edge of the village is another good choice. Some of the rooms have wonderful views of the towering peak of Mont Dolent on the other side of the valley.

The village is also home to a small **supermarket** and an **outdoor shop.** There is also an **ATM** and **free wi-fi** at the **tourist information centre** (☎ 027-775 2384, 🖥 www.lafouly.ch; daily 8.30am-noon & 1.30-5.30pm) which you will see on the right as you enter the village. There are **buses** from La Fouly to Orsières (for Champex) or you can get a **taxi**: Taxi Fen'yx (☎ 079-773 7740).

ROUTE GUIDE AND MAPS

LA FOULY TO CHAMPEX [Map 25 p125, Map 26 p128, Map 27 p129, Map 28 p130, Map 29 p131]

The route continues through the grounds of the campsite. Follow the metalled lane which turns into a rough 4WD track as it enters woodland. The path is easy to follow, keeping to the west bank of the river, **La Drance de Ferret**. There is some beautiful woodland along this stretch which is broken up by grassy glades with views of the imposing mountain wall to the left. In places you may cross some old avalanche debris – a jumble of smashed branches and twigs embedded in dirty ice and snow – that has spilled across the path. Look out for the spectacular **freefalling waterfall** on the cliffs above. A little beyond the falls there is a small stone shepherd's hut; a good spot for a break on a wet day.

Ignore the paths that branch off to the right which lead to the small hamlets of Prayon and Branche d'en Haut. At the next junction, by a bench on a bend, the Tour leaves the wide track and joins a narrow trail on the left. There is an airy section of path ahead which some folk may find a little unnerving; a chain attached to the cliff offers a little reassurance. If you do not have a head for heights you can stick to the main track (which is the route suggested on the 1:25,000 IGN maps). The two routes meet up again about a mile further on.

Once past this cliff-hugging section of the trail, things gets easier and you can concentrate on enjoying the hush of the spruce forest. We soon reach a junction. Take a right and follow the straight-as-an-arrow path along the narrow, forested **Crête de Saleina** ridge. This is actually the old lateral moraine wall left behind by the Glacier de Saleina, the snout of which now sits a mile and a half up the side valley.

At the foot of this moraine wall turn left to rejoin the main track. Five minutes later the trail enters a complex of holiday cottages, scattered higgledy-piggledy across trim lawns. Some of them seem to be pseudo-ancient whilst others have a genuinely ramshackle, aged look to them. The Swiss are famous for having some of the tidiest log piles in the world; you'll see some good examples here.

(cont'd on p132)

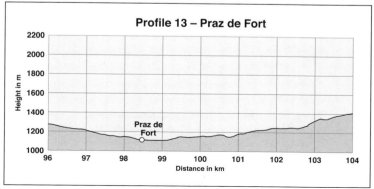

Profile 13 – Praz de Fort

ROUTE GUIDE AND MAPS

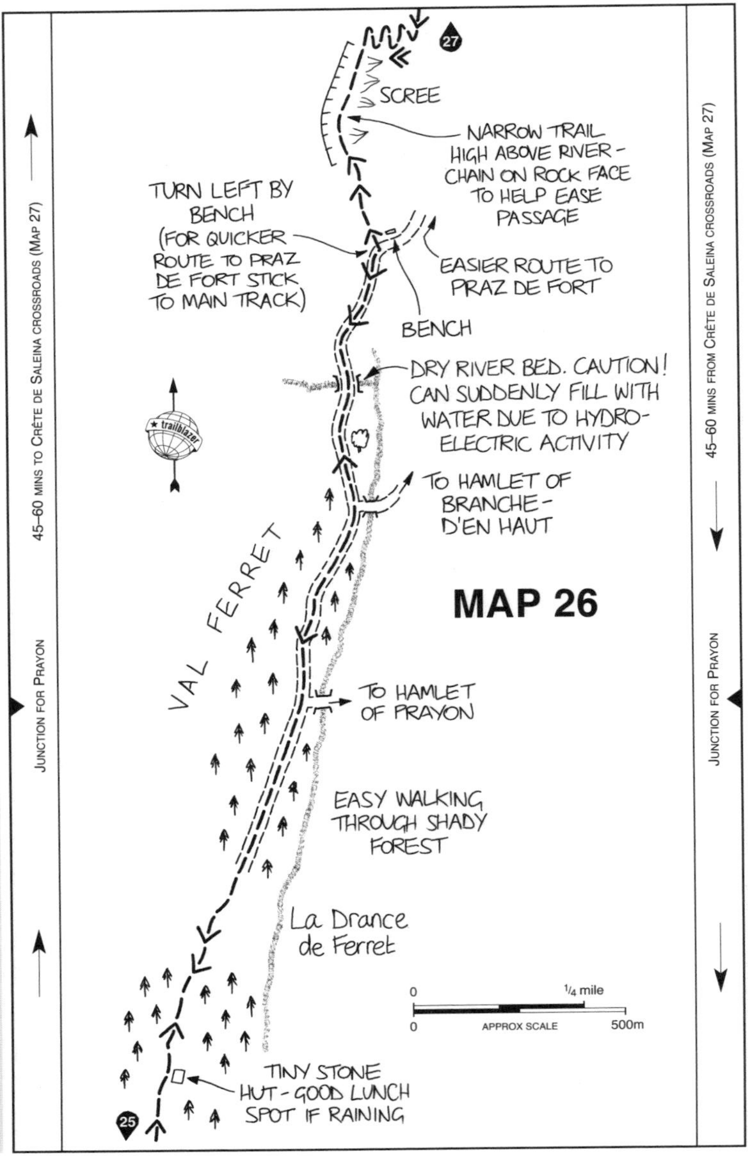

MAP 26

45–60 MINS TO CRÊTE DE SALEINA CROSSROADS (MAP 27)

45–60 MINS FROM CRÊTE DE SALEINA CROSSROADS (MAP 27)

JUNCTION FOR PRAYON

JUNCTION FOR PRAYON

trailblazer

SCREE

NARROW TRAIL HIGH ABOVE RIVER – CHAIN ON ROCK FACE TO HELP EASE PASSAGE

TURN LEFT BY BENCH (FOR QUICKER ROUTE TO PRAZ DE FORT STICK TO MAIN TRACK)

EASIER ROUTE TO PRAZ DE FORT

BENCH

DRY RIVER BED. CAUTION! CAN SUDDENLY FILL WITH WATER DUE TO HYDRO-ELECTRIC ACTIVITY

TO HAMLET OF BRANCHE-D'EN HAUT

VAL FERRET

TO HAMLET OF PRAYON

EASY WALKING THROUGH SHADY FOREST

La Drance de Ferret

0   1/4 mile
0   APPROX SCALE   500m

TINY STONE HUT – GOOD LUNCH SPOT IF RAINING

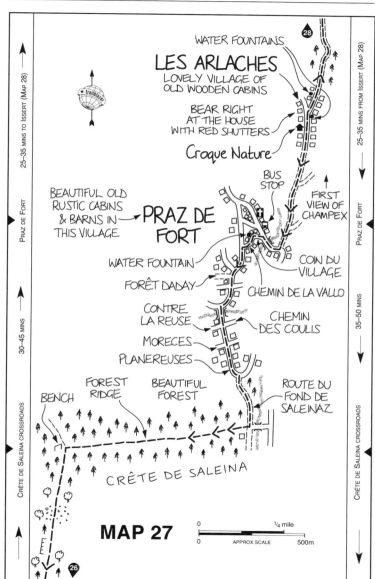

WATER FOUNTAINS

LES ARLACHES
LOVELY VILLAGE OF
OLD WOODEN CABINS

BEAR RIGHT
AT THE HOUSE
WITH RED SHUTTERS

Croque Nature

BEAUTIFUL OLD
RUSTIC CABINS
& BARNS IN
THIS VILLAGE

PRAZ DE FORT

BUS STOP

FIRST VIEW OF CHAMPEX

WATER FOUNTAIN

FORÊT DADAY

COIN DU VILLAGE

CHEMIN DE LA VALLO

CONTRE LA REUSE

CHEMIN DES COULIS

MORECES

PLANEREUSES

FOREST RIDGE

BEAUTIFUL FOREST

ROUTE DU FOND DE SALEINAZ

BENCH

CRÊTE DE SALEINA

MAP 27

0   ¼ mile
0   APPROX SCALE   500m

★ trailblazer

28

26

25–35 MINS TO ISSERT (MAP 28)

PRAZ DE FORT

30–45 MINS

CRÊTE DE SALEINA CROSSROADS

25–35 MINS FROM ISSERT (MAP 28)

PRAZ DE FORT

35–50 MINS

CRÊTE DE SALEINA CROSSROADS

ROUTE GUIDE AND MAPS

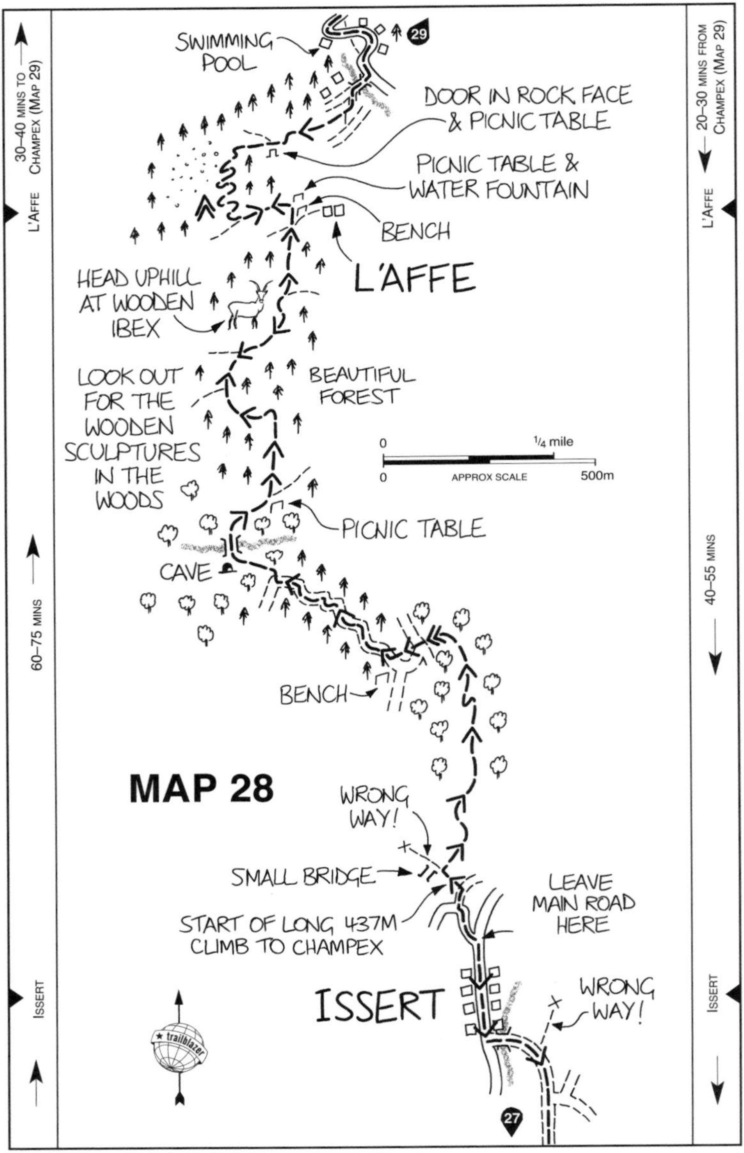

SWIMMING POOL

DOOR IN ROCK FACE & PICNIC TABLE

PICNIC TABLE & WATER FOUNTAIN

BENCH

L'AFFE

HEAD UPHILL AT WOODEN IBEX

LOOK OUT FOR THE WOODEN SCULPTURES IN THE WOODS

BEAUTIFUL FOREST

PICNIC TABLE

CAVE

0   ¼ mile
0   APPROX SCALE   500m

BENCH

MAP 28

WRONG WAY!

SMALL BRIDGE

START OF LONG 437M CLIMB TO CHAMPEX

LEAVE MAIN ROAD HERE

ISSERT

WRONG WAY!

★ trailblazer

30–40 MINS TO CHAMPEX (MAP 29)

L'AFFE

60–75 MINS

ISSERT

20–30 MINS FROM CHAMPEX (MAP 29)

L'AFFE

40–55 MINS

ISSERT

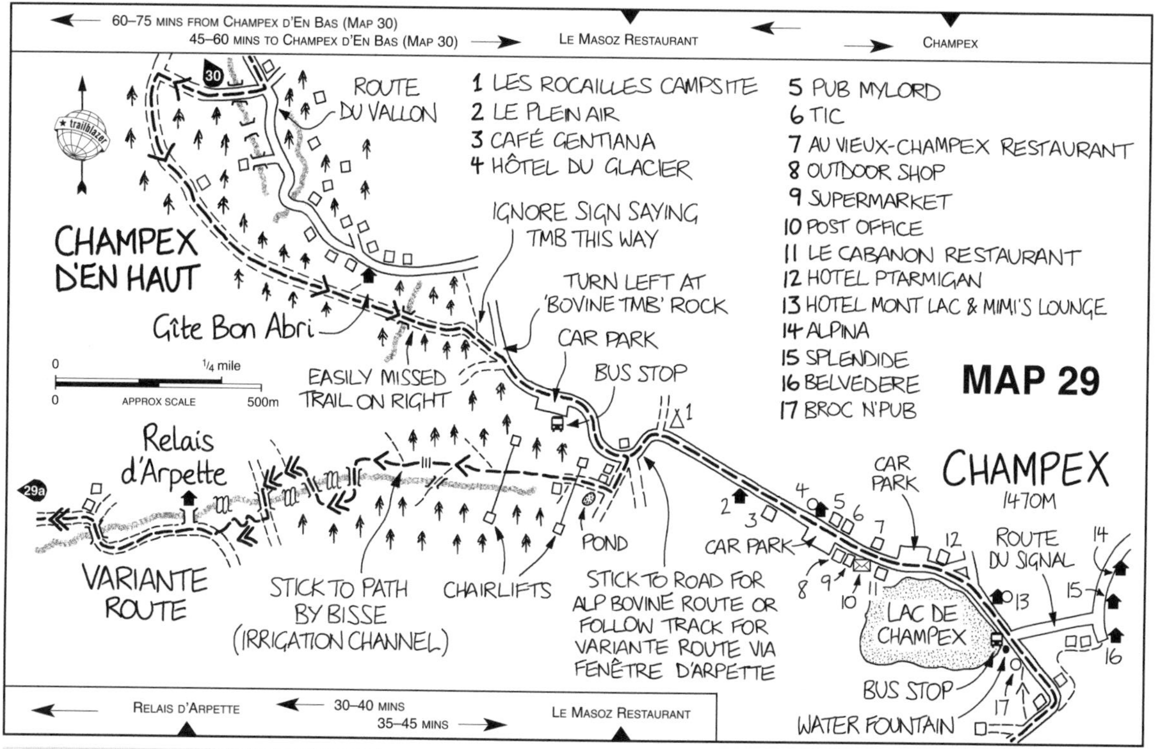

MAP 29

CHAMPEX 1470M

1 LES ROCAILLES CAMPSITE
2 LE PLEN AIR
3 CAFÉ GENTIANA
4 HÔTEL DU GLACIER
5 PUB MYLORD
6 TIC
7 AU VIEUX-CHAMPEX RESTAURANT
8 OUTDOOR SHOP
9 SUPERMARKET
10 POST OFFICE
11 LE CABANON RESTAURANT
12 HOTEL PTARMIGAN
13 HOTEL MONT LAC & MIMI'S LOUNGE
14 ALPINA
15 SPLENDIDE
16 BELVEDERE
17 BROC N'PUB

ROUTE DU SIGNAL

LAC DE CHAMPEX

CAR PARK

BUS STOP

WATER FOUNTAIN

CHAMPEX

Le Masoz Restaurant

60–75 MINS FROM CHAMPEX D'EN BAS (MAP 30)
45–60 MINS TO CHAMPEX D'EN BAS (MAP 30)

ROUTE DU VALLON

CHAMPEX D'EN HAUT

Gîte Bon Abri

EASILY MISSED TRAIL ON RIGHT

IGNORE SIGN SAYING, TMB THIS WAY

TURN LEFT AT 'BOVINE TMB' ROCK

CAR PARK

BUS STOP

CAR PARK

POND

STICK TO ROAD FOR ALP BOVINE ROUTE OR FOLLOW TRACK FOR VARIANTE ROUTE VIA FENÊTRE D'ARPETTE

CHAIRLIFTS

STICK TO PATH BY BISSE (IRRIGATION CHANNEL)

Relais d'Arpette

VARIANTE ROUTE

APPROX SCALE
0   500m
0   ¼ mile

30–40 MINS
35–45 MINS
RELAIS D'ARPETTE

Le Masoz Restaurant

ROUTE GUIDE AND MAPS

(cont'd from p127)   There is quite a maze of lanes around these holiday cottages and it is easy to take the wrong one. Keep right for the lane into **Praz de Fort**. There is little to keep you in this village, pretty as it is.

Follow the main road south across the bridge and turn left onto a farm track which meanders gently through lush fields. You can see Champex high on the hillside ahead. Next stop is **Les Arlaches**, a simply gorgeous Swiss village of creaking old wooden barns and buildings. As you tramp through the stone alleyways your boot-steps echo from the timber walls. You can stay in one of the old buildings at *Croque Nature* (☎ 027 565 2646, 🖳 www.croquenature.ch; chambre with breakfast CHF55).

From Les Arlaches head downhill to **Issert**, a less-inspiring village of concrete buildings hugging the main road. Just outside the village we turn left for a steep zigzagging climb through fields and woodland. This is just the start of an unforgiving 437-metre ascent to **Champex**. The pain in your calf muscles is somewhat compensated for by yet more wonderful woodland throughout the climb.

CHAMPEX   [Map 29, p131]

Champex is a popular lakeside resort where Swiss, French and Italians come to relax. Here you can hire a rowing boat, go fishing or simply sit by the lake and watch the world go by. While it is certainly a beguiling spot, slotted in between high mountains, some may be uncomfortable with the resort's touristy nature. The upside is the plethora of places offering accommodation and food so why not be a tourist and spend the night here.

Everything you need is laid out along the one street with most of interest to the north of the lake. Here you'll find a **tourist information office** (☎ 027 775 2383, 🖳 www.champex.ch; daily 8.30am-noon & 1.30-5.30pm) with free **wi-fi**, a **post office** with ATM and a small **supermarket** (Mon-Fri 7.30am-12.30pm & 2.30-6.30pm, Sat-Sun 7.30am-5.30pm). Next to the supermarket is an **outdoor shop**.

Where to stay and eat

At Champex's eastern end is *Hôtel Mont Lac* (☎ 026 565 6600, 🖳 www.hotel-mont-lac.ch; en suite demi-pension €40pp) where each of the four en suite rooms has a terrace overlooking the lake. There is a handful of grand hotels up Route du Signal, each with a fantastic view over the valley below. The first is *Belvedere* (☎ 027 783 1114, 🖳 www.le-belvedere.ch; 20 beds; demi-pension CHF220pp), followed by

Splendide (☎ 027 783 1145, 🖳 www.hotel-splendide.ch; €65-86pp) and *Alpina* (☎ 027 783 1892, 🖳 www.alpinachampex.ch; CHF160-180pp).

Down on the main drag is *Hôtel Ptarmigan* (☎ 027 783 1640, 🖳 www.ptarmigan.ch; chambre with breakfast CHF50pp) a small and homely place with three rooms sharing a bathroom. Two of the rooms have balconies with views over the lake.

At the far western end of the village is *Hôtel du Glacier* (☎ 027 782 6151, 🖳 www.hotelglacier.ch; from CHF60-70pp), with 20 rooms, tennis court and jacuzzi, and no-frills *Pension En Plein Air* (☎ 027 783 2350, 🖳 www.pensionenpleinair.ch; 73 beds; dortoir with breakfast CHF44, demi-pension dortoir CHF69pp, chambre with breakfast CHF57pp, demi-pension chambre CHF82pp) with its Fresian cow décor. It has small two-, three-, four- and six-bed rooms. *Les Rocailles Campsite* (☎ 027 783 1979, 🖳 www.champexcamping. ch) is 500 metres to the west by the big bend in the road. Pitches are CHF15.

For a meal out try *Le Cabanon Restaurant* with its lakeside terrace. They do beef dishes from CHF25 and fondue for CHF22. Opposite the post office is the rustic-looking *Au Vieux-Champex Restaurant* (☎ 027 783 1216, 🖳 vieux.champex@drans net.ch) with traditional fondue for CHF23 and smoked salmon for CHF21. They also do pizzas and spaghetti dishes from CHF16. One of the smarter restaurants is at *Hôtel du Glacier* (see opposite) where you can tuck into roast beef for CHF36 or spaghetti bolognese for CHF18. They also do pizzas and burgers from CHF15. At Hôtel Mont Lac (see opposite) there is a classy wine and tapas bar, *Mimi's Lounge*, where you can enjoy tapas as well as more substantial risotto (CHF24), quiche (CHF17) and lasagne (CHF19) dishes. For a snack try *Boulangerie Tearoom Café Gentiana* (☎ 027 783 1258) which has a variety of home-made pastries and does a great breakfast. Finally, if all you need is a drink, pull up a chair at *Pub Mylord*, which, as the name suggests, panders to an English clientele, or *Broc N'Pub* (closed Sun-Mon), a trendy bar with a giant flamingo and a cable car converted into seats.

CHAMPEX TO COL DE LA FORCLAZ
[Map 29 p131, Map 30 p134, Map 31 p136, Map 32 p137]

This official route, via Alp Bovine, while less spectacular than the Fenêtre d'Arpette variante (see p135), still offers plenty. Most of the walk passes through pine and larch forests but there are also some open stretches, particularly around Alp Bovine which offers sensational views down the Rhône Valley to Sion and Sierre; views which those taking the Fenêtre d'Arpette variante will miss.

Begin by heading along the road past Les Rocailles campsite, around the S-bend in the road and past the chairlift station. A few minutes further on there is a large rock on the left-hand side with the words 'Bovine TMB' painted on it. Turn left here, down the forestry track.

Across the meadows on the right is *Gîte Bon Abri* (☎ 027 783 1423, 🖳 www.gite-bon-abri.com; Jun-Sep; demi-pension dortoir €30-39pp, demi-pension chambre €45pp). As well as the rooms (2-, 4-, 6- and 18-bed rooms) there's also a teepee: €9pp. It's a peaceful place to stay, away from the hustle and bustle of the village.

The TMB route continues along the forestry track to **Champex d'en Bas**. Turn left here and keep on the main track as it bears right through the woodland, past a small pasture and on to the lane leading to the buildings at **Plan de l'Au**.

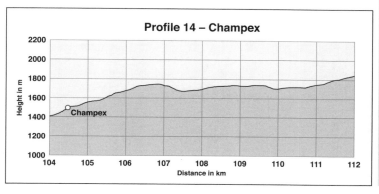

Profile 14 – Champex

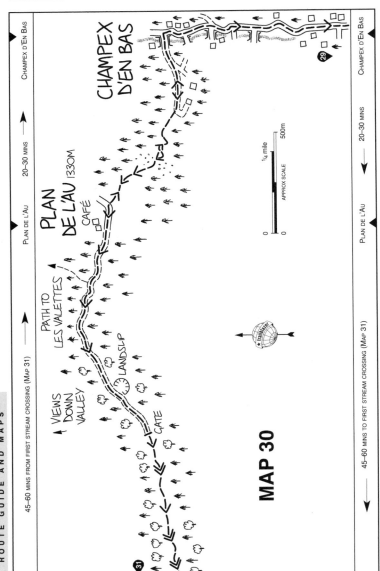

CHAMPEX D'EN BAS

CHAMPEX D'EN BAS

20–30 MINS

20–30 MINS

PLAN DE L'AU

PLAN DE L'AU

45–60 MINS FROM FIRST STREAM CROSSING (MAP 31)

45–60 MINS TO FIRST STREAM CROSSING (MAP 31)

PLAN DE L'AU 1330M

CHAMPEX D'EN BAS

CAFÉ

PATH TO LES VALETTES

VIEWS DOWN VALLEY

LANDSLIP

GATE

MAP 30

1/4 mile

APPROX SCALE

0   500m
0

29

31

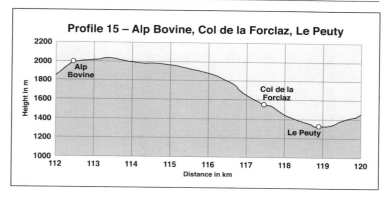

Profile 15 – Alp Bovine, Col de la Forclaz, Le Peuty

A small **café** here sells snacks and drinks. The track heads straight back into the thick forest and contours the mountainside as it enters **Le Barmay** valley. At the head of this valley the trail gets steeper and crosses some high Alpine pasture. There are a few streams to negotiate which are easy in dry weather but pose problems in heavy rain.

Now back in the forest the path climbs further still, eventually emerging onto the open mountainside where cattle graze. That's the steep stuff behind you. Now follow the well-worn path as it contours northwards to *Alp Bovine*. The garden at this rustic barn is a spectacular spot for lunch with wide-ranging views down the Rhone valley and over the peaks of the Bernese Alps. This is simply magnificent stuff. The towns of Martigny, Sion and Sierre can be picked out far below. You can also just about see the end of Lake Geneva. At Alp Bovine they serve tranche au fromage (€13) and rosti nature (€12) among other local specialities.

The path from Alp Bovine climbs to a gate and then descends through a beautiful larch forest to the farm at **La Giète**. Continue across the pasture and back into the forest. It's another mile and a half of pleasant walking along the forested mountainside to **Col de la Forclaz**.

Variante route via Fenêtre d'Arpette
[Map 29 p131, Map 29a p139, Map 29b p140, Map 33 p142]
This is the more spectacular, and more demanding of the two routes between Champex and Col de la Forclaz. If the weather is poor you would be wise to opt for the route described above. If, on the other hand, the sun is shining and you are feeling fit you will be well rewarded for the effort of climbing to the Fenêtre d'Arpette, a narrow col at 2665m on a dramatic rocky crest separating the Val d'Arpette from the neighbouring Trient valley.

Begin by following the road uphill from Champex. Just past Les Rocailles campsite there is a track. Head up here and almost immediately turn right next to a small pond. The path ducks under the chairlift wires and follows an irrigation channel through the pine forest. *(cont'd on p138)*

ROUTE GUIDE AND MAPS

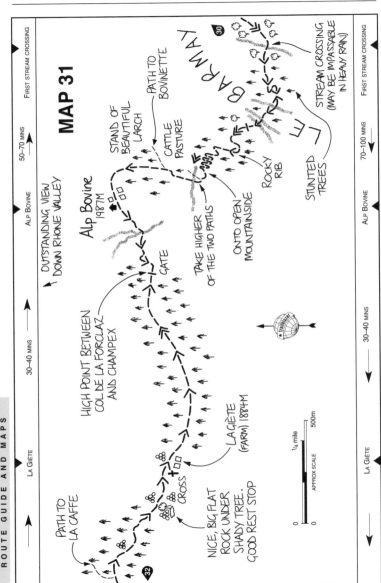

ROUTE GUIDE AND MAPS

MAP 31

FIRST STREAM CROSSING

50-70 MINS

OUTSTANDING VIEW DOWN RHONE VALLEY

ALP BOVINE

30-40 MINS

LA GIÈTE

STAND OF BEAUTIFUL LARCH

PATH TO BOVINETTE

CATTLE PASTURE

Alp Bovine 1987M

ROCKY RIB

STUNTED TREES

STREAM CROSSING (MAY BE IMPASSABLE IN HEAVY RAIN)

TAKE HIGHER OF THE TWO PATHS

ONTO OPEN MOUNTAINSIDE

GATE

HIGH POINT BETWEEN COL DE LA FORCLAZ AND CHAMPEX

LA GIÈTE (FARM) 1884M

CROSS

PATH TO LA CAFFE

NICE, BIG FLAT ROCK UNDER SHADY TREE. GOOD REST STOP

¼ mile
500m
APPROX SCALE
0
0

FIRST STREAM CROSSING

70-100 MINS

ALP BOVINE

30-40 MINS

LA GIÈTE

BARMAY

30

32

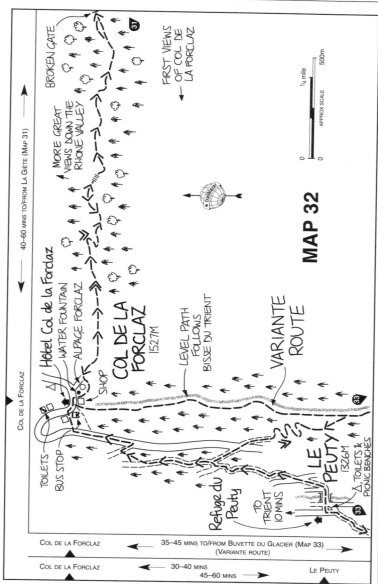

MAP 32

COL DE LA FORCLAZ

40–60 MINS TO/FROM LA GIÈTE (MAP 31)

BROKEN GATE

MORE GREAT
VIEWS DOWN THE
RHONE VALLEY

FIRST VIEWS
OF COL DE
LA FORCLAZ

31

Hotel Col de la Forclaz
Water Fountain
Alpage Forclaz

COL DE LA
FORCLAZ
1521M

SHOP

LEVEL PATH
FOLLOWS
BISSE DU TRIENT

VARIANTE
ROUTE

33

TOILETS
BUS STOP

Refuge du Peuty

TO
TRIENT 10MINS

LE PEUTY
1326M

TOILETS &
PICNIC BENCHES

33

APPROX SCALE

¼ mile
500m

trailblazer

COL DE LA FORCLAZ

35–45 MINS TO/FROM BUVETTE DU GLACIER (MAP 33)
(VARIANTE ROUTE)

COL DE LA FORCLAZ

30–40 MINS
45–60 MINS

LE PEUTY

(cont'd from p135)   Continue to a forest track where you cross a bridge and rejoin the path on the opposite bank. It is a short, steep climb to ***Relais d'Arpette*** (☎ 027 783 1221, 🖥 www.arpette.ch; May-Sep; 86 beds; demi-pension dortoir CHF69.50, demi-pension chambre CHF87-97pp, **camping** CHF13.50pp, picnic lunch CHF16) but once there it is pleasant walking through the valley which, in summer, is full of wildflowers, particularly orchids.

Enjoy the easy nature of the path while you can. It soon begins to climb again, at first through a rocky gully and then traversing the steep mountainside as it negotiates boulder-strewn slopes and patches of scree. The gradient eases a little as the path passes below savage black cliffs on either side before finally arriving at a bowl of rocks and boulders just below **Fenêtre d'Arpette**. A series of tight zigzags climb steeply to the col. Take care on this section; it's steep and the rocks and gravel are loose in places. You may also need to cross some semi-permanent snow patches in the hollows and gullies.

If you have good weather you will want to stop at the col to take in the magnificent view on the other side. The **Glacier du Trient** below you steals the show.

If you look at the recently scoured rock below the snout you can appreciate just how far the glacier has retreated in recent years. At the start of the 20th century the snout rested close to the village of Trient, about two miles down valley.

The descent is almost as steep as the ascent so tread carefully. Before long the steepest sections are behind you and the trail guides you through high mountain pasture above the glacier. There is a rudimentary stone **shepherd's 'hut'** about halfway down which offers a suggestion of shelter in bad weather. Soon the wild flowers and fields give way to stunted trees and then the trail follows the crest of the old lateral moraine ridge through the thick forest of the lower valley. There is a café, ***Buvette du Glacier de Trient***, in the forest where you can buy sandwiches for €5.50 and more filling dishes such as croute au fromage for €17. You have a choice of routes here. The main trail to **Col de la Forclaz** is straight on, or there is a shortcut to Col de Balme across the river (see p141).

From the café it is a long but easy walk along a good level path that follows an old irrigation channel, the Bisse du Trient (see box below), all the way to Col de la Forclaz. There is little here except for good views, a road and the historic ***Hôtel Col de la Forclaz*** (☎ 027 722 2688, 🖥 www.coldelaforclaz.ch; all year; 75 beds; dortoir CHF29pp, demi-pension dortoir CHF65pp, chambre CHF44-68 chambre demi-pension CHF72-94pp, **camping** CHF8pp and CHF6-9 per tent), a friendly establishment complete with stuffed local fauna but far from stuffy staff; this is an imposing old hotel with a warm welcome while the food is fresh and tasty. The fondue is CHF26 and croute au fromage is CHF13. Across the road there is a small shack, the ***Alpage Forclaz***, selling beer and snacks. There is also a small **shop** selling drinks, chocolate bars and ice cream.

❏ The Bisse du Trient
The 'bisse' or irrigation channel that flows from Trient Glacier to Col de la Forclaz was constructed in 1865 to carry meltwater from the snout of the glacier to irrigate the fields in the valleys below. In places the water flows through carefully constructed wooden aqueducts. Ice was also once transported from the glacier and carried to the hotel at Col de la Forclaz by tramway. The path follows the old route of this tramway and at one point you can still see a section of the track and an old ice wagon.

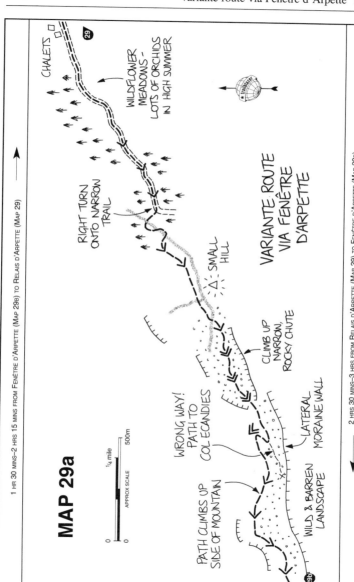

MAP 29a

0   ¼ mile
0   500m
APPROX SCALE

PATH CLIMBS UP SIDE OF MOUNTAIN

WRONG WAY! PATH TO COL ECANDIES

WILD & BARREN LANDSCAPE

LATERAL MORAINE WALL

CLIMB UP NARROW, ROCKY CHUTE

SMALL HILL

VARIANTE ROUTE VIA FENÊTRE D'ARPETTE (MAP 29b)

RIGHT TURN ONTO NARROW TRAIL

WILDFLOWER MEADOWS – LOTS OF ORCHIDS IN HIGH SUMMER

CHALETS

29

29b

1 HR 30 MINS–2 HRS 15 MINS FROM FENÊTRE D'ARPETTE (MAP 29b) TO RELAIS D'ARPETTE (MAP 29)

2 HRS 30 MINS–3 HRS FROM RELAIS D'ARPETTE (MAP 29) TO FENÊTRE D'ARPETTE (MAP 29b)

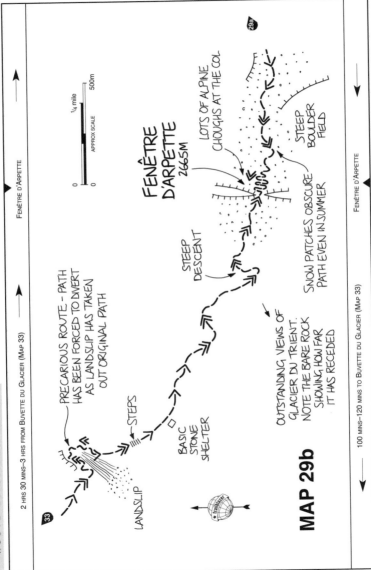

Short cut from Buvette du Glacier to Col de Balme via Refuge les Grands
[Map 33 p142, Map 34 p143]

If you are coming from Champex via the Fenêtre d'Arpette you can take a short cut to the Col de Balme. This route misses out on Col de la Forclaz and the villages in the Trient valley but the advantage is that you keep your altitude and you have less distance to cover.

Refuge les Grands (☎ 026 548 1323; 15 beds; late Jun-Sep), halfway along this route, offers an alternative, quieter spot to spend the night than Chalet-Refuge du Col de Balme. However, it is very small and has no catering facilities. Call ahead to check opening times and availability.

The short cut begins when you reach *Buvette du Glacier de Trient* after crossing the Fenêtre d'Arpette. The food here is tasty but expensive; the croute au fromage (a kind of cheese on toast) is CHF17 and the assiette Valaisanne (a local dish of hams and cheeses) is CHF24. Cross the bridge below the café and follow the path to the left. This climbs up the valley to a junction. Take a right here and climb up the sparsely forested side valley.

Glacier de Bron and **Glacier des Grands** hug the bare rocky slopes above. As the stunted trees give way to the open mountainside the path takes in a couple of large switchbacks, the second of which leads onto a spectacular stretch where the trail has been built into the cliff face. If you don't have a head for heights you will appreciate the metal cable bolted into the rock for security. Beyond this is **Refuge les Grands** (see above). It is a pleasant walk from here to Col de Balme; at first the trail clambers over rough terrain of rocky outcrops, shrubs and stunted trees and then round the shoulder of the mountain where it contours high above the Nant Noir valley. From here the trail offers easy walking to the **Col de Balme** ahead.

LE PEUTY & TRIENT
[MAP 32, p137]

The local authority has set aside an area for **camping** here (CHF4pp). There are no facilities except for the toilets and picnic tables. There is also *Refuge du Peuty* (☎ 027-722 0938; mid June to mid Sep; 37 beds; dortoir €20pp) which has a self-catering kitchen, showers and dormitory beds.

Half a mile north is **Trient.** Here you will find the *Auberge du Mont Blanc* (☎ 027 767 1505, 🖳 www.aubergemont-blanc.com), a large hotel run by the owners of the Refuge du Peuty. There are private rooms (€42pp, demi-pension €69pp) as well as large dormitories (€33pp, demi-pension €57pp). Nearby is *La Grande Ourse* (☎ 027 722 1754, 🖳 www.la-grande-ourse.ch; dortoir CHF35pp, dortoir demi-pension CHF68pp, chambre CHF52-62pp, chambre demi-pension CHF85-95pp) which offers a similar bed or dormitory deal.

COL DE LA FORCLAZ TO COL DE BALME
[Map 32 p137, Map 33 p142, Map 34 p143]

Before we can go up to Col de Balme we have to go down from the Col de la Forclaz to the floor of the Trient valley. The path starts opposite the hotel and passes a couple of old buildings to descend to the road. Follow the road for about 300 metres and then take the track on the right. The signs lead you down through the steep woodland to **Le Peuty**.

After crossing the river into Le Peuty turn left along the road and almost immediately take a right along a farm track. *(cont'd on p144)*

ROUTE GUIDE AND MAPS

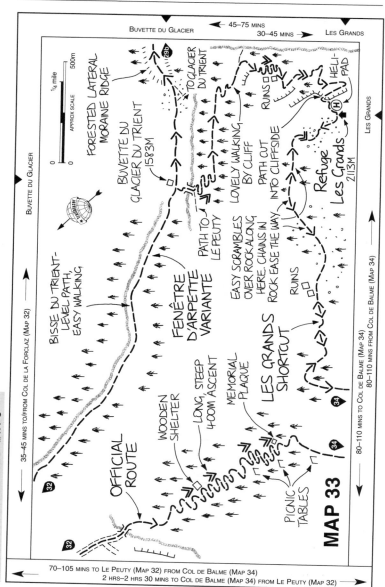

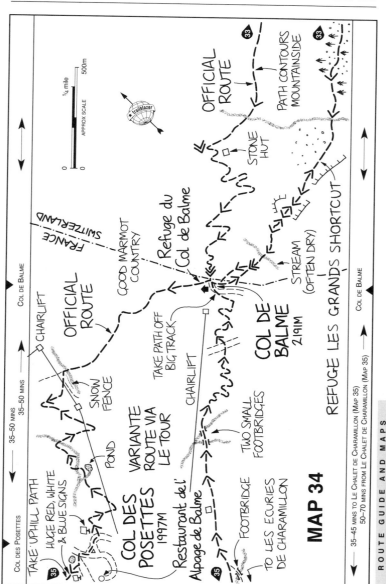

COL DE POSETTES

35-50 MINS ← → 35-50 MINS

COL DE BALME

TAKE UPHILL PATH

HUGE RED, WHITE & BLUE SIGNS

CHAIRLIFT

CHAIRLIFT

OFFICIAL ROUTE

POND

SNOW FENCE

FRANCE ——·—— SWITZERLAND

GOOD MARMOT COUNTRY

Refuge du Col de Balme

OFFICIAL ROUTE

PATH CONTOURS MOUNTAINSIDE

STONE HUT

¼ mile

APPROX SCALE

0   500m

0

trailblazer

COL DES POSETTES 1997M

Restaurant de l'Alpage de Balme

VARIANTE ROUTE VIA LE TOUR

TAKE PATH OFF BIG TRACK

TWO SMALL FOOTBRIDGES

COL DE BALME 2191M

STREAM (OFTEN DRY)

FOOTBRIDGE

TO LES ECURIES DE CHARAMILLON

MAP 34

COL DE BALME

REFUGE LES GRANDS SHORTCUT

35-45 MINS TO LE CHALET DE CHARAMILLON (MAP 35)
50-70 MINS FROM LE CHALET DE CHARAMILLON (MAP 35)

(cont'd from p141)   The path passes through some rough pasture before crossing a stream to reach the forest. Say goodbye to the views for now; the path ducks into the shady forest and begins to climb. This is one of the steepest and longest ascents on the Tour, on a par with the ascent out of Courmayeur.

Despite the lack of views there is some wonderful pine forest to enjoy as you climb ever upwards, and when you do finally climb past the last tree you are met with a wonderful panorama of the previous valley.

Ahead is the **Col de Balme**. For the most part, the gradient becomes more forgiving as the trail eases its way upwards, high above the **Nant Noir** below. At the Col de Balme we reach the border of Switzerland and France. It's a cold and rather barren place but the views of the **Aiguilles Rouges** beyond more than make up for it, not only for their beauty but for the realisation that you are looking at the very same mountains that you saw when you began the trek all those days ago; the circle is nearing completion – well, almost. If you wish to stay at this lofty spot there's *Refuge du Col de Balme* (☎ 04-50 54 23 33; 26 beds). Be aware, however, that it is very run-down and online reviews of this hostelry are almost universally scathing. You may wish to consider Le Chalet de Charamillon as an alternative (see opposite).

COL DE BALME TO TRÉ LE CHAMP
[Map 34 p143, Map 35 p146, Map 36 p147]

The route described here goes via Aiguillette des Posettes; see opposite for the Variante Route via Le Tour.

Follow the trail north-west from the col. This traverses the grassy hillside before dropping down in wide zigzags below the line of a chairlift to the broad **Col des Posettes**. There are a number of trails in this area so it is quite easy to lose your way; look out for the red-and-white painted waymarks on the rocks and study Map 34 (p143). Turn right on the wide ski track and then left onto a faint trail that climbs onto the ridge ahead. If you end up at Restaurant Alpage de Balme you have gone

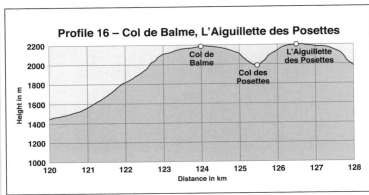

Profile 16 – Col de Balme, L'Aiguillette des Posettes

too far south, unless you are hungry, in which case make the detour. *Restaurant Alpage de Balme* (☎ 06-83 33 86 61; end Jun-end Sep, daily 9am-5pm) does excellent food which you can eat outside on the picnic benches. It's a sensational spot with far-reaching views down the valley to Chamonix.

The trail soon reaches the crest of the wide, **Aiguillette des Posettes** ridge with its rocky outcrops and pink alpenrose. This is a simply magnificent vantage point with views in every direction. To the south is the Chamonix valley and to the north the craggy peaks of the **Montagne de Loriaz** and **Barberine** on the Swiss border. At the summit cairn the twin peaks of **Aiguille Martin** and **Aiguille Morris** across the valley brood menacingly and tempt you onwards.

The descent begins benignly enough but once you reach the far end of the crest the path begins to drop sharply into the fir trees. There are a number of path junctions in the woods so, again, keep an eye on the trail maps in this book and look out for the red-and-white waymarks. Eventually the path hits the road just south of the **Col des Montets**. Around 400m south along the road is the village of **Tré le Champ** (see p148); take the left-hand lane (Chemin de Trélechamp) just after the old chapel to reach the village. There is accommodation here and in the nearby village of Le Tour (see below).

Variante route via Le Tour
[Map 34 p143, Map 35 p146, Map 36 p147]
This is certainly less scenic than the Aiguillette des Posettes route but in bad weather it offers a much safer and quicker descent to Tré le Champ. At Refuge du Col de Balme follow the path southwards and take the first right. This path descends steadily down the grassy ski pistes, following the line of a chairlift before traversing the open slope. At the path junction the left fork is for *Les Ecuries de Charamillon* (☎ 04-50 54 17 07, 🖳 www.restaurant-les-ecuries-de-charamillon.fr; dortoir €24pp, demi-pension €49pp, 19 beds, picnic lunch €11). To continue on the Tour take the right fork which drops down to the cable-car station and *Le Chalet de Charamillon*. You can get refreshments here including crêpes from €3.20 and sandwiches from €3.60.

You now have the choice of shamefacedly hopping on a cable car for a quick descent to **Le Tour** or proudly forging on by foot. The former will cost you €14 (last ride down varies through the summer but is usually around 4.45-5.30pm) while the latter is free and involves an easy if uninspiring walk below cablecar wires. Montroc is a 20-minute walk further down the only road.

LE TOUR & MONTROC
Le Tour and Montroc are both small villages at the northern extreme of the Chamonix valley. There is little to do in either but they are pretty enough with the icy backdrop of the Glacier du Tour.

Trains run from Montroc to Chamonix and Switzerland and the **Chamonix bus** runs as far as Le Tour; see pp22-6.

By the cable-car station in **Le Tour** is

L'Olympique Hôtel & Restaurant (☎ 04-50 54 01 04, 🖳 www.hotel-olympique-chamonix.com; 13 rooms; demi pension €75pp), a looming modern establishment and a few doors away is the intimate and rustic *Le Passon Restaurant* (☎ 04-50 54 33 04) with a beautiful wooden interior that was hand-crafted in nearby Argentière. The croûte au fromage is €13.50 and they do omelettes for €7.50.

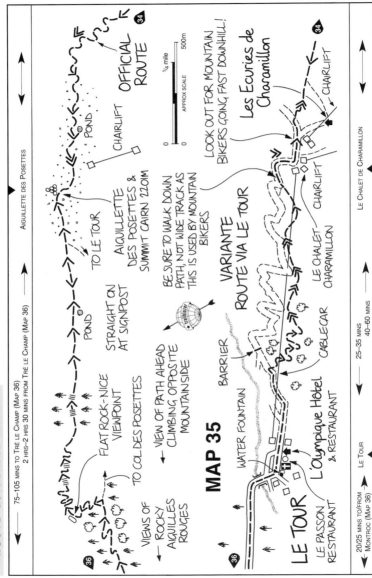

ROUTE GUIDE AND MAPS

MAP 35

LE TOUR

LE PASSON RESTAURANT

L'Olympique Hôtel & Restaurant

WATER FOUNTAIN

BARRIER

CABLECAR

VARIANTE ROUTE VIA LE TOUR

LE CHALET CHARAMILLON

CHAIRLIFT

VIEWS OF ROCKY AIGUILLES ROUGES

FLAT ROCK - NICE VIEWPOINT

TO COL DES POSETTES

VIEW OF PATH AHEAD CLIMBING OPPOSITE MOUNTAINSIDE

STRAIGHT ON AT SIGNPOST

POND

TO LE TOUR

AIGUILLETTE DES POSETTES & SUMMIT CAIRN 2201M

BE SURE TO WALK DOWN PATH, NOT WIDE TRACK AS THIS IS USED BY MOUNTAIN BIKERS

POND

CHAIRLIFT

OFFICIAL ROUTE

Les Ecuries de Charamillon

LOOK OUT FOR MOUNTAIN BIKERS GOING FAST DOWNHILL!

CHAIRLIFT

APPROX SCALE
0 — 500m
0 — ¼ mile

36

34

34

← 75-105 MINS TO TRÉ LE CHAMP (MAP 36) →
2 HRS-2 HRS 30 MINS FROM TRÉ LE CHAMP (MAP 36)

AIGUILLETTE DES POSETTES

LE CHALET DE CHARAMILLON

← 20/25 MINS TO/FROM MONTROC (MAP 36) →

LE TOUR

← 25-35 MINS →
40-60 MINS

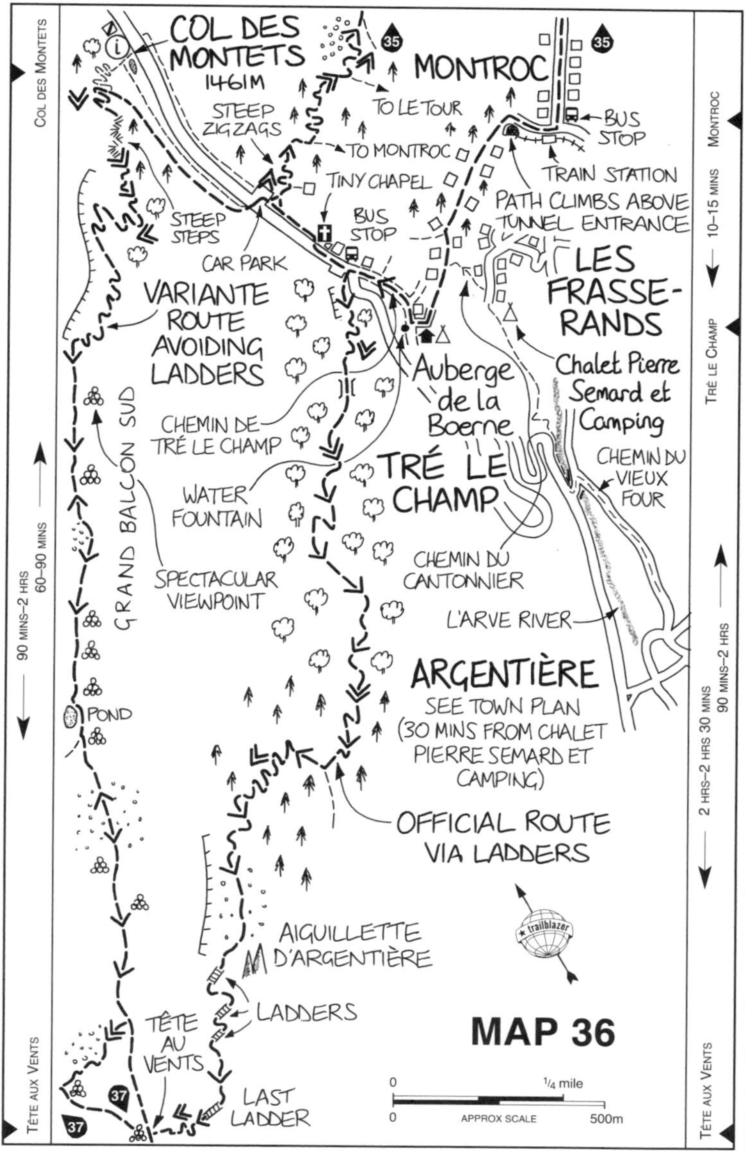

COL DES MONTETS 1461M

MONTROC

35

35

TO LE TOUR

BUS STOP

STEEP ZIGZAGS

TO MONTROC

TRAIN STATION

TINY CHAPEL

PATH CLIMBS ABOVE TUNNEL ENTRANCE

STEEP STEPS

BUS STOP

LES FRASSE-RANDS

CAR PARK

VARIANTE ROUTE AVOIDING LADDERS

Auberge de la Boerne

Chalet Pierre Semard et Camping

CHEMIN DE TRÉ LE CHAMP

TRÉ LE CHAMP

CHEMIN DU VIEUX FOUR

WATER FOUNTAIN

SPECTACULAR VIEWPOINT

CHEMIN DU CANTONNIER

L'ARVE RIVER

POND

ARGENTIÈRE

SEE TOWN PLAN (30 MINS FROM CHALET PIERRE SEMARD ET CAMPING)

OFFICIAL ROUTE VIA LADDERS

AIGUILLETTE D'ARGENTIÈRE

TÊTE AU VENTS

LADDERS

LAST LADDER

37

MAP 36

GRAND BALCON SUD

trailblazer

0   1/4 mile
0   APPROX SCALE   500m

COL DES MONTETS

MONTROC

10-15 MINS

TRÉ LE CHAMP

90 MINS-2 HRS   60-90 MINS

90 MINS-2 HRS

2 HRS-2 HRS 30 MINS

90 MINS-2 HRS

TÊTE AUX VENTS

37

TÊTE AUX VENTS

ROUTE GUIDE AND MAPS

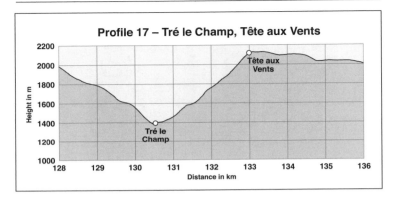

Profile 17 – Tré le Champ, Tête aux Vents

The quickest route to Tré le Champ from here is to turn right at Montroc train station. A path climbs up and over the entrance to a railway tunnel and, ten minutes later, emerges in Tré le Champ.

TRÉ LE CHAMP [Map 36 p147]

Despite being a few boot steps from the main road, Tré le Champ has a peaceful air thanks to the dip that it lies in below the road. It is a charming little place with a small stream flowing through the centre and flower-bedecked balconies on the timber-framed houses.

The main place to stay is the very pretty *Auberge de la Boerne* (☎ 04-50 54 05 14, 🖳 www.la-boerne.fr; all year; 31 beds; dortoir €20pp, demi-pension €44pp, chambre €32pp, chambre demi-pension €55pp, breakfast €10, picnic lunch €10). Their restaurant menu includes omelettes

for €11 and raclette for €17. Campers can pitch on the tiny lawn.

If you didn't manage to squeeze your tent in there then head to *Chalet Pierre Semard et Camping* (☎ 04-50 54 00 29; 🖳 chalet-hotel-psemard.com), ten minutes down the hill. There is plenty of space here but you will have to share it with campervans and pre-fab chalets. Pitches are €8.50pp and they have rooms for €35-45pp.

If no bed or pitches are available you can still catch the bus (or the train from Montroc) to Argentière or Chamonix and come back in the morning to continue the walk; see pp22-6.

ARGENTIÈRE

Argentière vies with Chamonix for the attention of skiers, mountaineers and hikers. It is smaller than Chamonix and has more of a village feel that isn't ruined by the main road running straight through it. It lies about a kilometre south of the trail so it is easy to reach on foot, or you can catch the train (from Montroc) or bus (from Tré le Champ or Col des Montets. The train continues on to Chamonix and Les Houches.

Argentière has a **tourist information**

centre (☎ 04-50 54 02 14; daily 9am-noon & 3-6pm) and a **bank** with an ATM next door. There are other useful services too including a **launderette** (daily 8am-10pm), a **pharmacy** (Mon-Sat 9am-noon, 2.30-7pm) and a handful of **outdoor equipment shops**. The **supermarket** (Mon-Sat 8am-7.30pm, Sun 8.30am-12.30pm) is well hidden between the main street and the river. You can reach it through an alleyway by the Sportech outdoor shop. Look for the big blue 'Marche U' sign.

Where to stay and eat

Two hotels on the main street offer smart, comfortable rooms: *Le Dahu* (☎ 04-50 54 01 55, 🖳 www.hotel-argentiere.com; 19 rooms; chambre €60-92pp) and *La Couronne* (☎ 04-50 54 00 02, 🖳 www.hotelcouronne.com; 39 rooms; chambre €44-64pp, breakfast €11.50).

There is no shortage of places to enjoy a good meal in Argentière. At the northern end of the village the street is lined with restaurants starting with *Stone Bar Pizzeria* (☎ 04-50 54 13 17) which has a vast range of pizzas with prices starting at €8.50. Next door is *Le Grenier* (☎ 04-50 54 06 00) where you can enjoy everything from crêpes from €3.50 to burgers from €15.50. *Les Voisines* (☎ 04-50 54 19 43, Tue-Sat noon-2pm & 7-9pm, Sun noon-2pm) has more sophisticated dishes such as rabbit leg for €17. You can also eat at *Le Dahu* hotel (see above) which does cheese burgers

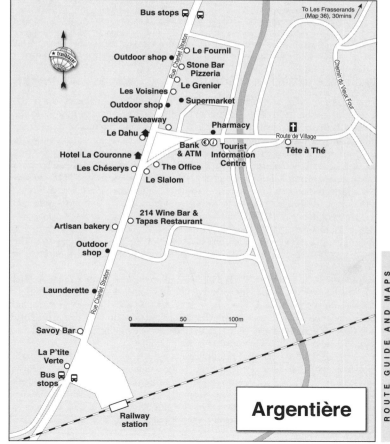

ROUTE GUIDE AND MAPS

(€16) and fondue (€18) among many other dishes. At *Les Cheserys* (☎ 04-50 18 23 48, noon-2pm, 6.30-9.30pm) there's a large outside terrace where you can enjoy a spaghetti dish for €13 and roast pork for €19.50.

On the other side of the road is *214 Wine Bar & Tapas Restaurant* (☎ 04-50 55 88 06) which does mini burgers for €6.50 and the more traditional assiette de fromage from €8.50. On Route du Village is *Tête à Thé* (☎ 09-53 15 28 39) a quiet spot for lunch away from the busy road. They do a dish of the day for €15.50 which includes pitta bread dishes. For food and beer a good bet is *The Office* (☎ 04-50 54 15 46), a bar and restaurant which attracts a mixed crowd to its terrace during the day but is mainly a 20-somethings' hangout

when the sun goes down. The food here is good value and plentiful; you can get a curry for €15. Down near the train station is an intimate restaurant *La P'tite Verte* (☎ 04-50 54 54 54) where you can indulge in their excellent steak tartare for €19 and tartiflette for €17.

For a quick snack, the *Ondoa Takeaway* (☎ 04-50 47 18 46) does sandwiches for €6.50. There are two **bakeries**: the *Artisan Bakery* and, at the top end of the high street, *Le Fournil*, where you can grab coffee and cake as well as pastries and sandwiches.

The Office (left) is a popular place for a beer, as is *Le Slalom*, a small bar next door serving burritos and sandwiches, and the *Savoy Bar* at the southern end of the street.

TRÉ LE CHAMP TO LA FLÉGÈRE   [Map 36 p147, Map 37]

The walk from Tré le Champ to La Flégère is five miles. This is where the Tour crosses the head of the Chamonix valley and begins its climb onto the **Grand Balcon Sud**, where the path contours the easy ground between steep mountain walls above and below. The remarkable view across the valley to the Mont Blanc massif, including the summit of Mont Blanc itself, is a fitting finale to a grand walk. But it doesn't end there. Turn 180 degrees and the cold black peaks of the Aiguilles Rouges vie for your appreciation. These mountains form the spine of the Aiguilles Rouges Nature Reserve (see the box on p153), one of France's most beautiful protected areas. Ibex, chamois and bearded vultures can all be seen here so take time to linger and look. The **ladder sections** on this route cannot be avoided so if you suffer from vertigo you should choose the variante route via Col des Montets, described on p153. The longest ladder is about 30 metres up a sheer rock face. It is very exposed in places.

To rejoin the trail from Tré le Champ head up the lane to the main road. The path begins on the other side of the road and immediately begins to climb through broken woodland. The ascent is a long one but is never too steep and there are some great views through the gaps in the trees of the **Glacier du Tour** and **Glacier d'Argentière** spilling down the opposite mountainsides. Soon, too, Mont Blanc comes into view further down the valley.

The first of the ladders is positioned opposite a spectacular needle of rock known as the **Aiguillette d'Argentière**. If the weather is good you will probably see climbers scaling its vertical sides or sitting precariously on the needle's tip, making the climb up the ladders seem distinctly ordinary. Go slowly on the ladders and don't feel rushed by others waiting below. Equally, be sure not to rush anyone ahead of you, especially if they appear not to be enjoying the experience.

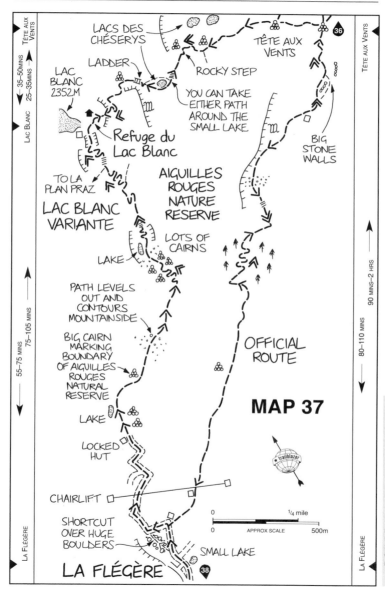

TÊTE AUX VENTS

35–50 MINS / 25–35MINS

LAC BLANC

LACS DES CHÉSERYS

LADDER

LAC BLANC 2352M

ROCKY STEP

TÊTE AUX VENTS

YOU CAN TAKE EITHER PATH AROUND THE SMALL LAKE

36

TÊTE AUX VENTS

Refuge du Lac Blanc

BIG STONE WALLS

TO LA PLAN PRAZ

AIGUILLES ROUGES NATURE RESERVE

LAC BLANC VARIANTE

LOTS OF CAIRNS

LAKE

75–105 MINS

PATH LEVELS OUT AND CONTOURS MOUNTAINSIDE

BIG CAIRN MARKING BOUNDARY OF AIGUILLES ROUGES NATURAL RESERVE

OFFICIAL ROUTE

55–75 MINS

90 MINS–2 HRS

80–110 MINS

LAKE

MAP 37

LOCKED HUT

trailblazer

CHAIRLIFT

SHORTCUT OVER HUGE BOULDERS

SMALL LAKE

0   ¼ mile

0   500m
APPROX SCALE

LA FLÉGÈRE

LA FLÉGÈRE

LA FLÉGÈRE

38

❏ Mer de Glace and the Montenvers mountain railway
No words can depict this remarkable scene, the ice being jammed and forced up, and broken into the most hideous gulfs and chasms. **J D Gardner**, 1851

The Mer de Glace is the second longest glacier in the Alps and by far the longest in the Mont Blanc massif. Thanks to the relatively easy access to the glacier from the valley below, it has been a place of sightseeing pilgrimage for over 250 years. This resulted in the construction of the Montenvers Hôtel, on the ridge above the ice. Since 1908 tourists have been carried up to the hotel and viewpoint by the mountain railway. The size of the glacier is almost overwhelming but you can get a real sense of its scale by looking for the tiny black figures of climbers crossing the ice on their way to the peaks in the heart of the Mont Blanc massif.

There is a long flight of stairs below the restaurant that leads right down to the glacier, or you can take a cablecar some of the way. Once you reach the ice the path continues right into the glacier. This man-made tunnel or 'ice grotto' goes under the blue ice and takes you past sculptures carved into the wall.

There is a sinister side to this experience. The glacier has been shrinking at an astonishing rate, so much so that the cablecar that once carried passengers down to the edge of the glacier no longer reaches far enough. In 1990 twelve steps had to be built below the cablecar station so sightseers could continue the journey to the ice. Every year more sections of steps have to be added as the ice retreats further and further. Today there are around 400 steps down the cliff face. As you descend the steps look out for the signs bolted into the rock, each one with a year written on it showing you the level of the glacier at that point in that given year. As an example of the impact of climate change there can be few sights more chilling; the retreating Mer de Glace is a canary in a coalmine.

The train leaves from the smaller railway station in Chamonix (see map p63; it's behind the main station). A return ticket costs €31.50 (for further information see 'S' p26 and the map pp24-5) .

The last of the ladders is the longest and will make your head spin the most. You will probably want to wait until you have climbed it before you sit down to enjoy the view of the **Mer de Glace** (see box above) winding its way between the serrated mountains on either side. Particularly impressive is the famous **Aiguille Verte**, the pyramidal peak on the eastern side of the glacier. On the other side is the **Aiguille du Grépon** and far in the distance creating the backdrop to it all are the ice-clad **Grandes Jorasses**. If you have been walking the whole trail you would have been walking on the far side of these mountains just a few days before.

A short climb beyond the last ladder is the **Tête aux Vents** (Windy Head!), a beautiful spot from which to appreciate the craggy sides of the Aiguilles Rouges. The official route from Tête aux Vents to La Flégère continues straight

❏ Phone and country codes
Phone numbers starting 06 and 04 are in France (+33); 01 and 03 are in Italy (+39); 026 and 027 are in Switzerland (+41).

ahead past some big stone walls. The route is obvious and while it offers fantastic views across the valley, it is no match for the variante route via Lac Blanc (see p154).

Variante route via Col des Montets   [Map 36 p147, Map 37 p151]

If you don't have a head for heights and the thought of iron ladders bolted into precipitous rock makes your stomach churn, don't fret; there is an alternative route without a ladder in sight. From Tré le Champ return along the main road to the point where you came down from the Aiguillette des Posettes. There is a car park here and across the road from it a path heads into the bushes.

This is the continuation of the route but before setting off, consider making the five-minute detour to **Col des Montets**. Here you will find the excellent **Chalet d'Accueil de la Réserve** (see box below), a visitor centre which is packed full of displays and information on the **Aiguilles Rouges Nature Reserve** that you are about to enter. If you do make the detour, you can pick up the main trail by following the path directly behind the centre.

It's 5½ miles from Col des Montets to La Flégère. The climb gets steeper above the col, eventually arriving at a spectacular viewpoint marked by a cairn. It's worth a stop here to admire the view down the length of the Chamonix valley with the **Glacier d'Argentière** and the **Aiguille Verte** dominating. From the viewpoint the path continues sharply upwards and then contours below a long sloping cliff face.

We're now deep into the **Aiguilles Rouges Nature Reserve**. This is an excellent place to see both chamois and ibex. It's an easy walk from here along the **Grand Balcon Sud** – the lap of the Aiguilles Rouges. To the west the black craggy peaks cast shadows over the lush green mountainsides. At **Tête aux Vents** we join the main trail and catch up with those who have just sweated their way up the ladders on the cliffs below.

There are two route choices at Tête aux Vents. An alternative path heads uphill towards the high-altitude **Lac Blanc** (see p154) but the quickest way to La Flégère is to turn left at the Tête aux Vents cairn and follow the high-rise trail on

---

❏ **Aiguilles Rouges Nature Reserve**
This protected area covers a large chunk of the Massif des Aiguilles Rouges, the mountains on the west side of the Chamonix valley. The dark rocky peaks that loom over the grassy slopes of alpenrose and dwarf rhododendron contrast greatly with the icy peaks of the Mont Blanc massif opposite. This is one of the best areas on the Tour to see wildlife, particularly chamois and ibex.

Before setting foot in the reserve take a trip to the interpretation centre at the Col des Montets, **Chalet d'Accueil de la Réserve** (☎ 04-50 54 02 24, 🖳 rnaiguillesrouges.org; daily, end May to Oct, 9.30am-6pm; free entry). You could spend an hour or two here looking at all the displays; there's a relief map of the area, stuffed birds and animals, microscopes for looking at bugs and leaves, and books in both French and English covering geology, weather and wildlife. They also host lectures and field trips during the summer (booking essential) and there is a **café** with hot and cold drinks and cakes.

its roller-coaster route high above the valley. The views to your left will draw your eye time and again. Mont Blanc is now in full view and the whole spectacular massif with its searing icy towers and pinnacles seems suspended in time.

At **La Flégère** there is a chairlift service in the summer. The last lift down to Les Praz de Chamonix (a short bus ride from Chamonix itself) is between 4.15 and 4.50pm and costs €14.50. There is also a **café** (wraps from €5.90 and baguettes from €4) here and *Refuge de la Flégère* (☎ 04-50 55 85 88; mid Jun to mid Sep; 65 beds; demi-pension €57pp). If you are discreet you can camp below the refuge and still book a table to eat at the restaurant in the refuge. Meals are typically local with tartiflette for €22 and a three-cheese fondue for €24.

Lac Blanc variante   [Map 37 p151]

This alternative route from Tête aux Vents to La Flégère involves more than 200m more climbing but the rewards are great. Lac Blanc is a beautiful lake surrounded by high rocky mountains and your chances of seeing ibex in this remote spot are good. If you don't want to walk all the way to La Flégère you have the option of stopping at *Refuge du Lac Blanc* (☎ 06 02 05 08 82, 🖳 www.refugedulacblanc.fr; mid Jun to Sep; 30 beds; demi pension €56). The hot food and drinks are very welcome at this chilly altitude. Soup is €6, bacon and fried eggs is €12 and omelettes are €10-12.

If you have come to Tête aux Vents from the ladder route the path to Lac Blanc continues straight ahead at the Tête aux Vents junction. If you have followed the alternative route from Col des Montets you can pick up the Lac Blanc trail about 200 metres before Tête aux Vents. Both paths soon merge into one before climbing to the **Lacs des Chéserys** which occupy a small glacial bowl. The path follows a small ridge above the lakes, crosses a spur and drops to another small lake. Cross the outlet stream of this lake and follow the path on its steep journey up to the **Refuge du Lac Blanc** (see above).

Lac Blanc sits in a barren rocky cirque below the shattered ridges of the Aiguille du Belvédère. On still days, the reflection of the Mont Blanc massif in the lake's milky waters is one of the most sensational sights on the whole Tour. It's no surprise that this vista can be seen on postcard stands all around Chamonix.

The descent to La Flégère begins by crossing the footbridge at the outflow from the lake and passing through a rocky cleft. Ignore the turning to Plan Praz and instead continue on the downhill path which soon meets a lower path. Bear right here past a small lake and down to a locked hut. Here the path widens into a 4WD track which soon leads to the cable-car station at La Flégère. You may have guessed from the bulldozed tracks, chairlifts and general destruction of the mountainside that you have now left the protected area of the Aiguilles Rouges Nature Reserve.

LA FLÉGÈRE TO LES HOUCHES
[Map 38 p156, Map 39 p157, Map 40 p158, Map 41 p160]

The scene is perfect, and, in all probability, few who have seen it have ever had or will ever have it equalled.   **Francis Trench**, 1847, describing the view from Le Brévent

It's a long 11 miles to Les Houches but every one is worth it. This is the climax of the whole journey and it ends in grandstand style with an ascent of 2525m

Le Brévent, a rocky pedestal high above the valley at the southern end of the Aiguilles Rouges ridge.

Begin by following the path from **Refuge de la Flégère** as it enters patchy pine forest. A steep drop through a cleft in the rock leads out to the edge of the forest and a wide glacial bowl. This then continues for some time as the path dips into shady forest and out onto clear grassy slopes dotted with stunted pines. After the path crosses a wide track it ducks beneath a chairlift cable and negotiates a precipitous cliff. No climbing is involved but in places the path is narrow and hugs the sheer rock, so watch your step.

Ahead we cross another wide track, ploughed through the mountainside by the ski industry, and across boulder fields and scree. At the ski track junction take the steep track straight ahead. This heads to the ski installations at **Plan Praz**. There is a large **café** here (daily, 11am-5pm). They serve *it better be good at that price* burger and fries for €20.50 and *there must be some mistake* orange juice for an eye-watering €6.10. If you are dying of thirst, as I was when researching this edition, and don't want to empty your wallet for a few glugs of OJ then you will be as pleased as I was to find the **drinking water tap** hidden on the back wall of the café building.

Just beyond the chairlift station take a right on a narrow path, the start of the climb to Le Brévent. A long zigzag leads to a steeper section which brings you onto **Col de Brévent** at 2368m, marked by a cairn. This is a cold, inhospitable spot, windy and often with late snow lying about in the hollows, but is also savagely beautiful. There is a great view to the west of rocky castellated mountains and green valleys – a contrast from the snowbound Mont Blanc massif to the east.

Take the rocky ridge to the west-south-west and after about five minutes follow the trail as it contours around the western side of the ridge. *(cont'd on p158)*

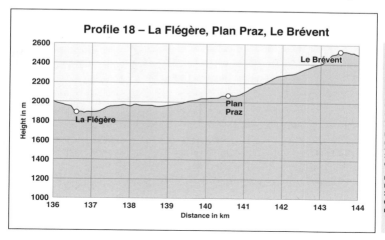

Profile 18 – La Flégère, Plan Praz, Le Brévent

Height in m / Distance in km

La Flégère, Plan Praz, Le Brévent

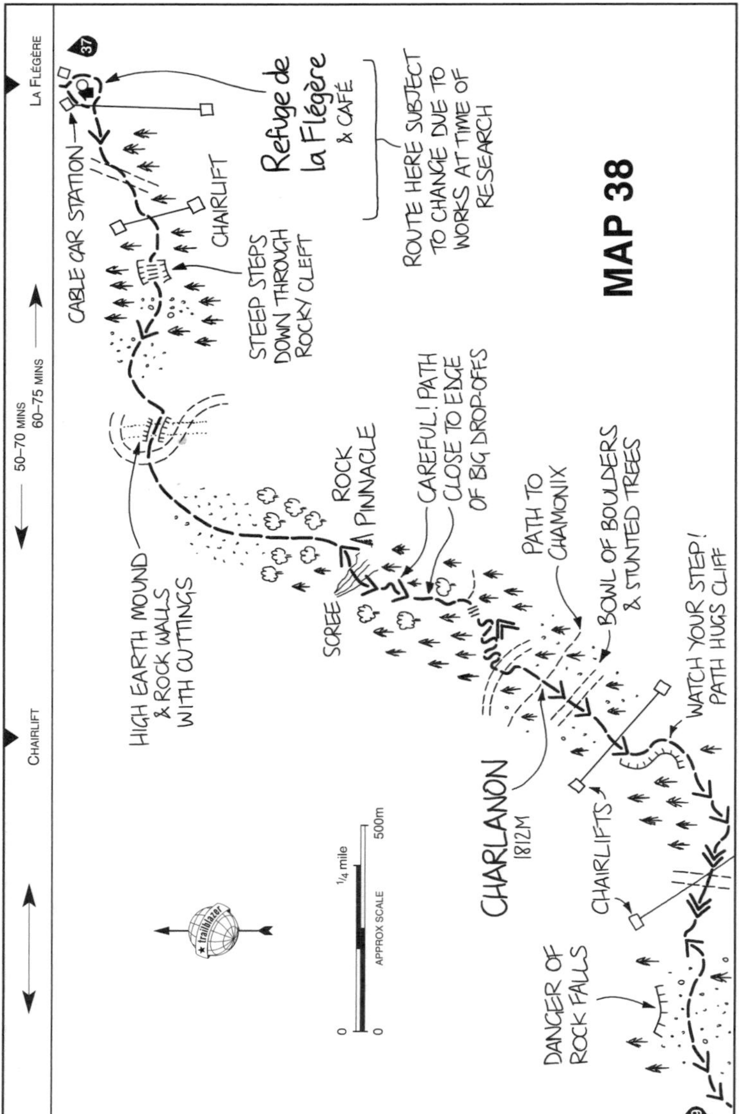

MAP 38

La Flégère

Refuge de la Flégère & CAFÉ

ROUTE HERE SUBJECT TO CHANGE DUE TO WORKS AT TIME OF RESEARCH

CABLE CAR STATION

CHAIRLIFT

STEEP STEPS DOWN THROUGH ROCKY/CLEFT

50–70 MINS
60–75 MINS

HIGH EARTH MOUND & ROCK WALLS WITH CUTTINGS

ROCK PINNACLE

SCREE

CAREFUL! PATH CLOSE TO EDGE OF BIG DROP-OFFS

PATH TO CHAMONIX

BOWL OF BOULDERS & STUNTED TREES

WATCH YOUR STEP! PATH HUGS CLIFF

CHARLANON 1812M

CHAIRLIFTS

DANGER OF ROCK FALLS

CHAIRLIFT

¼ mile
500m

0
0
APPROX SCALE

ROUTE GUIDE AND MAPS

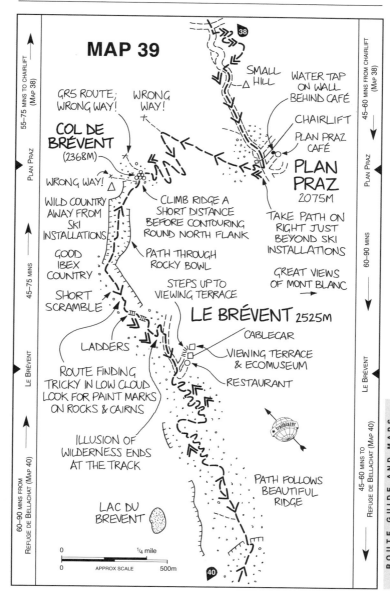

(cont'd from p155)   The path continues through a moonscape of rocky bowls and jagged ridges. Route finding can be tricky in mist so keep an eye out for the red-and-white paint splashes that mark the route. Just below the ridge there is a short section of **ladders** up the steep rock. These are unavoidable but they're not as frightening as the ones above Argentière. A little further and we reach the ski track to the summit of **Le Brévent**. This is a magnificent viewpoint with Mont Blanc looming just across the valley. A good eye can pick out tiny specks on the snowy summit ridge – climbers approaching the top.

The summit of Le Brévent is home to a **restaurant** (lasagne €19, salad €6) with an overhanging terrace that has one of the finest views of Mont Blanc to be had from a restaurant table. On top of the crag, above the restaurant, there is a small **ecomuseum** (free entry) with displays on the local fauna and flora. You

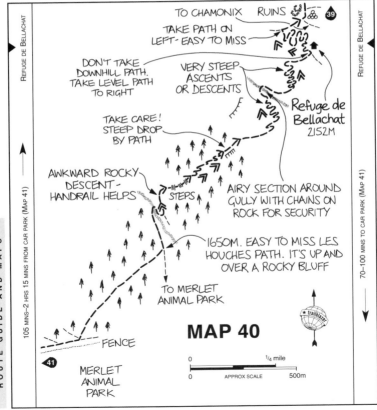

TO CHAMONIX RUINS **39**

TAKE PATH ON
LEFT- EASY TO MISS

DON'T TAKE
DOWNHILL PATH.
TAKE LEVEL PATH
TO RIGHT

VERY STEEP
ASCENTS
OR DESCENTS

Refuge de
Bellachat
2152M

REFUGE DE BELLACHAT

TAKE CARE!
STEEP DROP
BY PATH

AWKWARD ROCKY
DESCENT-
HANDRAIL HELPS

STEPS

AIRY SECTION AROUND
GULLY WITH CHAINS ON
ROCK FOR SECURITY

1650M. EASY TO MISS LES
HOUCHES PATH. IT'S UP AND
OVER A ROCKY BLUFF

TO MERLET
ANIMAL PARK

MAP 40

105 MINS–2 HRS 15 MINS FROM CAR PARK (MAP 41)

70–100 MINS TO CAR PARK (MAP 41)

FENCE

41

MERLET
ANIMAL
PARK

0   ¼ mile
0   500m
APPROX SCALE

ROUTE GUIDE AND MAPS

can also get a **cable car** (€15; mid Jun to mid July & Sep 9am-4pm, mid Jul to Aug 8am-5pm) down to Plan Praz and from there down to Chamonix. Tour walkers, however, need to do it on foot!

The descent begins on the west side of the summit where a path snakes down through a beautiful landscape of undulating ridges decorated with shrubs and boulder fields. It's a drawn-out descent so it's worth taking a break at *Refuge de Bellachat* (☎ 04-50 53 46 99, 🖳 www.refuge-bellachat.com; end Jun-mid Sep; 24 beds). A bed here costs €52pp for demi-pension. Ignore the path that drops down from the hut and instead follow the level one to the west. After negotiating a couple of very steep sections – eased by the tight zigzagging path – we enter the cool forest.

While it may feel like the end is fast approaching, there is still some way to go. Continue past **Merlet Animal Park** (see p167) to a car park. About one hundred metres down the road from the car park pick up the trail again on the left.

This heads down to the 70-year-old, 17-metre-high **Christ Roi** statue (you can stay in a beautiful old farm building, *Tupilak*, in the woods here – see under Les Houches, p74, plus Map 1 p76) and down to a wide track, past some houses to the road.

Cross the railway and the river and climb the road into **Les Houches**. Well done! You've circumnavigated the Mont Blanc massif. That calls for a celebration – you can either stay in Les Houches (see p74) or, if you prefer, head for the bright lights and bustle of Chamonix. You can catch a train there from the station you passed as you approached the village or a bus from the stop near the tourist information centre.

See p22 for public transport details and pp61-8 for all the essential information on Chamonix.

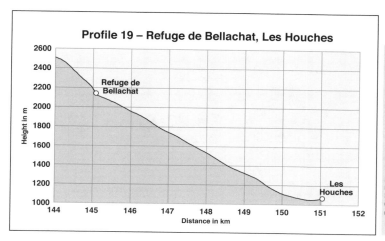

Profile 19 – Refuge de Bellachat, Les Houches

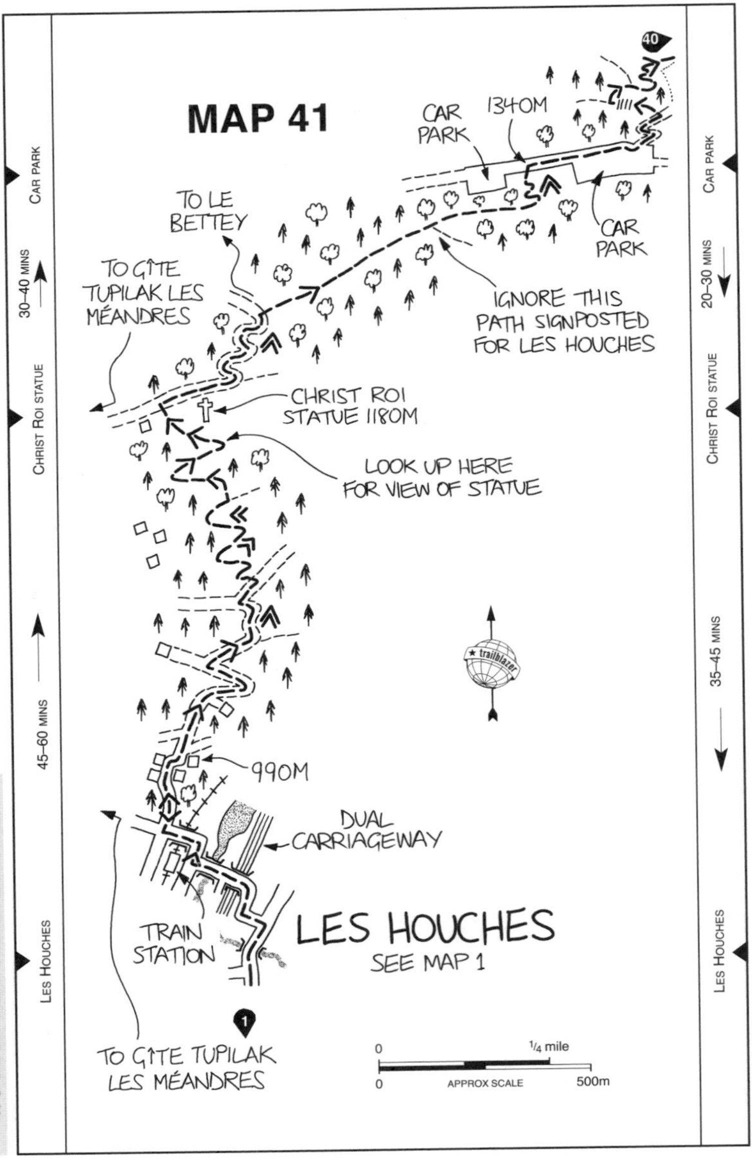

MAP 41

CAR PARK

1340M

TO LE BETTEY

CAR PARK

CAR PARK

TO GÎTE TUPILAK LES MÉANDRES

IGNORE THIS PATH SIGNPOSTED FOR LES HOUCHES

CHRIST ROI STATUE 1180M

LOOK UP HERE FOR VIEW OF STATUE

990M

DUAL CARRIAGEWAY

LES HOUCHES
SEE MAP 1

TRAIN STATION

TO GÎTE TUPILAK LES MÉANDRES

CAR PARK

30-40 MINS

CHRIST ROI STATUE

45-60 MINS

LES HOUCHES

CAR PARK

20-30 MINS

CHRIST ROI STATUE

35-45 MINS

LES HOUCHES

ROUTE GUIDE AND MAPS

0   ¼ mile

0   APPROX SCALE   500m

Above: The airy terrace at Le Brévent (2525m, see p157) offers what must be one of the best views of Mont Blanc from a restaurant table. Diners and day-trippers from Chamonix reach it using the cable car from Plan Praz. **Below left**: The street cafés of Chamonix are the perfect place to relax before or after your trek. **Below right**: The statue of Dr Michel Paccard, in Chamonix, who shares the conquest of Mont Blanc with Jacques Balmat (see photo opp p161), reaching the summit in 1786. **Overleaf**: Mont Blanc seen from the trail near La Flégère (see p154).

Above: Professor HB de Saussure and Jacques Balmat gaze upon Mont Blanc from their monument in Chamonix. On 8th August 1786, with Dr Paccard (see photo opp p160), Balmat became the first person to scale Mont Blanc (see pp57-9). **Below**: The summit of Mont Blanc is capped in a thick layer of ice and snow, the depth of which varies through the year, making exact measurements difficult. From the 19th century its official elevation was 4807m (15,771ft) but in 2007 IGN (the French mapping agency) put it at 4810m (15,781ft). This was revised to 4808.73m (15,777ft) in 2015.

THE ASCENT OF
MONT BLANC

Having wandered around Mont Blanc's hem for a week or two you
might feel lured to her icy summit. This is not an expedition to be
taken lightly and is a long way from the world of trekking. That so
many people climb the mountain (20,000 people do so each year)
makes it appear easy to inexperienced mountain travellers. Seasoned
alpine climbers may refer to the ascent as nothing more than a snow
plod but this is nothing more than elitist talk. In reality, climbing
Mont Blanc is a serious Alpine mountaineering expedition that
involves at least three days of preparation on lesser peaks. You
should have at least some winter mountaineering experience before
even considering the ascent.

Mont Blanc poses few technical difficulties, depending on your
route choice, but she will regularly pick off folk who set off with no
understanding of how fierce and unpredictable she can be. People
come a cropper on the mountain every year. A lack of experience
leads to death through exposure, exhaustion, falling through crevass-
es, triggering of avalanches and rockfalls. You should certainly not
attempt an ascent of Mont Blanc without first climbing one or two
other mountains of between 3000 metres and 4000 metres. This will
help build up your fitness, help you acclimatise to the altitude and
help prepare you for the physical and mental effort required.

For advice on climbing Mont Blanc head for the **Office de
Haute Montagne de Chamonix** (☎ 04 50 53 22 08, 🖳 chamoni-
arde.com; Mon-Sat 9am-noon & 3-6pm) in Maison de la Montagne,
at 190 place de l'Eglise, 74400, Chamonix (see map, p62-3).

WITH OR WITHOUT A GUIDE?

Mountaineers with plenty of experience of climbing in the Alps will
know what to expect and will not need a guide. If you are wondering
whether you have enough experience or not, you need a guide. Even
if you have a guide you should still have some experience of climbing mountains in winter conditions, be it in the Alps or elsewhere.
Most guiding companies charge around €1000-2000pp which also
includes the cost of food, accommodation and lift passes. There
should be no more than two people per guide on the summit attempt.

Before climbing Mont Blanc your guide should lead you up a
couple of smaller peaks to help you acclimatise and build your fit-

ness. This should be included in the overall cost. Any attempt to climb Mont Blanc without first acclimatising and building up fitness on some lower peaks is doomed to failure. For this reason most mountain guides will charge you for a five- or six-day course with only the final two days spent on Mont Blanc. The usual route of ascent is on the relatively easy, and consequently most popular, Goûter Route (see opposite).

Mountain guides

Chamonix is unofficially known as the world capital of mountaineering and has plenty of outfits offering guided mountaineering trips including ascents of Mont Blanc. For a list of mountain guides contact **Office de Haute Montagne de Chamonix** (see p161) or peruse the non-exhaustive list below.

Compagnie des Guides de Mont Blanc (☎ 04-50 53 00 88, 🖳 www.chamonix-guides.com), based in Office de Haute Montagne de Chamonix (see p161) is a good place to start when looking for a guide. Founded in 1821 they are the oldest and largest guides company in the world. An ascent of Mont Blanc, via the Goûter Route, with one of their 200 professional guides costs €1265. This includes transport costs (cable car and mountain train to Nid d'Aigle), lunches and half-board at the Goûter Refuge. Most importantly, it also includes two days in which you familiarise yourself with an ice axe and crampons on the Mer de Glace, and climb Mont Blanc du Tacul (4248m) to help you acclimatise to the altitude. They also offer the ascent via the Cosmiques Route.

Other guiding companies based in the **Chamonix valley** (see opposite for companies based in Courmayeur, Italy) include:
● **Allibert Trekking** (☎ 04-76 45 84 84; 🖳 www.allibert-trekking.com; l'Aiguille du Midi, 74400, Chamonix) Six-day course for €1645 per person.
● **Bureau des Guides du Mont Blanc** (☎ 04-50 53 27 05, 🖳 www.guides-du-montblanc.com; 9 Passage de la Varlope, 74402, Chamonix) Five-day course is €990-1360pp including half board in Goûter Refuge and transport to Nid d'Aigle.
● **Chamonix Experience** (☎ 04-50 93 23 14, 🖳 www.chamex.com; 610 Route Blanche, 74400, Chamonix) Six-day courses for €2050 for up to four people (includes five nights half board in a chalet, plus two nights half board in the mountain refuge, lunches and transport).
● **Chamonix Ski Guide** (☎ 06-12 22 04 82, 🖳 www.chamonixskiguide.com) Six-day course with ascent of Mont Blanc for €1150 for guiding only.
● **Evolution 2** (☎ 04-50 55 53 57, 🖳 www.evolution2-chamonix.com; 130 Rue des Moulins, Chamonix) Three-day course via the Goûter Refuge for €980 per guide for up to two people.
● **Exodus Travels** (☎ +44 (0)203 553 9076, 🖳 www.exodus.co.uk) Eight-day course for £2559 per person.
● **High Mountain Guides** (☎ +44 (0)115 888 2994, 🖳 www.highmountain-guides.com) A well-established outfit offering a six-day course for €1495 per person (guiding only).
● **Michel Bordet** (☎ 677 345 429, 🖳 www.michelbordet.com; 2720 Route de Coupeau, 74310, Les Houches) An independent guide with 30 years' experience. Offers four-day courses for €1285 per person.

- **Mont Blanc Guides** (☎ +44 (0)117 230 0144, 💻 www.montblanc guides.com) Six-day courses for €2150; includes half-board accommodation through the week and transport but not lunches.
- **Mountain Adventure Guides** (☎ +44 (0)330 321 1017, 💻 www.moun- tainadventureguides.co.uk) Six-day courses for €1575 per person which includes half-board accommodation in the mountain huts and self-catering accommodation in the valley but not transport or meals in the valley.
- **Stages et Expeditions** (☎ 450 559 426, 💻 www.stagexpe.com; 319 Rue Ravanel-le-Rouge, 74400, Chamonix) Three-day courses for €1095 per person and five-day courses for €1565 per person.

For mountain guides based in **Courmayeur, Italy**, contact **Società delle Guide Alpine Maestri di Alpinismo di Courmayeur** (☎ +39 0165 842064, 💻 www.guidecourmayeur.com; opposite the church on Via Roma, Courmayeur; daily 9am-12.30pm & 4-7pm, closed Mon). They offer six-day courses culmi- nating in an ascent of Mont Blanc for €990 for up to four people. The price includes guiding and transfers only.

WEATHER AND CLIMATE

The most popular months for the ascent are June to September; this is when most guiding companies offer their ascent courses. There is good reason for this: the weather is usually more reliable and there is less snow. However, it is possible to climb Mont Blanc at any time of year, depending on the weather. If you wish to do so with a guide, contact **Office de Haute Montagne de Chamonix** (see p161) to find out which guides are willing to take clients out- side the main climbing season.

WHAT TO TAKE

This is not a trek so you can forget the trail shoes. This is a mountaineering expedition so you will need the following: ice axe and crampons, rope and har- ness, four-season mountaineering boots and clothing, goggles, helmet, flask, water bottle and sun block. You might want to take some of the items listed on pp28-31 too.

THE ROUTE

There are a number of routes to the summit. Most mountain guides use the Goûter Route which is described below along with a couple of alternatives. These general overviews are intended as brief summaries and not detailed descriptions of the routes. Other routes are possible but are not described here.

The Goûter Route

This is the most popular and least difficult approach although it does involve a dan- gerous crossing of the Grand Couloir which is renowned for its incessant rockfalls.

Sometimes referred to as **Voie des Cristalliers** or **Voie Royale**, this route begins by climbing aboard the mountain train from St Gervais to Nid d'Aigle, situated at 2372m. You can also get the cable car (see N p23) from Les Houches to Bellevue and pick the train up from there. From Nid d'Aigle you have to go on foot; it's about five to six hours to the overnight stop at the Goûter Refuge. From Nid d'Aigle, begin by climbing to *Tête Rousse Refuge* (☎ 04-50 58 24 97; mid Jun to mid Sep) at 3167m. Beyond the hut is the infamous Grand Couloir. Some call it a bowling alley because of the frequent rockfalls. Climbers are injured and killed here every year so be aware. It's a bit of a scramble on the final 500 metres to the Goûter Refuge (3817m) but once there you can relax and enjoy the outstanding views from the balcony. It's very important to book a bed in advance at *Goûter Refuge* (☎ 04-50 54 40 93; end May-end Sep) as this is a busy hut.

You should start the climb to the summit early the next day and that means well before sunrise. Most climbers set off between 2am and 3am. If you leave too late the snow softens up with the afternoon sun and the going becomes harder if not impossible. It takes about five hours to the summit from the Goûter Refuge via Dôme du Goûter (4304m) and the Vallot Hut (4262m) which is nothing more than an emergency shelter. The final push follows the Bosses Ridge which is quite exposed but not technically difficult.

The Cosmiques Route

Also known as the **Traverse Route** or **Three Monts Route**, this is a relatively short but strenuous approach. While some may consider it not technically difficult, it is harder than the Goûter Route thanks to the steeper ground that necessitates a sound knowledge of crampon techniques; you will need to front point on some sections. For this reason it is best left to those with some Alpine climbing experience. The Cosmiques Route is a bit of a rollercoaster, taking in the summits of Mont Blanc du Tacul (4248m) and Mont Maudit (4465m) en route.

Begin by taking the cable car to the Aiguille du Midi (3842m). This is a rapid ascent from the valley and you should be prepared to feel quite ill with the effects of acute mountain sickness (AMS) or altitude sickness. Do not even think about setting off towards the summit as soon as you arrive. Instead you should descend to, and cross, the Aiguille du Midi arête, and spend the night at *Cosmiques Refuge* (☎ 04 50 54 40 16; mid Feb to mid Oct) at 3613m, an hour's walk from the Aiguille du Midi cable-car station.

If you are not suffering from the effects of AMS, the following day you can begin the ascent which takes about six hours. Start by climbing the snow slopes to the summit of Mont Blanc du Tacul (4248 metres). From here, cross Col Maudit before negotiating the steep slopes of Mont Maudit (4465 metres) and descending again to Col de la Brenva. Finally, you can begin to climb Mont Blanc itself via the Petits Mulets.

The Cosmiques Route is technically more difficult than the Goûter Route and you should attempt it only if you have experience of climbing in the Alps with ice axe and crampons.

> '*Mont Blanc is the monarch of mountains;*
> *They crowned him long ago*
> *On a throne of rocks, in a robe of clouds,*
> *With a diadem of snow*'.
> (**Byron Manfred**)

The Grands Mulets Route

The route that Paccard and Balmat (see p58) took to become the first men to stand on Mont Blanc's summit, the Grands Mulets Route is still used but is not as popular as it once was. It starts at the middle station on the Aiguille du Midi cable-car and traverses the Glacier des Bossons before coming to the overnight stop at *Refuge des Grands Mulets* (☎ 04-50 53 57 10; Apr-Sep) at 3051m. The following day involves a lot of ascent so you will need to be very fit. From the hut you continue up the glacier to join the Goûter Route between Dôme du Goûter and Vallot Emergency Hut.

MOUNTAIN SAFETY

There is detailed information on mountain safety in Part 1 (see pp38-46) but there is one particular illness that is specific to climbing at high altitude: acute mountain sickness, or AMS, which is dealt with here.

Acute mountain sickness (AMS)

This is commonly referred to as altitude sickness and is a serious threat to anyone climbing above 3000 metres, particularly those who are inexperienced at high-altitude climbing because they are less aware of just how lethal it can be. AMS is caused by too rapid an ascent and a failure of the body to adapt quickly enough to the decrease in oxygen that occurs with altitude. It affects about three in ten people to a significant degree and has nothing to do with fitness. AMS itself does not kill but, if ignored, it can lead to high altitude cerebral edema (HACE; usually spelt HACO – high altitude cerebral oedema – in Britain) or high altitude pulmonary oedema (HAPE or HAPO) which is the build up of fluid in the brain and lungs respectively. Both of these conditions are fatal if ignored.

To avoid AMS, HAPE and HACE it is important to look out for the symptoms and act on them. The symptoms of AMS include headache, dizziness, nausea and loss of appetite. If you suspect AMS it's important to stop climbing any higher. Take plenty of rest and consider spending an extra night at a hut rather than attempting to climb higher. If the symptoms get worse you should descend.

Symptoms of HAPE include severe headache, lack of coordination, slurring of speech and blurred vision while the symptoms of HACE include breathlessness (even when resting), blue tinges to the lips and fingertips and drowsiness. These are serious symptoms and the only course of action that should be countenanced is to descend and get medical attention as soon as possible.

For more information on AMS look at the excellent *First Aid and Wilderness Medicine* by Dr Jim Duff and Dr Peter Gormley (Treksafe Publishing).

7

OTHER ACTIVITIES

You've photographed, admired, circumnavigated, and maybe even conquered Mont Blanc – but there are still plenty of other things to do on or near the mountain to help you fill those last few days of your trip.

AIGUILLE DU MIDI

The Aiguille du Midi is a pinnacle of rock on a snowbound mountain ridge high above the Chamonix valley. The summit of the Aiguille is 3842m above sea level and it is nearly 3000m above the valley floor. When you take these figures into consideration it seems all the more remarkable that in 1956 engineers successfully finished construction of a cable car from Chamonix to the top of the mountain. It would not have been possible were it not for the vision of the Italian engineer Count Monte Dino Lora Totino or the thirty mountain guides who hauled a cable nearly two kilometres long and weighing over a tonne from Chamonix to the summit of that rocky needle.

The journey takes you from the bustle of Chamonix's streets in the warmth of the valley floor to a world of ice, crumbling black peaks and heart-stopping views. This is the kind of mountain scenery that is usually enjoyed only by mountaineers.

The cable car (☎ 04-50 53 22 75, 🖳 www.compagniedumont-blanc.fr) takes just 10 minutes to reach the lower station at Plan de l'Aiguille before arriving, another 10 minutes later, at Aiguille du Midi station at 3777m. The cable car leaves you inside a vast metallic building that clings to the rocky pinnacle. Here you will find a café, snack bar and restaurant but it is surely the views you will have come to see. There are four terraces facing in different directions but it is the summit terrace that gives the all-round panorama and a real on-top-of-the-world feeling. A lift takes you up through the pinnacle to this summit terrace where you can amble about safely and gawp at the mesmerising views. There is a barrier around the terrace to stop you from falling back to Chamonix.

While the 360° panorama includes the likes of the Matterhorn and Monte Rosa, it is Mont Blanc, just three and a half miles away as the alpine chough flies, that will command most of your attention. From the valley the summit of the mountain appears to be in a different world but here it feels conquerable.

The cable car (see 'T' p26 and map pp24-5) runs daily at regular intervals depending on the weather. The fares are as follows:

Chamonix–Aiguille du Midi €61.50 return/€49.50 one way. See p23 for details of the Mont Blanc Multipass.

SKYWAY MONTE BIANCO

Italy's answer to the Aiguille du Midi is the Skyway Monte Bianco. From Pontal, just outside Courmayeur, a cable car whisks you up to Punta Helbronner at 3462m. A new cable car station opened here in 2015 and from its terrace there are extraordinary views of the Grandes Jorasses and Dent du Géant (Giant's Tooth), a magnificent pinnacle of rock high on the ridge above the Glacier du Géant. The cable car (see 'V' p26 and map pp24-5) runs regularly throughout the summer when the weather is fine.

The fares are: Pontal–Pointe Helbronner €49 return/€37 one way.

MONT BLANC GONDOLA

The cable cars that hoist you from Chamonix to Aiguille du Midi and from Pontal to Pointe Helbronner are remarkable enough but the crowning glory is the gondola (for details see 'V' p26) that links the two. Since 1958 it has been possible to traverse the Mont Blanc massif, from France to Italy, by gondola and cable car. This remarkable journey takes you across the vast Glacier du Géant in the heart of the massif. For those with no experience of mountaineering it is a chance to savour the extraordinary beauty of the high mountains that is usually the preserve of those who are prepared to bust a gut to climb and see them.

Due to the inhospitable weather at these high altitudes the gondola is susceptible to closures because of high winds. July and August are when you're most likely to find it operational.

You can buy a trans-Mont Blanc ticket from Chamonix to Helbronner for €76 one-way and €89 return.

MERLET ANIMAL PARK

Wildlife around the Mont Blanc massif is plentiful, particularly in Aiguilles Rouges Natural Reserve. Just take a walk along the Tour du Mont Blanc between Tré le Champ and La Flégère and you may well see ibex, chamois and possibly even a lammergeier.

For an easier introduction to a whole array of indigenous Alpine fauna, Merlet Animal Park (☎ 04-50 53 47 89, 🖳 www.parcdemerlet.com) is the place to go. It's conveniently placed right on the route of the Tour du Mont Blanc, just an hour before the finish at Les Houches. So, if you have just completed the whole circuit and you haven't seen so much as a marmot, you could do worse than pay a visit.

The park is host to some of the most iconic Alpine species including ibex, chamois, marmots and the very rare mouflon. The park is open from Tuesday to Sunday 10am-6pm (May, Jun & Sep) and daily 9.30am-7.30pm (Jul & Aug). Entry costs €8.

MONTENVERS RAILWAY AND MER DE GLACE

The rack and pinion mountain railway that climbs from Chamonix to the view-point at Montenvers (1913m) has been in operation since 1908, making it the longest-running purpose-built tourist attraction in the Chamonix valley. It remains hugely popular, but it is not the train journey itself that draws the crowds; it is the Mer de Glace.

The Mer de Glace is possibly the best-known glacier in the Alps and is certainly, at between five and nine miles long (depending on who you ask), the longest in France. This is a true valley glacier, not one of those small icy glaciers that cling to the cirques. This glacier occupies a deep valley and is fed by the high-altitude ice fields of the Glacier du Géant and Glacier du Leschaux. Its snout almost spills out into the main Chamonix valley. Indeed in the 19th century it once did; the snout was clearly visible from Chamonix until 1820. It has since retreated and is now diminishing rapidly. Since the first edition of this book the glacier has shrunk to a shadow of its former self (see p152). Nevertheless, it is still a colossal tongue of ice over 200m thick, two miles wide and with a surface area of around 40 sq km. Seeing it up close is the only way to appreciate the immense power of this slow-moving giant.

The view from Montenvers is magnificent and includes not just the Mer de Glace but the peaks of the Grandes Jorasses, Les Drus, Aiguille Verte and Aiguille du Grépon, all of them peaks of extraordinary beauty and renowned in mountaineering circles as some of the finest in the Alps.

You can get a closer look at the glacier by taking the short trip on the cable car that descends from the station at Montenvers to the ice grotto, a cavern that is dug out every year to allow you to wander into the glacier itself.

If all this natural wonder is too much to bear there are other distractions at Montenvers. The café and restaurant are open all day and there are a number of small museums. The Alpine Fauna museum has a variety of stuffed animals including ibex, chamois and foxes. It's all very educational but it's certainly nicer to see them gambolling about, with their hearts beating, on the mountain-sides. There's also a Crystal Museum with displays of quartzite and amethyst and other natural treasures found in the region.

The mountain railway (see 'S' p26 and map pp24-5) departs frequently from Chamonix; not from the main train station but from the smaller mountain railway station (see map p62-3) just behind. A ticket costs €31.50 return.

PARAGLIDING

Any trekker who walks along the Grand Balcon Sud, the section of the Tour that runs along the hem of the Aiguilles Rouges, cannot fail to notice paragliders gracefully circling like giant gaudy birds high above the valley. Paragliding is a hugely popular activity in the Alps; indeed, the Chamonix valley is where some of the world's best paragliders take to the sky.

I have tried paragliding only once, on the benign slopes of the Touch Hills in Scotland. Launching oneself from that hillside was thrilling enough but to jog down an Alpine mountainside and find your legs whirling into space, 100 metres above the valley floor, must be a truly exhilarating experience.

Far from being the preserve of experts with a serious head for heights, anyone can have a go at paragliding. It is surely the closest man will ever get to the sensation of true flight; there's no aluminium sheet like you get with a plane or glider; nor is there the noise of a whirring engine such as that which accompanies every flight with a microlight. Unless you look up, there isn't even a sense of the vast wing above you. It can be a curious sensation of relaxation mixed with blind fear.

There are a number of companies offering tandem rides and paragliding lessons. Prices for a tandem flight are generally around €110. For the ultimate thrill you can take a tandem flight from the 3842-metre summit of the Aiguille du Midi for around €290. For one-to-one tuition the price is high at around €900. The following companies offer tuition and tandem flights:

● **Les Ailes du Mont Blanc** ☎ 06-20 46 55 57, ⌨ www.lesailesdumont-blanc.com; 117 chemin des Chosalets, 74400, Chamonix
● **Alpine Flying Centre** ☎ 04-50 54 59 63, ⌨ www.flyers-lodge.com; 799 route de la Grangeat, 7470, Domancy
● **Evolution 2** ☎ 07-60 82 10 12, ⌨ www.evolution2.com; 130 rue des Moulins, 74400, Chamonix
● **Kailash Parapente** ☎ 07-69 68 25 85, ⌨ www.kailash-parapente.com; 31 avenue Michel Croz, 74400, Chamonix
● **Summits** ☎ 04-50 53 50 14, ⌨ www.summits.fr; 81 rue Joseph Vallot, 74400, Chamonix

WHITE-WATER RAFTING AND HYDROGLISSE

Rafting is popular on the Arve, the fast-flowing river that occupies the Chamonix valley, and so is hydroglisse. **Hydroglisse** is a more recent phenomenon which involves swimming down the river with the aid of a float, flippers and helmet. First-timers will find the Arve offers plenty of thrills without being too dangerous.

Rafting and hydroglisse trips both cost in the region of €35 to €45 per person for a two to three-hour trip. The following outfits in Chamonix can all introduce you to the thrill of white water:

● **ChamAventure** ☎ 04-50 53 55 70, ⌨ www.cham-aventure.com; 190 place de l'Eglise, 74400, Chamonix
● **Chamonix Hydroglisse** ☎ 06-80 73 97 73, ⌨ www.hydroglisse.com; 540 Prom du Fori, 74400, Chamonix
● **Evolution 2** ☎ 07-60 82 10 12, ⌨ www.evolution2.com; 130 rue des Moulins, 74400, Chamonix
● **Session Raft** ☎ 04-50 93 63 63, ⌨ www.sessionraft.fr; 1871 chemin des Peupliers, 74190, Passy

OTHER ACTIVITIES

MOUNTAIN-BIKING

The Chamonix valley is ideal for mountain biking with plenty of chairlifts and a web of trails through the steep forests. The maintained trails offer plenty of scope for exploring, whether that's pootling along at 5mph or bombing downhill on a dirt trail. Advanced riders will find a lifetime's worth of downhill trails on the steep valley sides but there are also easier routes for the beginner. If you don't have your own bike you can hire one from one of the following outlets:

● **ChamAventure** ☎ 04-50 53 55 70, 🖵 www.cham-aventure.com; 190 place de l'Eglise, 74400, Chamonix
● **Evolution 2** ☎ 07-60 82 10 12, 🖵 www.evolution2.com; 130 rue des Moulins, 74400, Chamonix
● **High Hills MTB** ☎ 663-329639, 🖵 www.highhillsmtb.com
● **Legend'Chx Bike and Board Shop** ☎ 04-50 90 22 25; 218 avenue Aiguille du Midi, 74400, Chamonix

Once you have hired your bike you can head for those dirt tracks. The following areas have dedicated downhill trails that are faithfully maintained and accessible by lift. A one-day lift pass for bikers is available for €20 for one lift, €30.50 for all lifts.

Some trails are for advanced riders only so choose your route carefully. A good place to search for a route that suits you is at this website: 🖵 www.chamonet.com/biking/trails.

Mountain biking can be dangerous if underestimated. Always wear a helmet, make sure your bike has a bell and carry a repair kit with you. Stick to the trails and always be aware of, and give way to, walkers.

Trails for beginners and intermediate riders The Petit Balcon Sud and Petit Balcon Nord offer dedicated trails through the lower slopes of the Chamonix valley, passing through cool larch and pine forests and offering superb views down the full length of the valley. The Petit Balcon Sud trail runs from Argentière to Chamonix (this is the easiest direction because it's downhill) while the Petit Balcon Nord trail runs from Chamonix to Le Tour (ie uphill).

The terrain is easy-going and is ideal for those new to mountain biking. There are a few trickier sections but these are easily avoided by getting off the bike!

It's well worth combining the two *balcons* by riding up one and down the other. Bear in mind that you may encounter walkers on both these routes. I would recommend the Petit Balcon Sud for the uphill section since the views are better from here and you will be more inclined to stop to appreciate them as you pedal slowly uphill.

For advanced riders The descent from Plan Praz to Chamonix is a popular ride, easily accessible via the Chamonix–Plan Praz cable car (see 'P' p26). The descent takes about one hour. It is steep and in places technically demanding.

Alternatively, try the track that descends from La Flégère, accessible by cable car from Les Praz. There are countless other route possibilities.

CLIMBING

Chamonix is often called the birth-place of mountaineering but it also has a long history of climbing, blessed as it is with superb granite and limestone and reliably good weather to boot. There are of course some magnificent winter climbs at high altitude but there are also plenty of crags and bouldering sites in the Chamonix valley. Beginners will need to get some tuition. Many of the mountain guides listed on pp162-3 offer climbing instruction.

Those who already know their figures of eight from their pieces of eight will be spoilt for choice. Try one of the following sites (there are many more):

Climbers on L'Aiguillette d'Argentière

● **Les Gaillands** Situated just outside the village of Les Pèlerins, on the outskirts of Chamonix, this is a very popular crag with bolted routes for everyone from beginner to rock jock. A perfect place for those who like an audience; tourists often congregate to gawp and point.

● **Le Brévent** Take the cable car from Chamonix and you will find yourself with plenty of multi-pitch routes.

● **La Joux** A small crag halfway between Chamonix and Argentière with 20m pitches and some bouldering opportunities too.

● **L'Aiguillette d'Argentière** This sharp needle of rock high above Argentière offers breathtaking views. Trekkers on the Tour du Mont Blanc will be familiar with it as it stands right by the trail on the way up to Tête aux Vents in the Aiguilles Rouges. Getting to the needle involves walking along, and up, the Tour du Mont Blanc for about two hours from Tré le Champ. There are enough bolted routes up this majestic rocky appendage to keep you entertained throughout the day.

● **Le Col des Montets** Not far from the road at Col des Montets are a number of gneiss boulders offering routes for beginners and experienced climbers alike. This is a very popular spot, probably because it gets a lot of sun! There is another good bouldering spot a short hop along the road into Switzerland.

Indoor climbing walls are the perfect places to learn to climb in a safe environment. They also offer a dry place to climb when the weather turns foul,

OTHER ACTIVITIES

although it can get busy at such times. There are some excellent indoor walls in the area. **Richard Bozon Sports Centre** (☎ 04-50 53 23 70; 214 avenue de la Plage, 74400, Chamonix), on the northern edge of Chamonix, is small but worth a look. Open daily it costs €6.40 per person.

In Les Houches there's **Mont Blanc Escalade** (☎ 04-50 54 76 48, 🖳 www.montblancescalade.com), one of the biggest walls in France with over 1000 square metres of wall, some as high as 16m. It's €14.50 per person.

APPENDIX A – BIBLIOGRAPHY AND MAPS

BIBLIOGRAPHY

Ascent and Tour of Mont Blanc and Passage of the Col du Geant between Sept 2nd and 7th 1850 J D Gardner (Chiswick, 1851)

A Short Account of an Expedition to the Summit of Mont Blanc Prof HB de Saussure (1788)

A Walk Round Mont Blanc Francis Trench (1847)

The First Ascent of Mont Blanc Brown, Thomas, Graham and de Beer (Oxford University Press, 1957)

Killing Dragons: The Conquest of the Alps Fergus Fleming (Granta, 2001)

Wildflowers of Britain and Europe W Lippert and D Podlech (Collins, 2001)

RECOMMENDED READING

First Aid and Wilderness Medicine Dr Jim Duff and Dr Peter Gormley (Cicerone, 2017) A useful pocket-sized book that offers first-aid advice to trekkers and mountaineers.

Killing Dragons: The Conquest of the Alps Fergus Fleming (Granta, 2001) An in-depth history of mountaineering in the home of mountaineering. Has some very interesting detail on the first attempts on, and ascents of, Mont Blanc.

Mont Blanc – Discovery and Conquest of the Giant of the Alps Stefano Ardito (White Star, 2006) A coffee-table book packed with stunning photographs from the high ridges and peaks of the Mont Blanc massif.

Flowers of the Alps Ansgar Hoppe (Pelagic, 2013).

MAPS

The maps in this guidebook are designed to keep you going in the right direction on the trail but it is well worth taking the two 1:25,000 IGN maps that cover the area: sheets *3630OT Chamonix/Massif du Mont Blanc* and *3531ET St-Gervais-les-Bains/Massif du Mont Blanc*. These will give you a sense of where you are in relation to the land further afield. If you intend to walk anywhere off route these maps become essential. You can buy them in most newsagents and bookshops in Chamonix and other towns in the area. In the UK they are available from Stanfords (☎ 020-7836 1321, 🖥 www.stanfords.co.uk) and The Map Shop (☎ 01684-593146, 🖥 www.themapshop.co.uk).

For **digital mapping** there's an IGN app available (outdoors-gps-france) and a subscription of £19.99 will give you access to IGN's range of maps for a year on a smartphone or tablet. You can download the area you need and use the maps offline.

APPENDIX B – USEFUL WORDS AND PHRASES

General	FRENCH	ITALIAN
Do you speak English?	*Parlez-vous Anglais?*	*Parlate inglese?*
I can't speak French	*Je ne parle pas Français*	*Non parlo italiano*
Please speak slowly	*Parlez plus lentement s'il vous plait*	*Parli prego lentamente*
How are you?	*Comment allez-vous?*	*Come sta?*
Fine thanks and you?	*Bien merci, et vous?*	*Bene, grazie*
Hello	*Salut*	*Ciao*
Good morning	*Bonjour*	*Buongiorno*
Good evening	*Bonsoir*	*Buona sera*
Goodnight	*Bon nuit*	*Buona notte*
Goodbye	*Au revoir*	*Arrivederci*
See you tomorrow	*à demain*	*A domani*
See you later	*à bientôt*	*A più tardi*
Please	*S'il vous plait*	*Per favore*
Thank you	*Merci*	*Grazie*
You're welcome/Don't mention it/That's okay	*De rien*	*Prego*
Excuse me	*Excusez-moi*	*Mi scusi*
I'm sorry	*Je suis désolé*	*Mi perdoni*
Closed	*Fermé(e)*	*Chiuso*

Accommodation

Do you have a room with one/two/three beds?	*Avez vous une chambre avec un/deux/trois lit/s?*	*Avate una stanza con una base/ due basi/tre basi?*
I'd like a single room/ a room with two beds	*Je voudrais une chambre pour une personne/deux personnes*	*Vorrei una camera singola/ doppia matrimoniale*
Can I leave my luggage here?	*Puis-je laisser mes bagages ici?*	*Posso lasciare I mei bagagli qui?*
How much is it…?	*C'est combien…?*	*Quanto è…?*
Accommodation	*Hébergement*	*Allogio*
Shelter	*Abri*	*Riparo*
Inn/guesthouse	*Auberge/Gîte*	*Pensione*
Room	*Chambre*	*Stanza*
Half board	*Demi-pension*	*Mezza-pensione*
Dormitory	*Dortoir*	*Dormitorio*
Mountain Hut/Shelter	*Refuge/Cabane*	*Rifugio*
Bath	*Bain*	*Bagno*

Eating out

A table for one/two/ three please	*Une table pour une/deux/trois personne(s) s'il vous plaît*	*Un tavolo per una/due/ tre per favore*
The menu please	*Le menu s'il vous plaît*	*Il menu per favore*
What is this?	*Qu'est-ce que c'est?*	*Che cosa è questo?*
I'll have that	*Je prends ça*	*Prendo quello*
Starter	*Entrée*	*Il primo*
Main course	*Plat principal*	*Piatto principale*
Pudding	*Dessert*	*Dolce*
The bill please	*L'addition s'il vous plaît*	*La fattura per favore*

Food and drink | FRENCH | ITALIAN (see also p39)

Food and drink	FRENCH	ITALIAN (see also p39)
Bread	*Pain*	*Pane*
Sugar	*Sucre*	*Zucchero*
Egg	*Oeuf*	*Uovo*
Cheese	*Fromage*	*Formaggio*
Fish	*Poisson*	*Pesci*
Meat	*Viande*	*Carne*
Vegetables	*Légumes*	*Verdure*
Vegetarian	*Végétarien*	*Vegetariano*
Breakfast	*Petit déjeuner*	*La prima colazione*
Lunch	*Déjeuner*	*Pranzo*
Dinner	*Dîner*	*Cena*
Water	*Eau*	*Acqua*
Milk	*Lait*	*Latte*
Tea	*Thé*	*Tè*
Coffee	*Café*	*Caffè*
Wine	*Vin*	*Vino*
Beer	*Bière*	*Birra*

Directions

Where is..	*Ou est..*	*Dove e..*
the train station?	*la gare?*	*la stazione ferroviaria?*
the supermarket?	*le supermarché?*	*il supermercato?*
the mountain hut?	*le refuge?*	*il rifugio?*
the tourist information office?	*l'office de tourisme?*	*il ente del turismo?*
the grocery?	*l'alimentation?*	*il negozio di alimentari?*
the butcher's?	*la boucherie?*	*la pizzicheria?*
the bakery?	*la boulangerie?*	*la panetteria?*
the town centre?	*le centre ville?*	*il centro città?*
the crepe shop?	*la crêperie?*	*la crêperie?*
the delicatessen?	*la charcuterie?*	*la pizzicheria?*
the bank?	*la banque?*	*la banca?*
the museum?	*le musée?*	*il museo?*
How far is it to... ?	*A quelle distance est il à...?*	*Fin dove e...?*
How do I get to... ?	*Pour aller à...?*	*Come ottengo...?*
Left/Right	*Gauche/Droit*	*Sinistra/Destra*
Straight ahead	*Tout droit*	*Va sempre derreto*
North	*Nord*	*Nord*
South	*Sud*	*Sud*
East	*Est*	*Est*
West	*Ouest*	*Ovest*
Street	*Rue*	*Via*
Road	*Route*	*Strada*
Town	*Ville*	*Città*
(Bus) Stop	*Arrêt*	*Fermata*

Time	**FRENCH**	**ITALIAN**
What time is it?	*Quelle heure est-il?*	*Che ora è?*
It's two o'clock	*Il est deux heures*	*Sono le due*
It's half past two	*Il est deux heures et demie*	*Sono le due e mezzo*
It's quarter past two	*Il est deux heures et quart*	*Sono le due e quarto*
It's quarter to two	*Il est deux heures moins le quart*	*Sono le due meno un quarto*
Today	*Aujourd'hui*	*Oggi*
Tomorrow	*Demain*	*Domani*
Yesterday	*Hier*	*Ieri*

Weather	**Temps**	**Tempo**
Fog	*Brouillard*	*Nebbia*
Storm	*Orage/Tempête*	*Tempesta*
Cloud/Cloudy	*Nuage/Nuageaux*	*Nube/Nuvoloso*
Wind	*Vent*	*Vento*
Sunny	*Soleil*	*Soleggiato*
Snow	*Neige*	*Neve*
Hot	*Chaud*	*Caldo*
Avalanche	*Avalanche*	*Valanga*
Weather forecast	*Météo*	*Tempo*

Numbers		
1	*un/une*	*un*
2	*deux*	*due*
3	*trois*	*tre*
4	*quatre*	*quattro*
5	*cinq*	*cinque*
6	*six*	*sei*
7	*sept*	*sette*
8	*huit*	*otto*
9	*neuf*	*nove*
10	*dix*	*dieci*
11	*onze*	*undici*
12	*douze*	*dodici*
13	*treize*	*tredici*
14	*quatorze*	*quattordici*
15	*quinze*	*quindici*
16	*seize*	*sedici*
17	*dix-sept*	*diciasette*
18	*dix-huit*	*diciotto*
19	*dix-neuf*	*diciannove*
20	*vingt*	*venti*
30	*trente*	*trenta*
40	*quarante*	*quaranta*
50	*cinquante*	*cinquanta*
60	*soixante*	*sessanta*
70	*soixante-dix*	*settanta*
80	*quatre-vingts*	*ottanta*

On the path	FRENCH	ITALIAN
Mountain rescue	*Secour en Montagne*	*Secour in montagna*
Lane/Way	*Chemin*	*Strada*
Mountain pass	*Col*	*Col*
Crest/Ridge	*Crête*	*Cresta*
Cross	*Croix*	*Croce*
Church	*Église*	*Chiesa*
Mountain/Mount	*Mont/Montagne*	*Montagna*
Valley	*Val/Vallée*	*Val*
Small valley	*Vallon*	*Valle*
Rock	*Pierre*	*Pietra*
Path	*Sentier*	*Via*
Cable car	*Téléphérique/Télécabine*	*Funivie*
Chairlift	*Télésiège*	*Funivie*
Ice axe	*Piolet*	*Piolet*
Hike/walk	*Randonée*	*L'escursionismo*
Dangerous	*Dangereux*	*Pericoloso*
Difficult	*Difficile*	*Difficile*
Easy	*Facil(e)*	*Facile*
White	*Blanc*	*Bianco/a*
Black	*Noir*	*Nera/o*
Red	*Rouge*	*Rosso*
Green	*Vert*	*Verde*
Head	*Tête*	*Testa*
Needle	*Aiguille*	*Ago*
Eagle	*Aigle*	*Aquila*
Window	*Fenêtre*	*Finestra*
Ice/Glacier	*Glace/Glacier*	*Ghiaccio*
Lake	*Lac*	*Lago*
House	*Maison*	*Casa*
Sea	*Mer*	*Mare*

APPENDIX C – GLOSSARY

Alp	High pasture
Alpage	Alpine meadow
Arête	A sharp, narrow mountain ridge or spur between corries in glacially eroded mountainous regions
Avalanche	Sudden snow slip
Balcon	A level or gently sloping terrace above a valley
Bisse	Mountain viaduct or irrigation channel
Buvette	Simple rustic mountain restaurant
Cairn	Pile of stones often used as a marker
Cirque	Steep-sided crescent-shaped basin formed by the action of ice
Col	Mountain pass
Combe	A short valley or deep hollow formed by the action of ice
Couloir	A deep mountainside gorge or gully forming a breach in a cliff-face
Crevasse	Deep crack or fissure in a glacier
Föhn	Warm southerly wind
Massif	High mountain range with a series of connected peaks
Montagnard	From the mountains (a mountain dweller)
Moraine	Mounds of debris carried and deposited by a glacier
Névé	Upper part of a glacier where the snow turns to ice; it refers in particular to a type of snow that has been partially melted, refrozen and compacted
Scree	Slopes of accumulated frost-shattered rock, often unstable
Serac	Pinnacle or ridge of ice among crevasses on a glacier

APPENDIX D – MOUNTAIN PHOTOGRAPHY

The art of mountain photography is in the ability to capture, in a two-dimensional image, the essence of these wild places; quite a challenge when one considers that mountains are not just a visual treat but a stimulus to all our senses. The trick therefore is to use the visual element to convey the sounds, scents and overall mood.

Light is a key consideration in this. The best time to photograph mountains is at dawn and dusk when the sun is low in the sky, casting shadows that capture the topography of the land. For the same reason, autumn and spring often throw up some beautifully subtle light, although these aren't the best seasons to walk the TMB as the huts are closed and the passes blocked by snow.

There are ways to improve your photography and learn from your own mistakes and successes. In the old pre-digital days of film each shot was expensive and you couldn't see it until days or weeks later; photographers would make sure they got the shot right first time. In today's world of digital photography we can take lots of shots, see the results instantly and keep tweaking the settings until we are happy. The disadvantage of this is we can become lazy and not put enough effort into getting the shot right first time but the advantage is you can experiment with different exposures, compositions and camera angles.

Anyone who takes landscape photography seriously will use a tripod. These are essential for holding the camera steady in low-light conditions when a slow shutter speed is needed. Using a slow shutter speed also helps bring out the natural colours in a photograph.

Composing a picture is down to personal taste. Most photographers agree that having a background, middle and foreground, works best. Having something in the foreground, a rock or stream for example, complements the mountains in the background, while natural lines leading to a focal point also work well.

But sticking to rules is the way to stem creativity. If the sky is full of beautiful cloud patterns then why not fill most of the frame with sky? And why not shoot into the sun with a small aperture? Doing so can create dramatic silhouettes of the mountains or your fellow trekkers. Many people put their cameras away when it's raining and grey but, if you know what to shoot, then this can be a great time to get some moody shots. Dark clouds swirling around granite peaks can make for a dramatic image. Experimenting with different techniques is the best way to learn what works for you.

1000m	3280ft	3600m	11,736ft
1200m	3936ft	3800m	12,388ft
1400m	4592ft	4000m	13,040ft
1600m	5248ft	4200m	13,692ft
1800m	5904ft	4400m	14,344ft
2000m	6560ft	4600m	14,996ft
2200m	7216ft	4800m	15,648ft
2400m	7872ft	5000m	16,300ft
2600m	8528ft	5200m	16,952ft
2800m	9184ft	5400m	17,604ft
3000m	9840ft	5600m	18,256ft
3200m	10,496ft	5800m	18,908ft
3400m	11,152ft	6000m	19,560ft

1km	⁵/₈ mile	80km	49½ miles
5km	3 miles	85km	52¾ miles
10km	6¼ miles	90km	55¾ miles
15km	9¼ miles	95km	59 miles
20km	12½ miles	100km	62 miles
25km	15½ miles	105km	65 miles
30km	18½ miles	110km	68¼ miles
35km	21¾ miles	115km	71¼ miles
40km	24¾ miles	120km	74½ miles
45km	28 miles	125km	77½ miles
50km	31 miles	130km	80½ miles
55km	34 miles	135km	83¾ miles
60km	37¼ miles	140km	86¾ miles
65km	40¼ miles	145km	90 miles
70km	43½ miles	150km	93 miles
75km	46½ miles	155km	96 miles

APPENDIX F – MAP KEYS

Trail map key

	Walking Trail		Fence	☐	Building
	Minor Trail		Gate	✦	Accommodation
	Track		Bridge	Δ	Campsite
	Road		Lake	✝	Church
	Steps		River	⊘	Public Toilet
	Slope		Stones	🚌	Bus Stop
	Steep Slope		Trees	18	Map Continuation

Town plan key

✦	Where to stay	📖	Library/bookstore	☐	Building
O	Where to eat and drink	@	Internet	●	Other
Δ	Campsite	🏛	Museum/gallery	CP	Car park
⊠	Post Office	✝	Church/cathedral	🚌	Bus station/stop
©	Bank/ATM	☏	Telephone	▭	Rail line & station
ⓘ	Tourist Information	⊘	Public toilet	▓	Park

INDEX

Page references in bold type refer to maps or pictures

TRAILBLAZER TREKKING GUIDES
Europe
British Walking Guides – 18-title series
Scottish Highlands – The Hillwalking Guide
Tour du Mont Blanc
Walker's Haute Route: Mt Blanc – Matterhorn

South America
Inca Trail, Cusco & Machu Picchu
Peru's Cordilleras Blanca & Huayhuash

Africa
Kilimanjaro
Moroccan Atlas – The Trekking Guide
Asia
Nepal Trekking & The Great Himalaya Trail
Sinai – the trekking guide
Trekking in the Everest Region
Australasia
New Zealand – The Great Walks

Kilimanjaro – the trekking guide
Henry Stedman, 5th edn, £14.99
ISBN 978-1-905864-95-9, 368pp, 40 maps, 50 colour photos
At 5895m (19,340ft) Kilimanjaro is the world's tallest freestanding mountain and one of the most popular destinations for hikers visiting Africa. Route guides & maps – the 6 major routes. City guides – Nairobi, Dar-es-Salaam, Arusha, Moshi & Marangu.

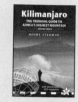

Peru's Cordilleras Blanca & Huayhuash
The Hiking & Biking Guide
Neil & Harriet Pike, 1st edn, £15.99
ISBN 978-1-905864-63-8, 242pp, 50 maps, 40 colour photos
This region, in northern Peru, boasts some of the most spectacular scenery in the Andes, and most accessible high mountain trekking and biking in the world. This practical guide contains 60 detailed route maps and descriptions covering 20 hiking trails and more than 30 days of paved and dirt road cycling.

Sinai – the trekking guide *Ben Hoffler,* 1st edn, £14.99
ISBN 978-1-905864-41-6, 288pp, 74 maps, 30 colour photos
Trek with the Bedouin and their camels and discover one of the most exciting new trekking destinations. The best routes in the High Mountain Region (St. Katherine), Wadi Feiran and the Muzeina deserts. Once you finish on the trail there are the nearby coastal resorts of Sharm el Sheikh, Dahab and Nuweiba to enjoy.

Moroccan Atlas – the trekking guide
Alan Palmer, 2nd edn, £14.99
ISBN 978-1-905864-59-1, 420pp, 86 maps, 40 colour photos
The High Atlas in central Morocco is the most dramatic and beautiful section of the entire Atlas range. Towering peaks, deep gorges and huddled Berber villages enchant all who visit. With 73 detailed trekking maps, 13 town and village guides including Marrakech.

Trekking in the Everest Region
Jamie McGuinness 6th edn, £15.99
ISBN 978-1-905864-81-2, 320pp, 95 maps, 30 colour photos
Sixth edition of this popular guide to the world's most famous trekking region. Covers not only the classic treks but also the wild routes. Written by a Nepal-based trek and mountaineering leader. Includes: 27 detailed route maps and 52 village plans. Plus: Kathmandu city guide

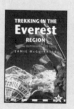

TRAILBLAZER'S LONG-DISTANCE PATH (LDP) WALKING GUIDES

We've applied to destinations which are closer to home Trailblazer's proven formula for publishing definitive practical route guides for adventurous travellers. Britain's network of long-distance trails enables the walker to explore some of the finest landscapes in the country's best walking areas. These are guides that are user-friendly, practical, informative and environmentally sensitive.

'The same attention to detail that distinguishes its other guides has been brought to bear here'.
THE
SUNDAY TIMES

● **Unique mapping features** In many walking guidebooks the reader has to read a route description then try to relate it to the map. Our guides are much easier to use because walking directions, tricky junctions, places to stay and eat, points of interest and walking times are all written onto the maps themselves in the places to which they apply. With their uncluttered clarity, these are not general-purpose maps but fully edited maps drawn by walkers for walkers.

● **Largest-scale walking maps** At a scale of just under 1:20,000 (8cm or 3¹/₈ inches to one mile) the maps in these guides are bigger than even the most detailed British walking maps currently available in the shops.

● **Not just a trail guide – includes where to stay, where to eat and public transport** Our guidebooks cover the complete walking experience, not just the route. Accommodation options for all budgets are provided (pubs, hotels, B&Bs, campsites, bunkhouses, hostels) as well as places to eat. Detailed public transport information for all access points to each trail means that there are itineraries for all walkers, for hiking the entire route as well as for day or weekend walks.

● **Includes dowloadable GPS waypoints** – Marked on our maps and downloadable from the Trailblazer website.

Cleveland Way *Henry Stedman*, 1st edn, ISBN 978-1-905864-91-1, 208pp, 56 maps
Coast to Coast *Henry Stedman*, 8th edn, ISBN 978-1-905864-96-6, 268pp, 110 maps
Cornwall Coast Path (SW Coast Path Pt 2) *Stedman & Newton*, 5th edn, ISBN 978-1-905864-71-3, 352pp, 142 maps
Cotswold Way *Tricia & Bob Hayne*, 3rd edn, ISBN 978-1-905864-70-6, 204pp, 53 maps,
Dales Way *Henry Stedman*, 1st edn, ISBN 978-1-905864-78-2, 192pp, 50 maps
Dorset & South Devon (SW Coast Path Pt 3) *Stedman & Newton*, 2nd edn, ISBN 978-1-905864-94-2, 336pp, 88 maps
Exmoor & North Devon (SW Coast Path Pt I) *Stedman & Newton*, 2nd edn, ISBN 978-1-905864-86-7, 224pp, 68 maps
Great Glen Way *Jim Manthorpe*, 1st edn, ISBN 978-1-905864-80-5, 192pp, 55 maps
Hadrian's Wall Path *Henry Stedman*, 5th edn, ISBN 978-1-905864-85-0, 224pp, 60 maps
Norfolk Coast Path & Peddars Way *Alexander Stewart*, 1st edn, ISBN 978-1-905864-98-0, 224pp, 75 maps,
North Downs Way *Henry Stedman*, 2nd edn, ISBN 978-1-905864-90-4, 240pp, 98 maps
Offa's Dyke Path *Keith Carter*, 4th edn, ISBN 978-1-905864-65-2, 240pp, 98 maps
Pembrokeshire Coast Path *Jim Manthorpe*, 5th edn, ISBN 978-1-905864-84-3, 236pp, 96 maps,
Pennine Way *Stuart Greig*, 4th edn, ISBN 978-1-905864-61-4, 272pp, 138 maps
The Ridgeway *Nick Hill*, 4th edn, ISBN 978-1-905864-79-9, 208pp, 53 maps
South Downs Way *Jim Manthorpe*, 6th edn, ISBN 978-1-905864-93-5, 204pp, 60 maps
Thames Path *Joel Newton*, 2nd edn, ISBN 978-1-905864-97-3, 256pp, 99 maps
West Highland Way *Charlie Loram*, 6th edn, ISBN 978-1-905864-76-8, 218pp, 60 maps

'The Trailblazer series stands head, shoulders, waist and ankles above the rest. They are particularly strong on mapping ...'
THE SUNDAY TIMES

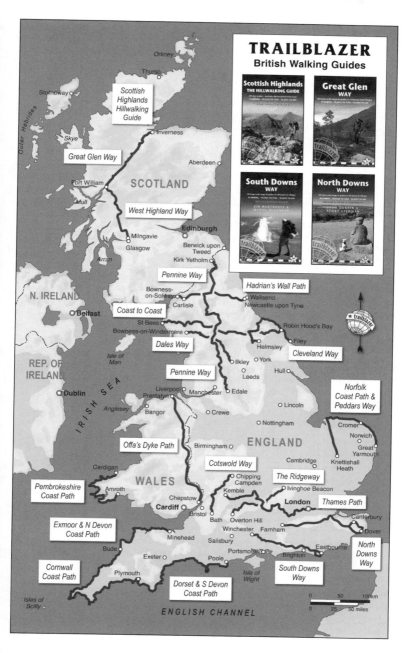

TRAILBLAZER TITLE LIST

For more information about Trailblazer and our
expanding range of guides, for guidebook updates or
for credit card mail order sales visit our website:

www.trailblazer-guides.com

Mont Blanc Region

The Aiguille Verte (4122m) appears through the clouds above Chamonix

Tour du Mont Blanc

0   5   10km